Orion Books Ltd
Orion House
5 Upper St Martin's Lane
London WC2H 9EA

First published by Orion in 2003

Drawings by Michael Martin

Cover illustrations by Alex Graham

© Associated Newspapers plc 2003

ISBN 0 75285 789 4

Printed and bound in Great Britain by
Butler & Tanner Ltd, Frome and London

ALEX GRAHAM'S FRED BASSET 2003

HAPPY BIRTHDAY FRED!

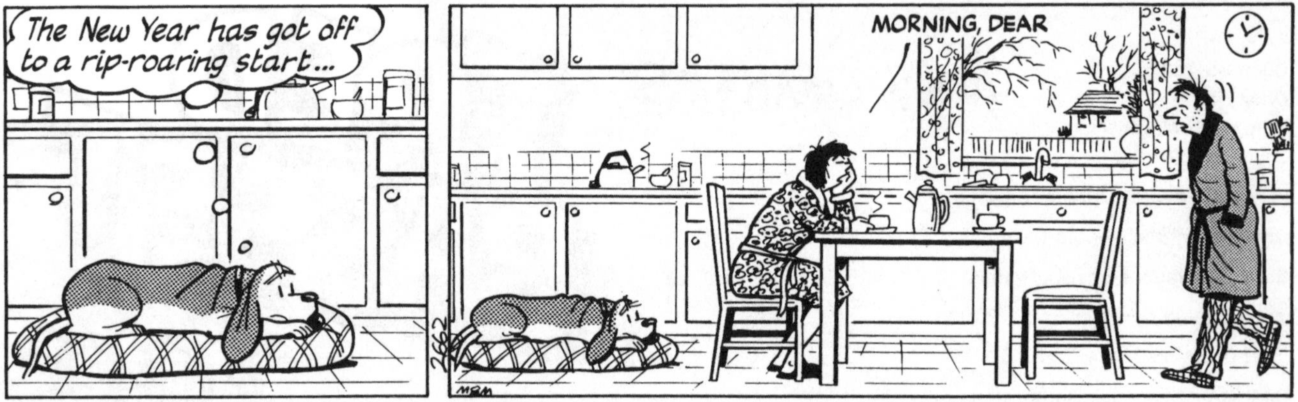
The New Year has got off to a rip-roaring start...
MORNING, DEAR

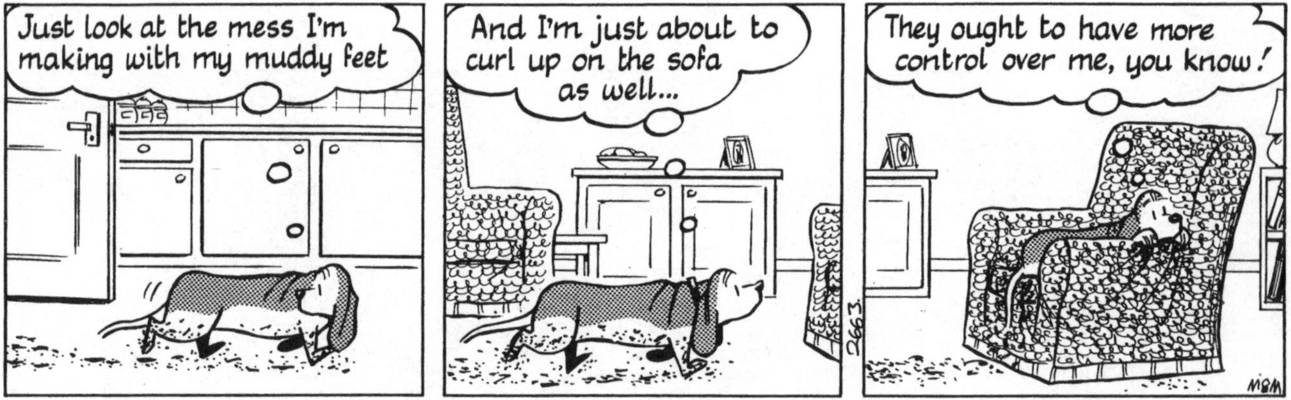
Just look at the mess I'm making with my muddy feet
And I'm just about to curl up on the sofa as well...
They ought to have more control over me, you know!

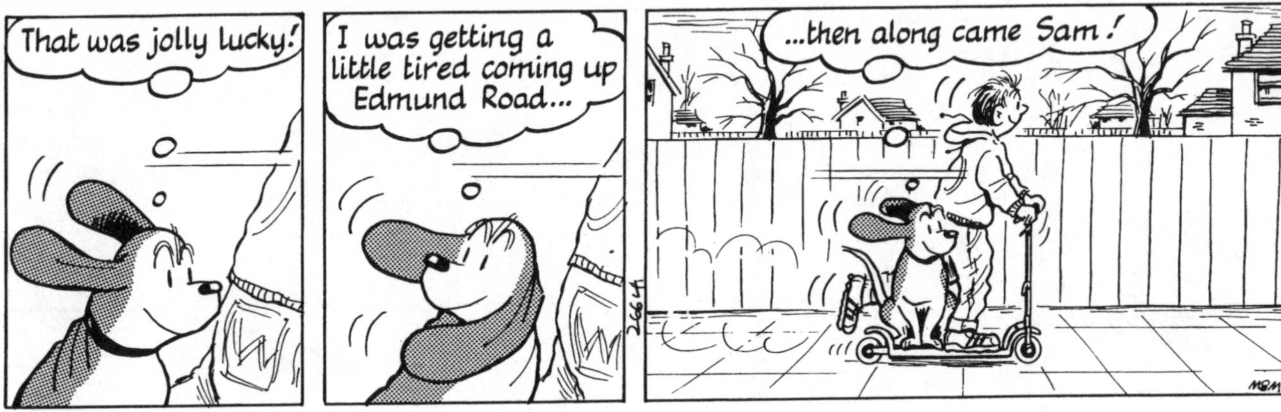
That was jolly lucky!
I was getting a little tired coming up Edmund Road...
...then along came Sam!

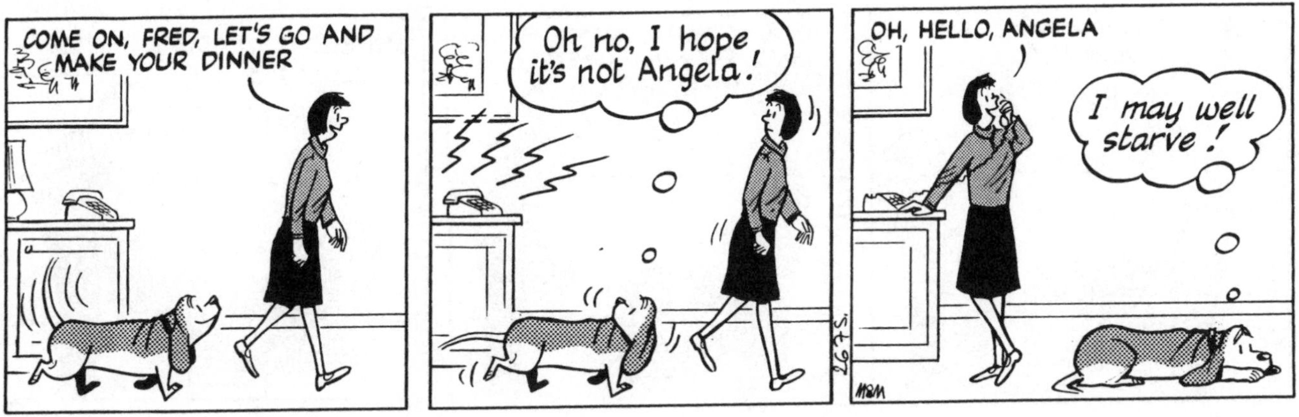
COME ON, FRED, LET'S GO AND MAKE YOUR DINNER
Oh no, I hope it's not Angela!
OH, HELLO, ANGELA
I may well starve!

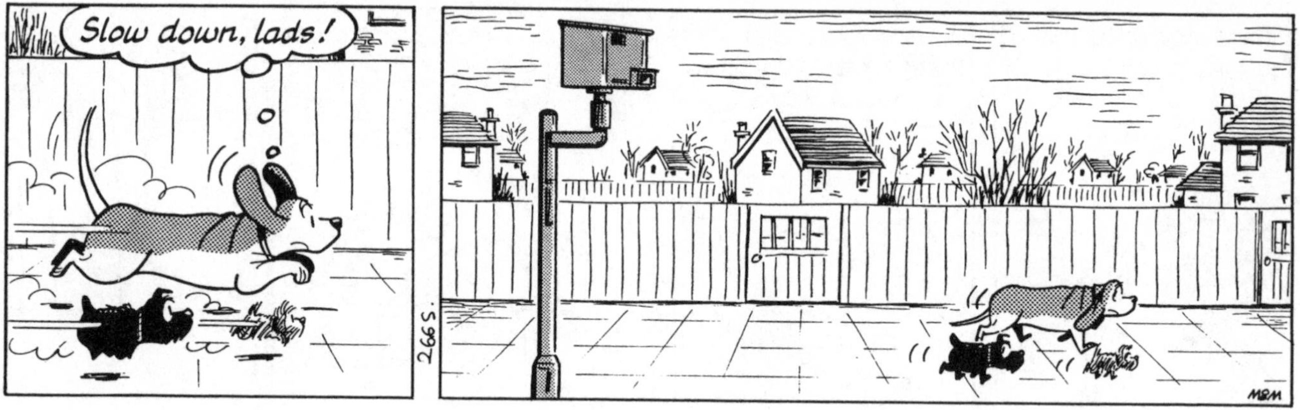
Slow down, lads!
2665.

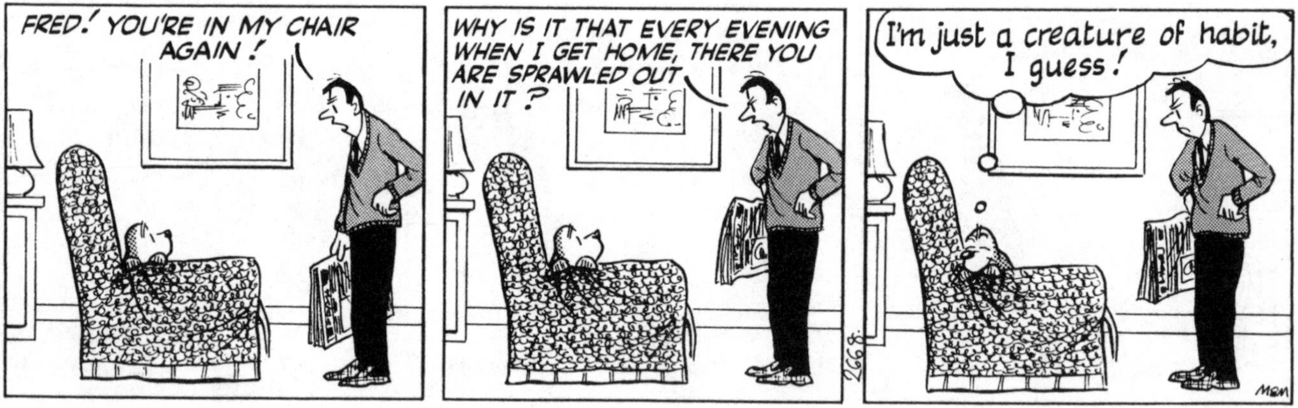
FRED! YOU'RE IN MY CHAIR AGAIN!
WHY IS IT THAT EVERY EVENING WHEN I GET HOME, THERE YOU ARE SPRAWLED OUT IN IT?
I'm just a creature of habit, I guess!
2668.

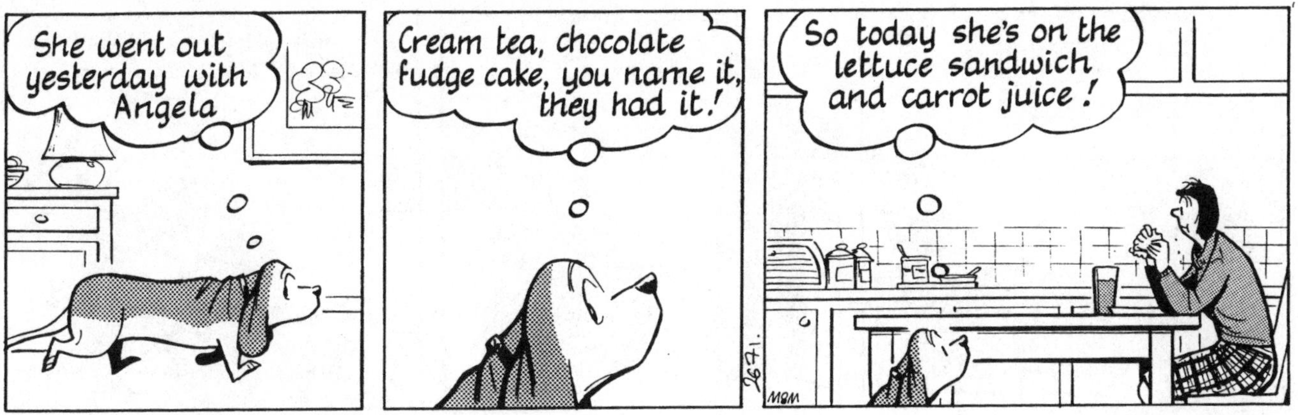
She went out yesterday with Angela
Cream tea, chocolate fudge cake, you name it, they had it!
So today she's on the lettuce sandwich and carrot juice!

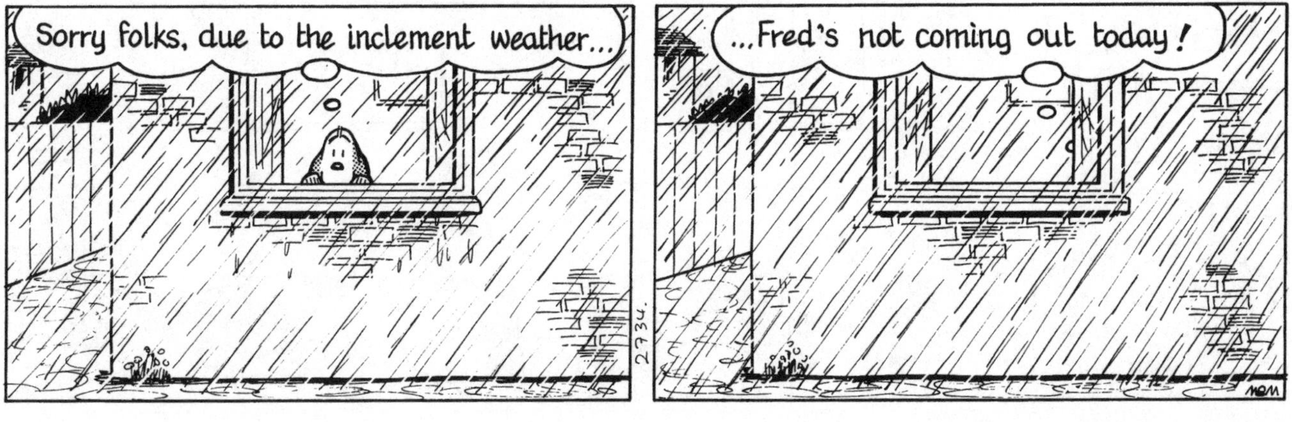
Sorry folks, due to the inclement weather...
...Fred's not coming out today!

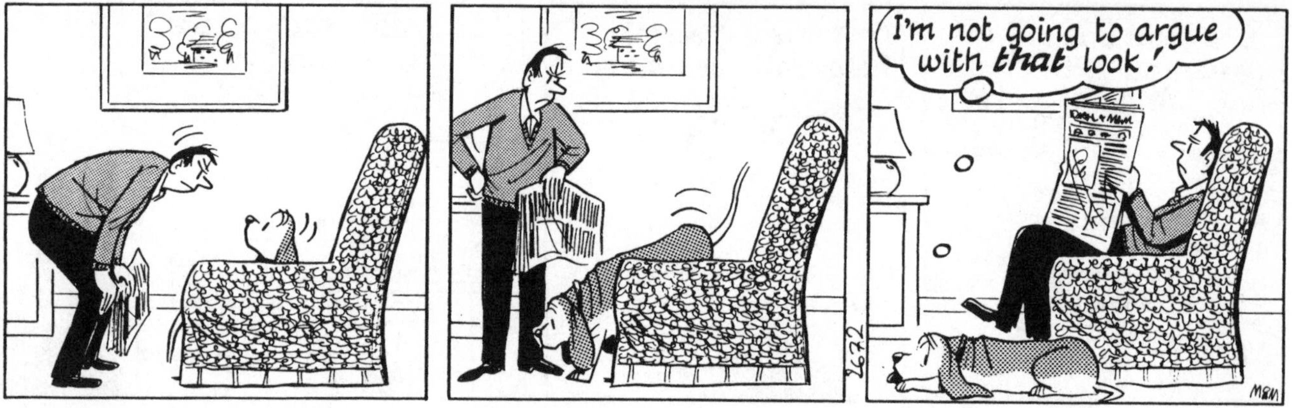
I'm not going to argue with *that* look!

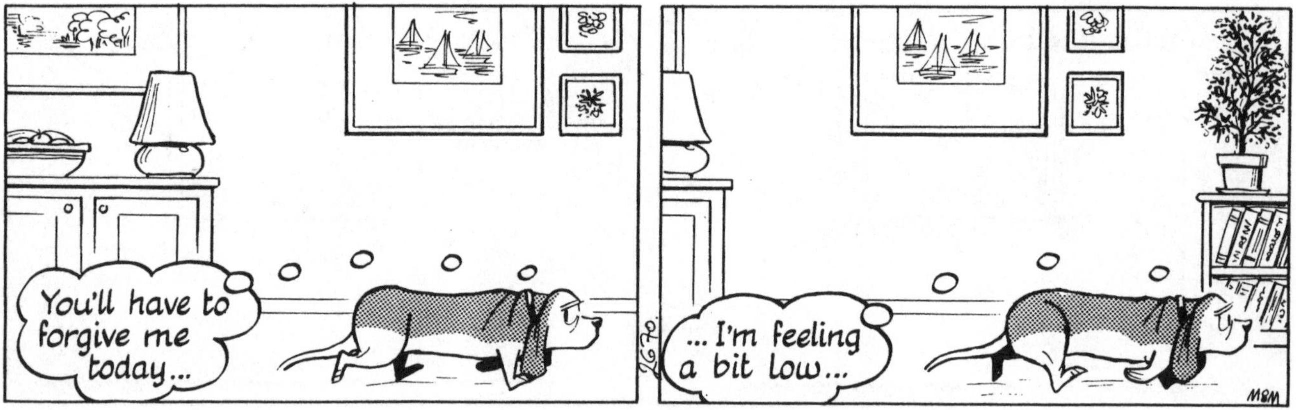
You'll have to forgive me today...
... I'm feeling a bit low...

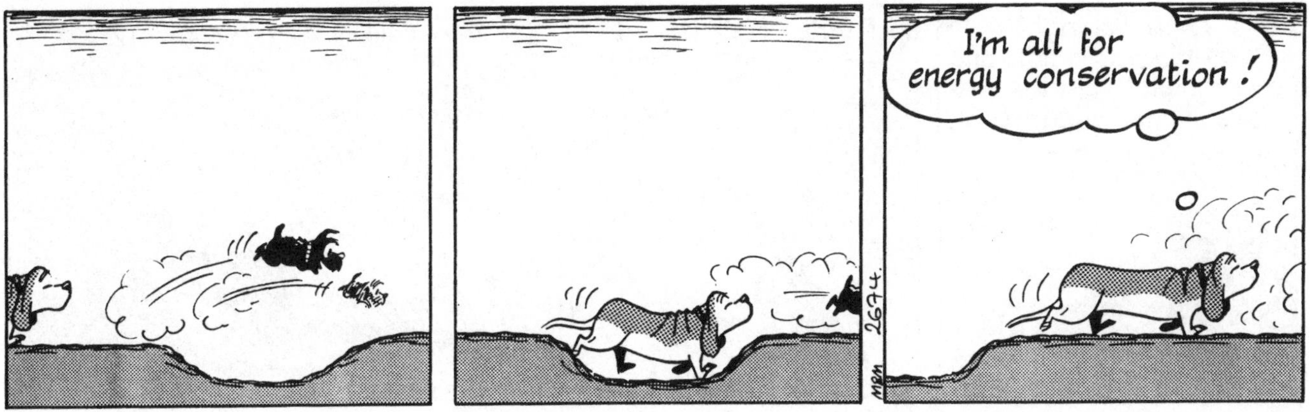
I'm all for energy conservation!

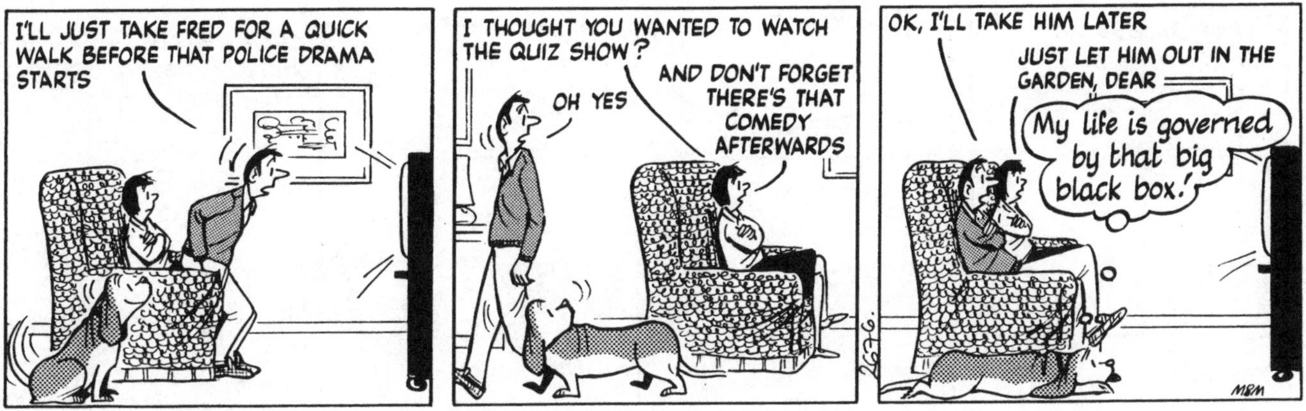
I'LL JUST TAKE FRED FOR A QUICK WALK BEFORE THAT POLICE DRAMA STARTS
I THOUGHT YOU WANTED TO WATCH THE QUIZ SHOW?
OH YES
AND DON'T FORGET THERE'S THAT COMEDY AFTERWARDS
OK, I'LL TAKE HIM LATER
JUST LET HIM OUT IN THE GARDEN, DEAR
My life is governed by that big black box!

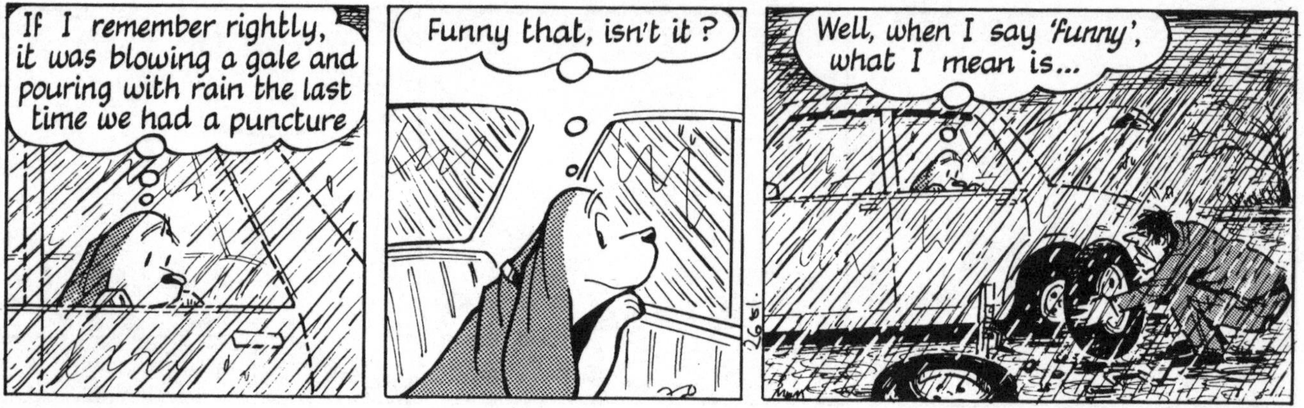
If I remember rightly, it was blowing a gale and pouring with rain the last time we had a puncture
Funny that, isn't it?
Well, when I say 'funny', what I mean is...

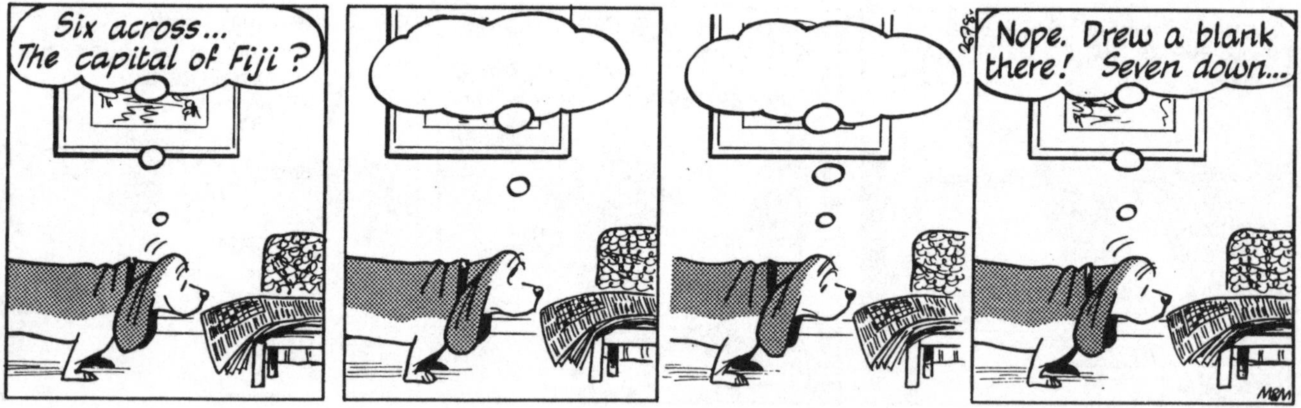
Six across... The capital of Fiji?
Nope. Drew a blank there! Seven down...

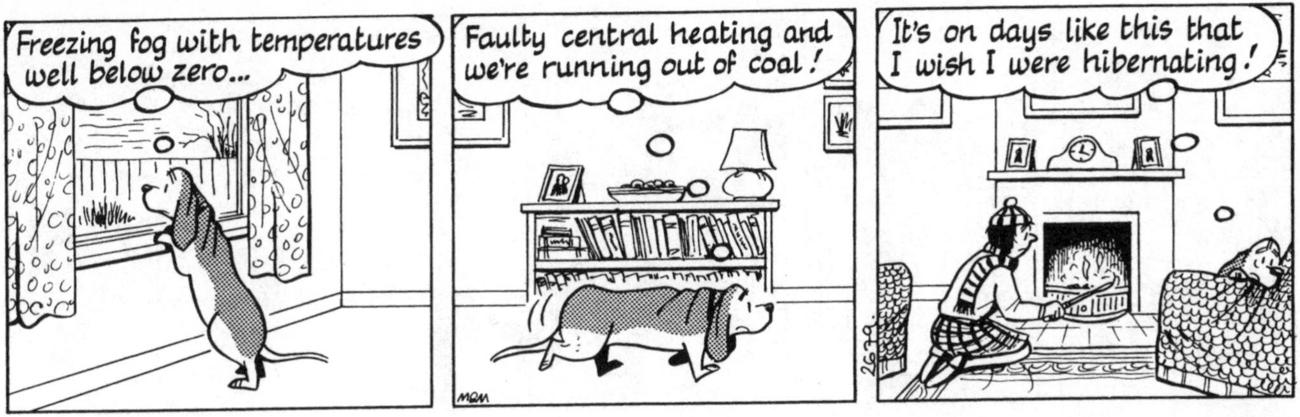
Freezing fog with temperatures well below zero...
Faulty central heating and we're running out of coal!
It's on days like this that I wish I were hibernating!

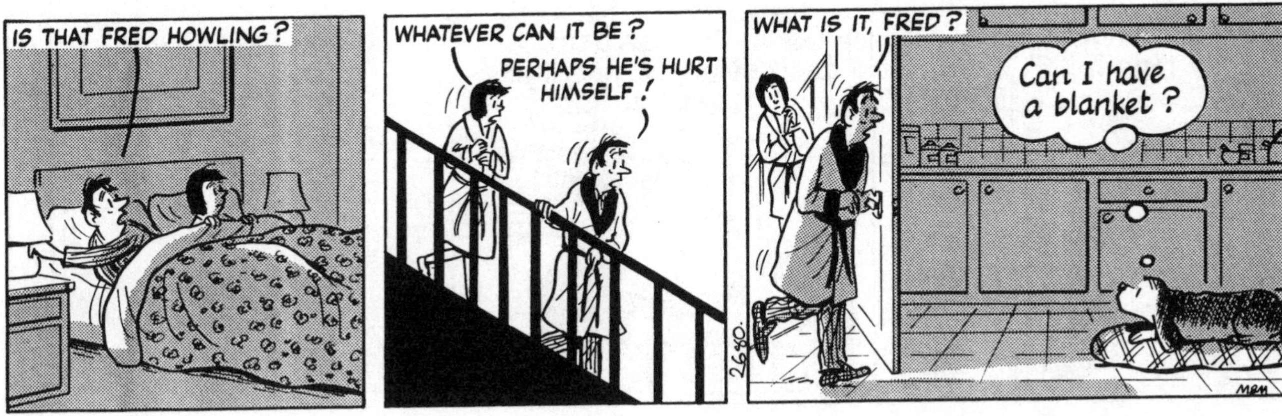
IS THAT FRED HOWLING?
WHATEVER CAN IT BE?
PERHAPS HE'S HURT HIMSELF!
WHAT IS IT, FRED?
Can I have a blanket?

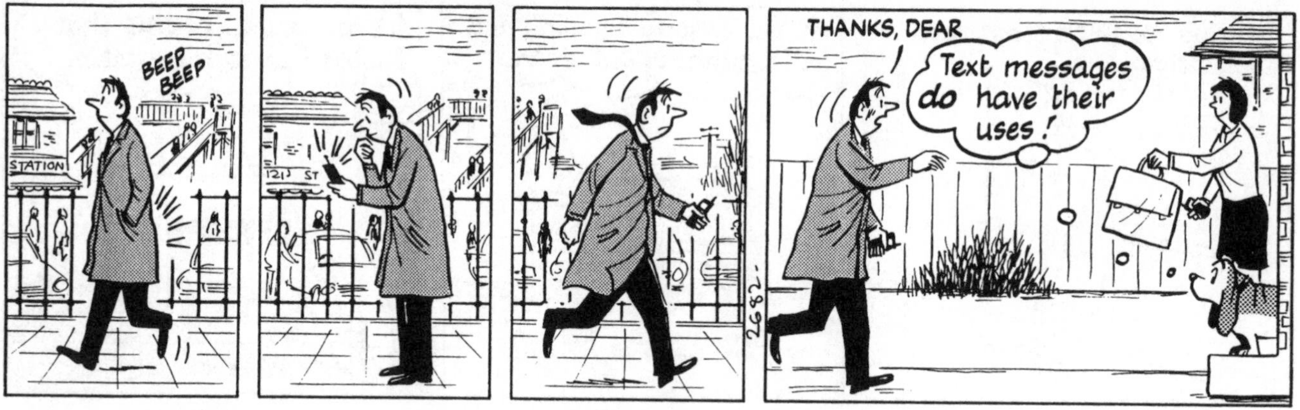
BEEP BEEP
STATION
THANKS, DEAR
Text messages do have their uses!
2682.

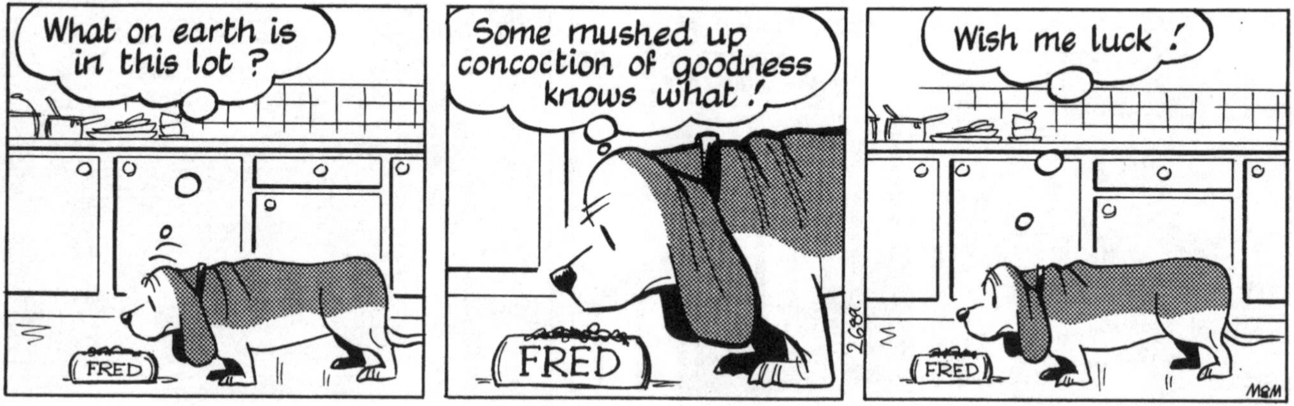
What on earth is in this lot?
FRED
Some mushed up concoction of goodness knows what!
FRED
2683.
Wish me luck!
FRED
MGM

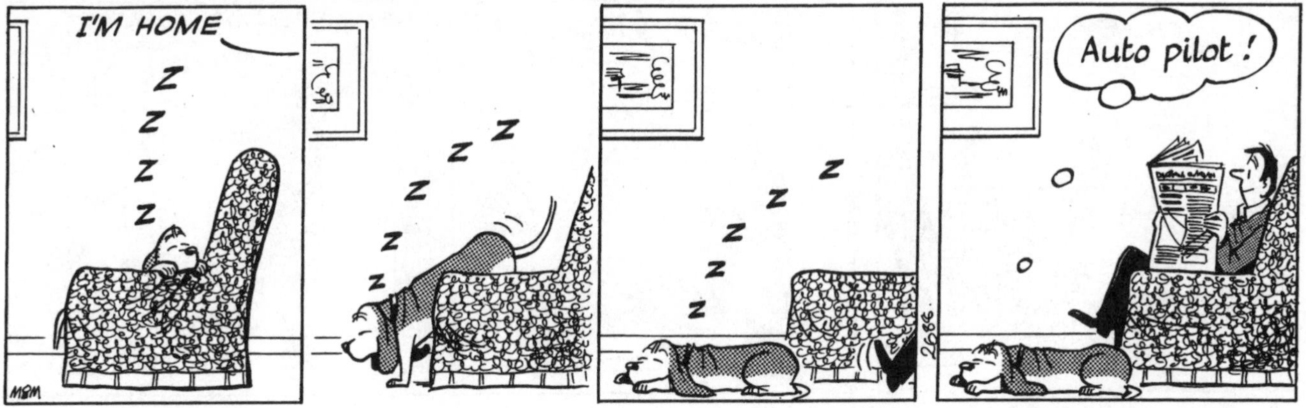
I'M HOME
Auto pilot !
MBM

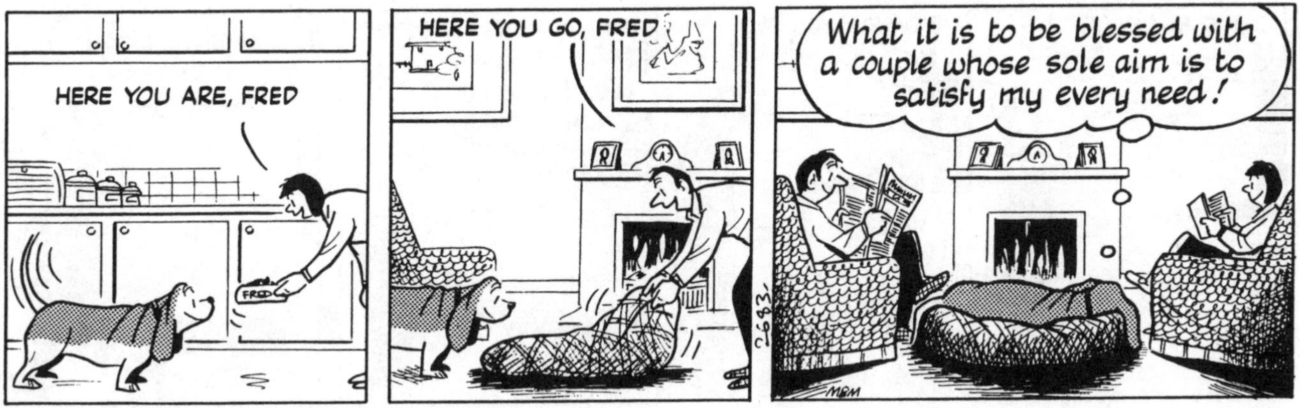
HERE YOU ARE, FRED
FRED
HERE YOU GO, FRED
What it is to be blessed with a couple whose sole aim is to satisfy my every need !
MBM

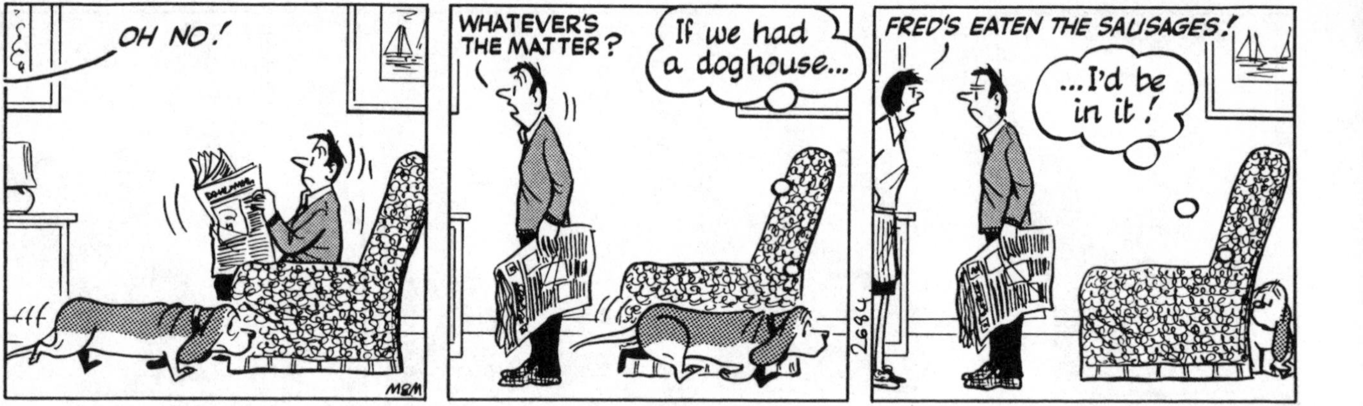
OH NO!
WHATEVER'S THE MATTER?
If we had a doghouse...
FRED'S EATEN THE SAUSAGES!
...I'd be in it!

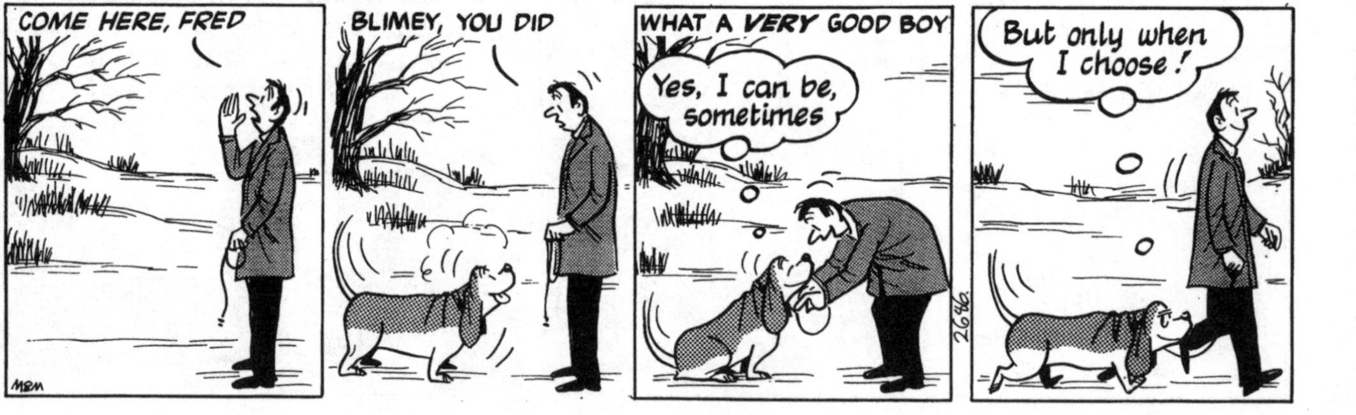
COME HERE, FRED
BLIMEY, YOU DID
WHAT A VERY GOOD BOY
Yes, I can be, sometimes
But only when I choose!

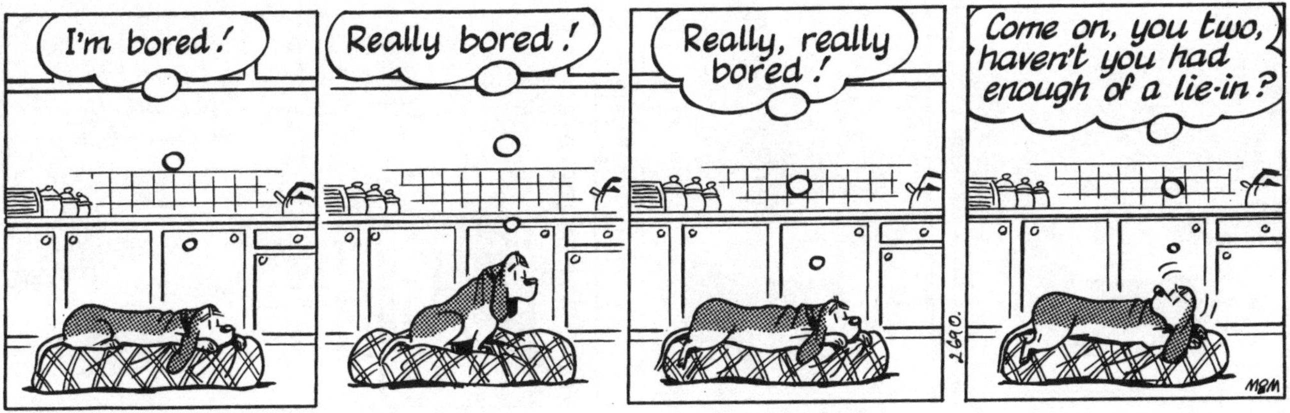
I'm bored!
Really bored!
Really, really bored!
Come on, you two, haven't you had enough of a lie-in?
2690.
MBM

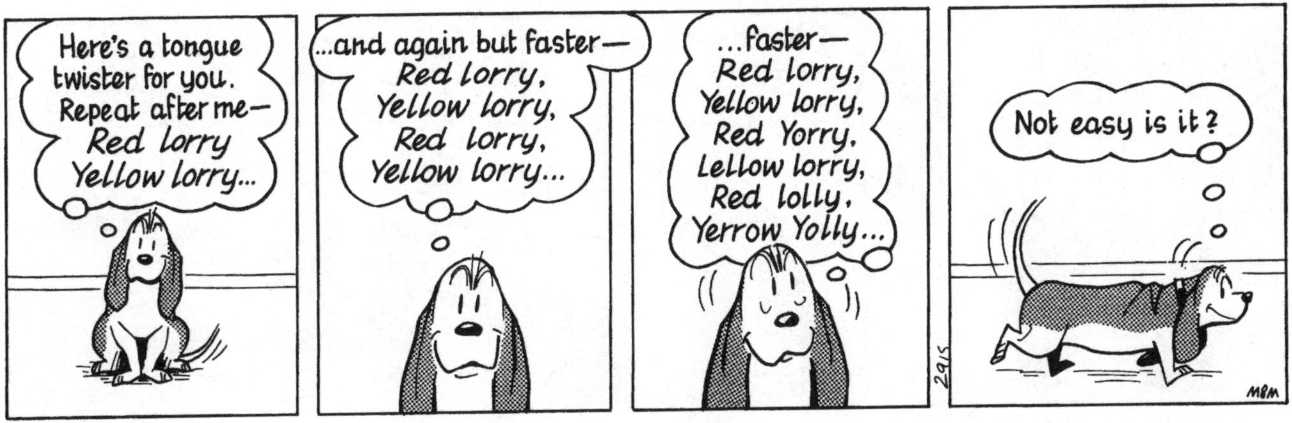
Here's a tongue twister for you. Repeat after me— Red lorry Yellow lorry...
...and again but faster— Red lorry, Yellow lorry, Red lorry, Yellow lorry...
...faster— Red lorry, Yellow lorry, Red Yorry, Lellow lorry, Red lolly, Yerrow Yolly...
Not easy is it?
2915
MBM

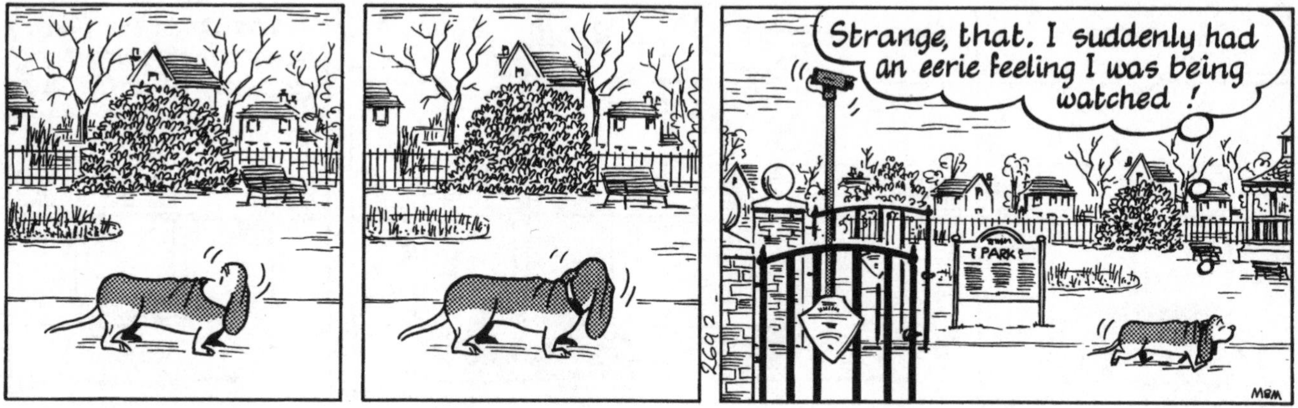
PARK
Strange, that. I suddenly had an eerie feeling I was being watched !

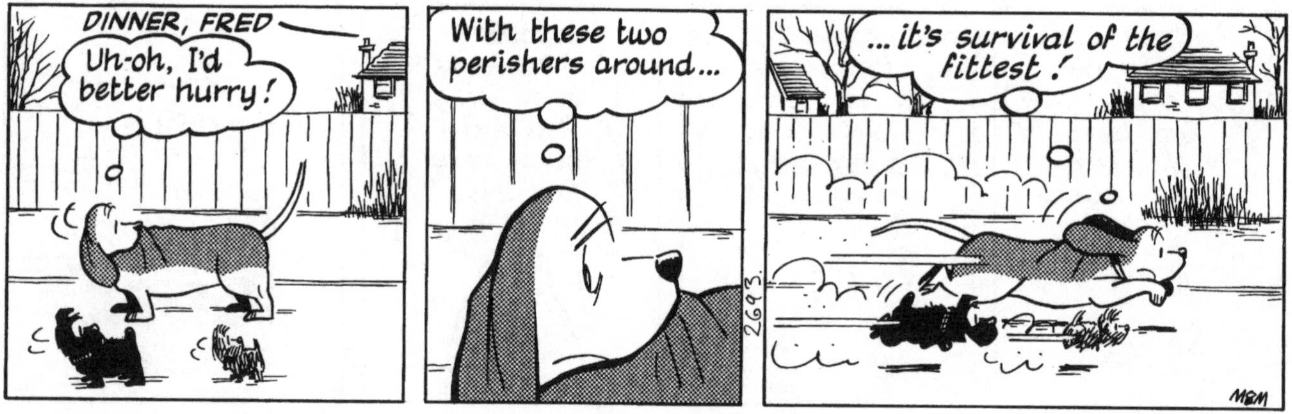
DINNER, FRED
Uh-oh, I'd better hurry !
With these two perishers around...
... it's survival of the fittest !

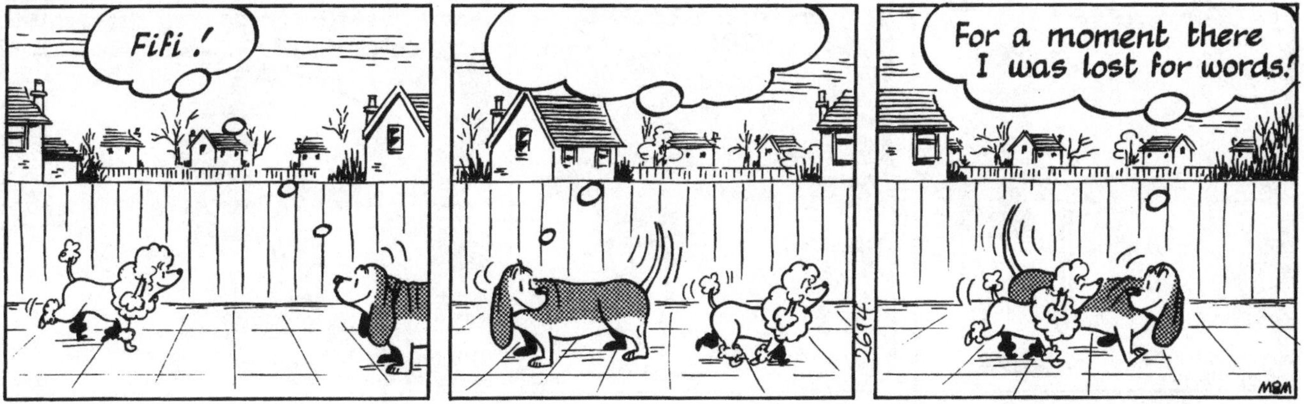
Fifi !
For a moment there I was lost for words!

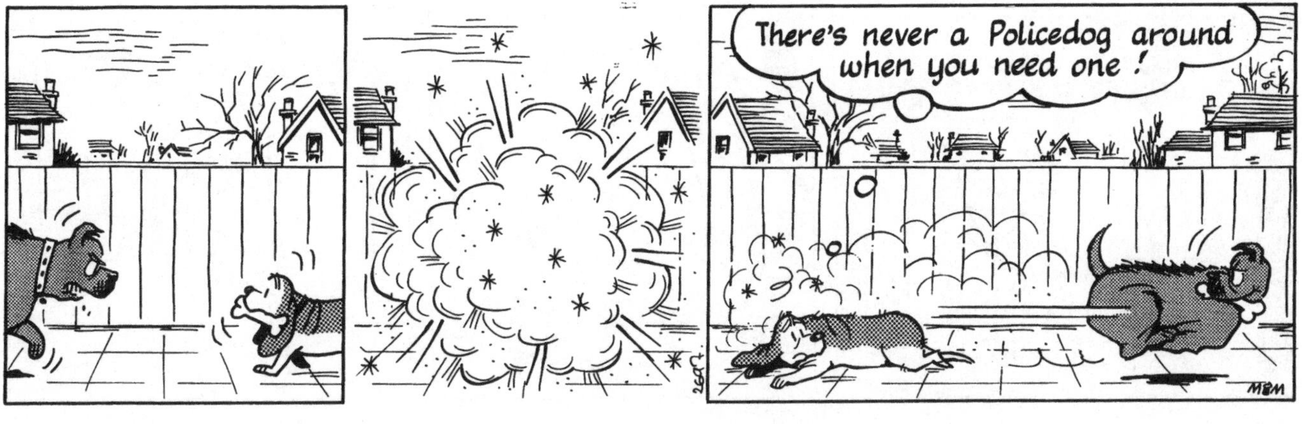
There's never a Policedog around when you need one !

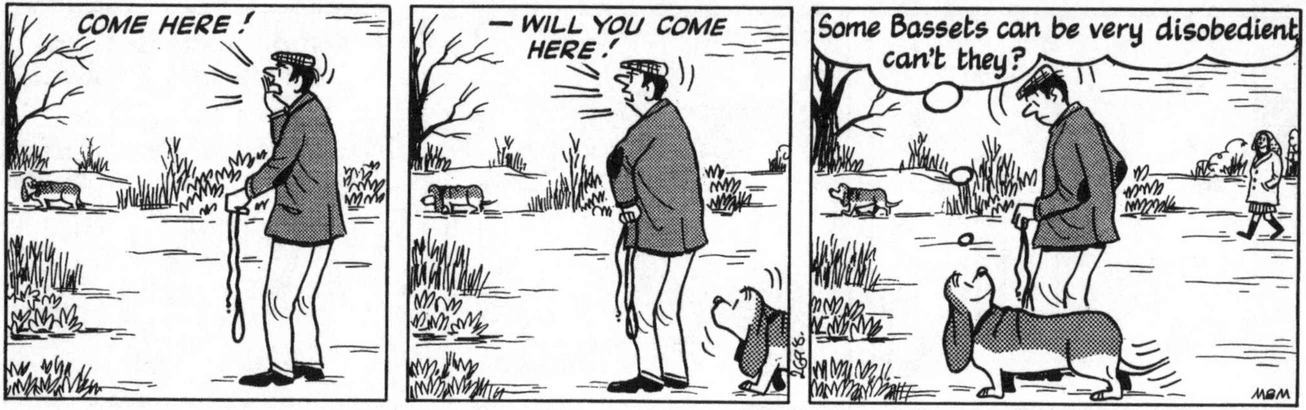
COME HERE !
— WILL YOU COME HERE !
Some Bassets can be very disobedient can't they?

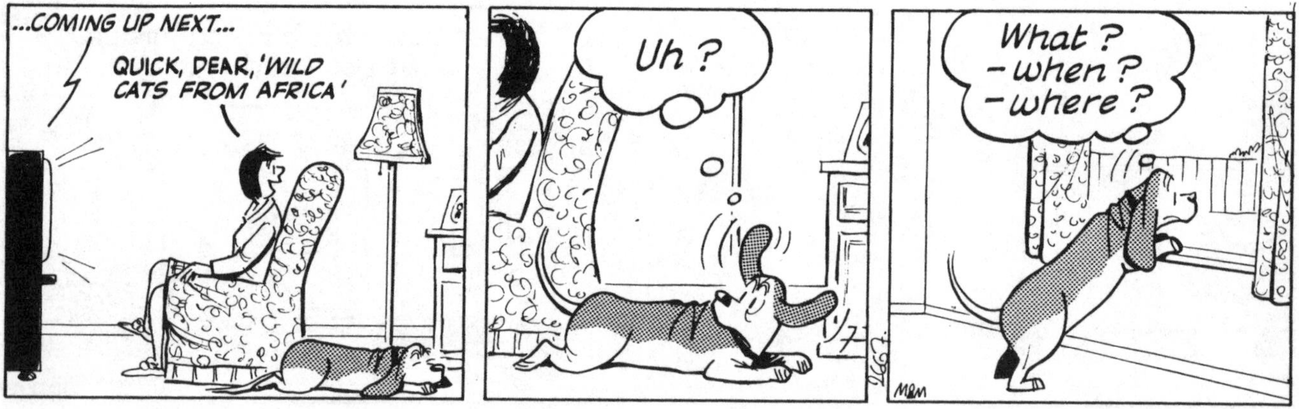
...COMING UP NEXT...
QUICK, DEAR, 'WILD CATS FROM AFRICA'
Uh ?
What ? -when ? -where ?

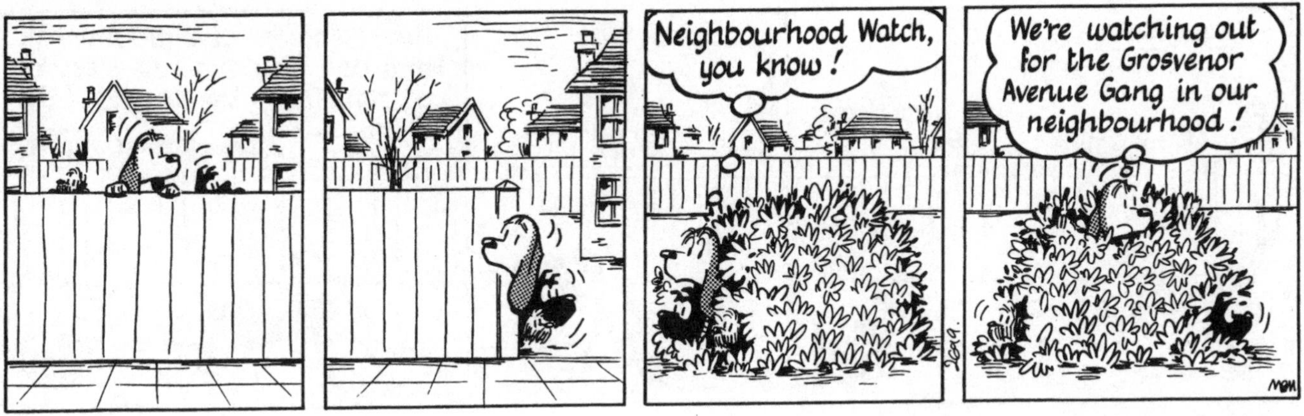
Neighbourhood Watch, you know!
We're watching out for the Grosvenor Avenue Gang in our neighbourhood!

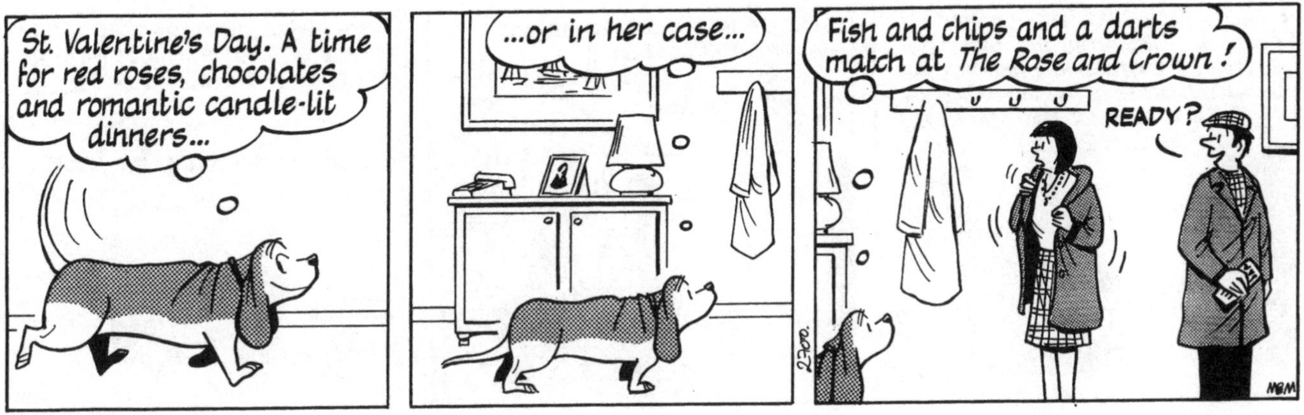
St. Valentine's Day. A time for red roses, chocolates and romantic candle-lit dinners...
...or in her case...
Fish and chips and a darts match at The Rose and Crown!
READY?

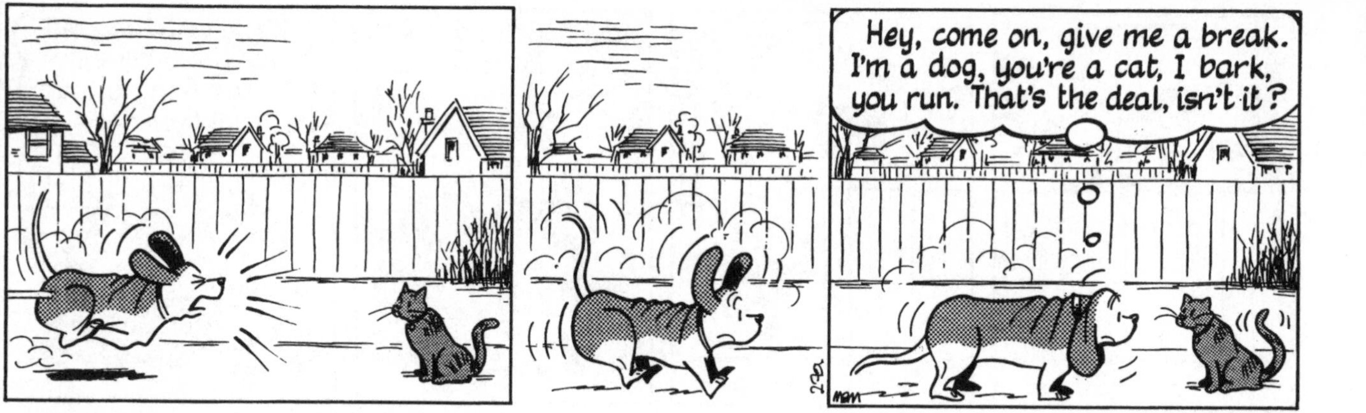
Hey, come on, give me a break. I'm a dog, you're a cat, I bark, you run. That's the deal, isn't it?

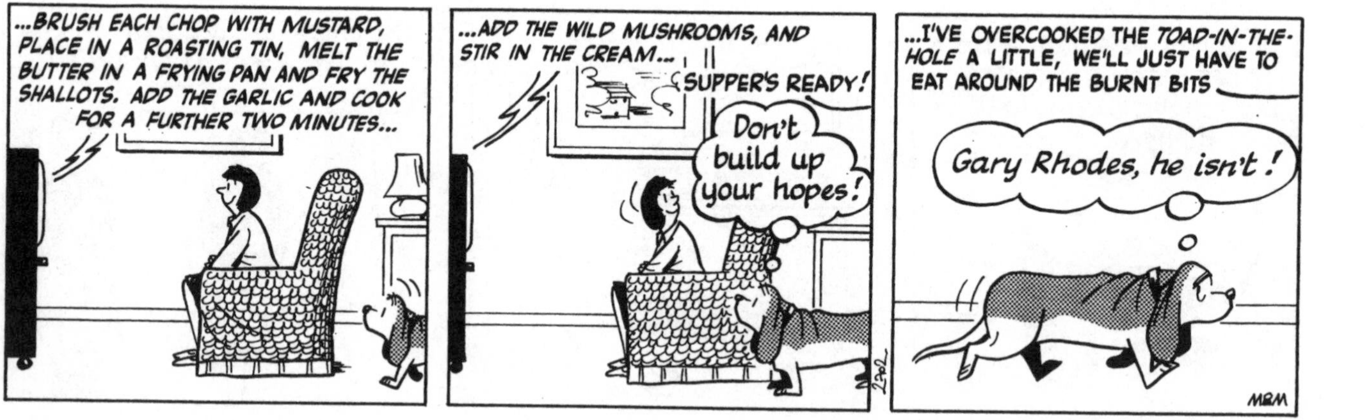
...BRUSH EACH CHOP WITH MUSTARD, PLACE IN A ROASTING TIN, MELT THE BUTTER IN A FRYING PAN AND FRY THE SHALLOTS. ADD THE GARLIC AND COOK FOR A FURTHER TWO MINUTES...
...ADD THE WILD MUSHROOMS, AND STIR IN THE CREAM...
SUPPER'S READY!
Don't build up your hopes!
...I'VE OVERCOOKED THE TOAD-IN-THE-HOLE A LITTLE, WE'LL JUST HAVE TO EAT AROUND THE BURNT BITS
Gary Rhodes, he isn't!
MBM

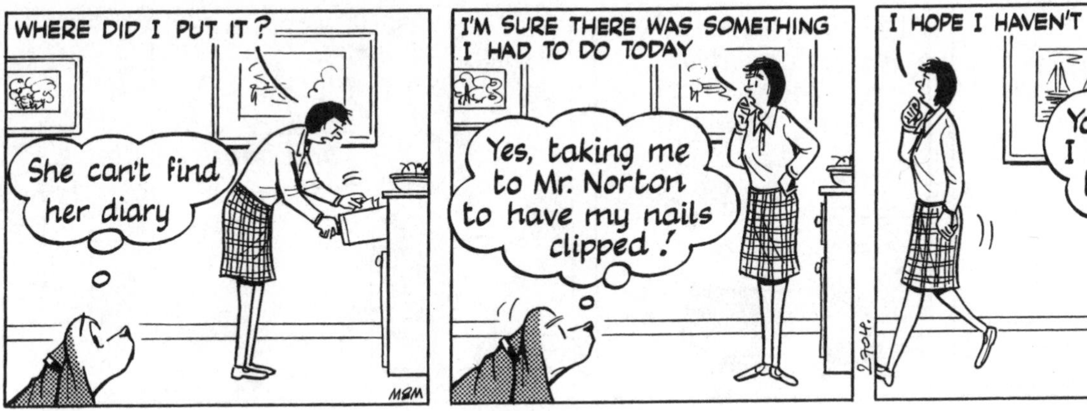
WHERE DID I PUT IT?
She can't find her diary
MBM
I'M SURE THERE WAS SOMETHING I HAD TO DO TODAY
Yes, taking me to Mr. Norton to have my nails clipped!
2704.
I HOPE I HAVEN'T LOST IT
You have, dear. I buried it in the garden!

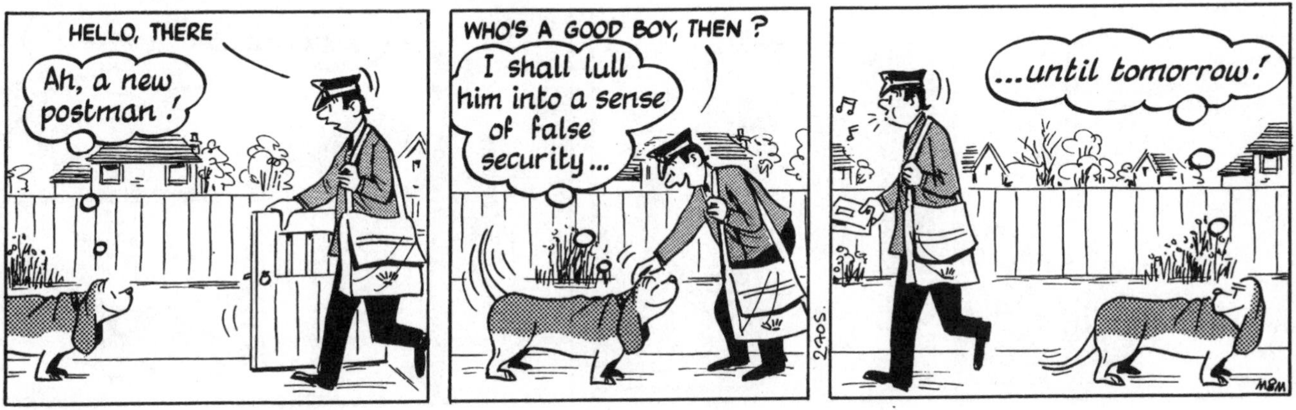
HELLO, THERE
Ah, a new postman!
WHO'S A GOOD BOY, THEN?
I shall lull him into a sense of false security...
2705.
...until tomorrow!
MBM

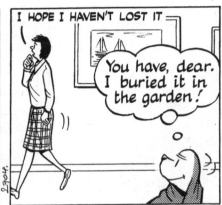

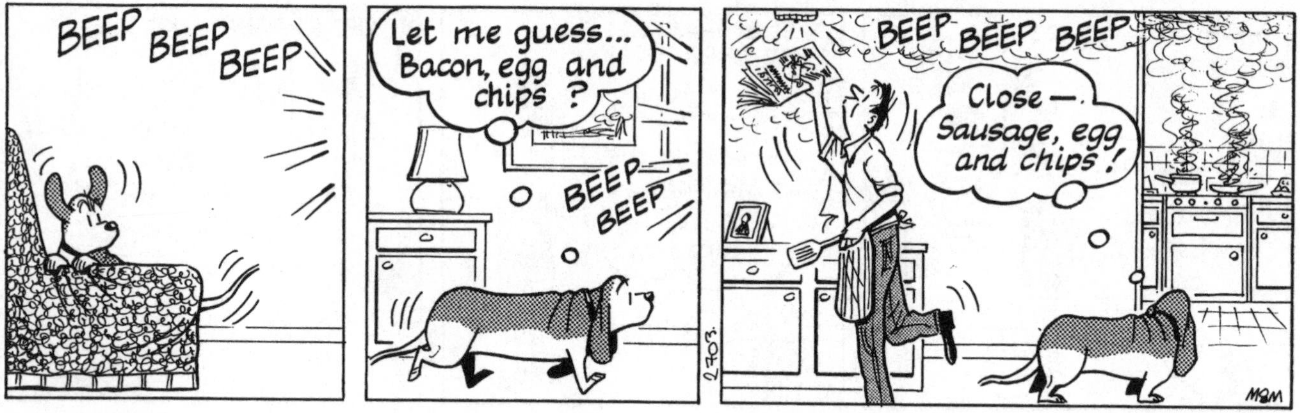
BEEP BEEP BEEP
Let me guess... Bacon, egg and chips ?
BEEP BEEP
2703.
BEEP BEEP BEEP
Close — Sausage, egg and chips !
MGM

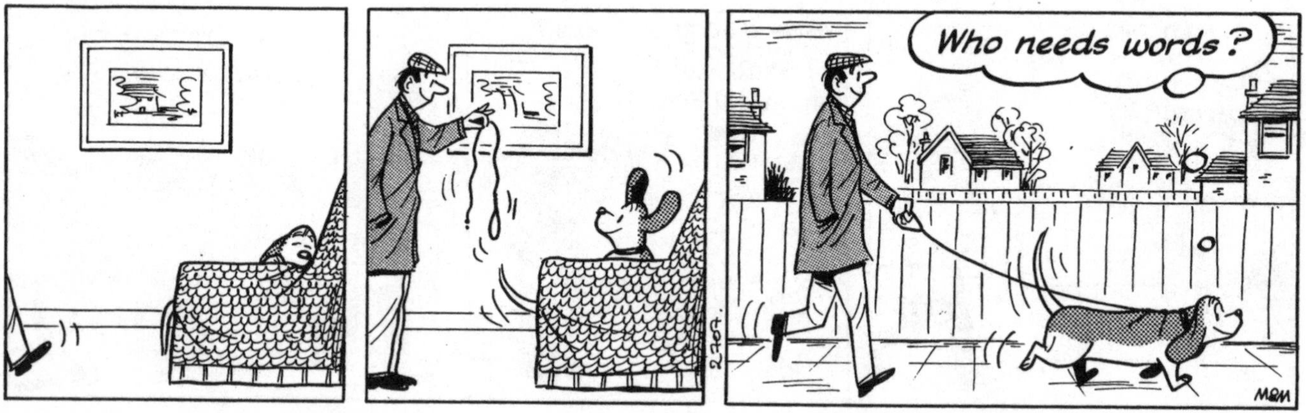
2707.
Who needs words ?
MGM

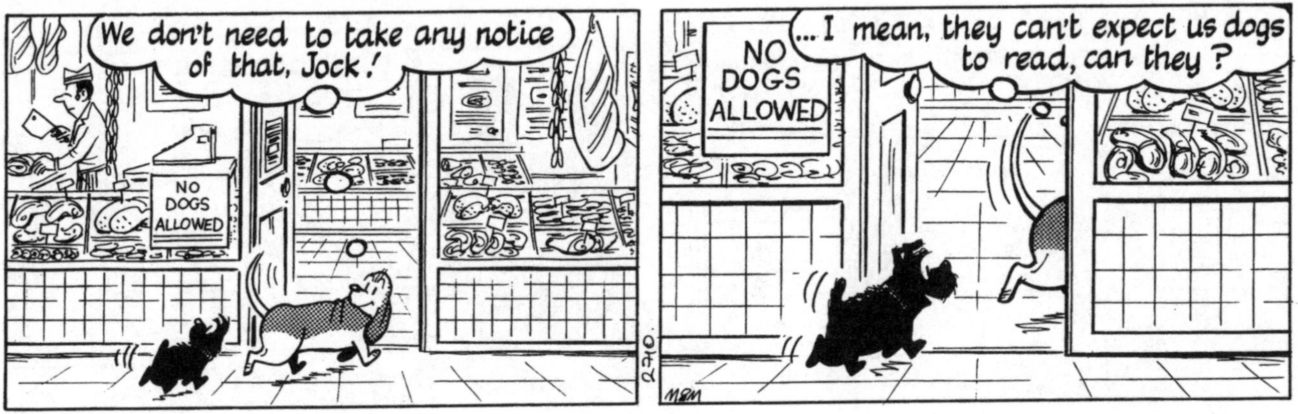
We don't need to take any notice of that, Jock!
NO DOGS ALLOWED
NO DOGS ALLOWED
... I mean, they can't expect us dogs to read, can they?

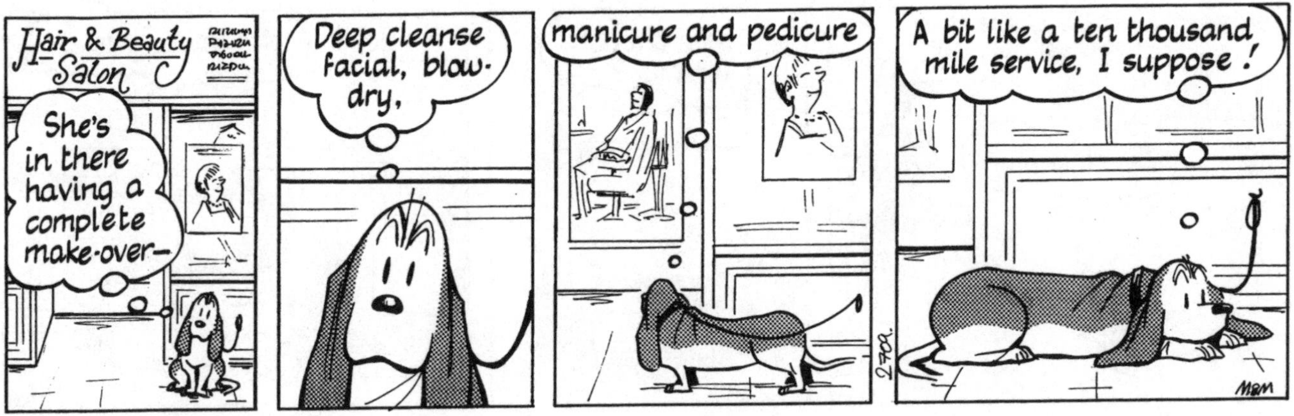
Hair & Beauty Salon
She's in there having a complete make-over—
Deep cleanse facial, blow-dry,
manicure and pedicure
A bit like a ten thousand mile service, I suppose!

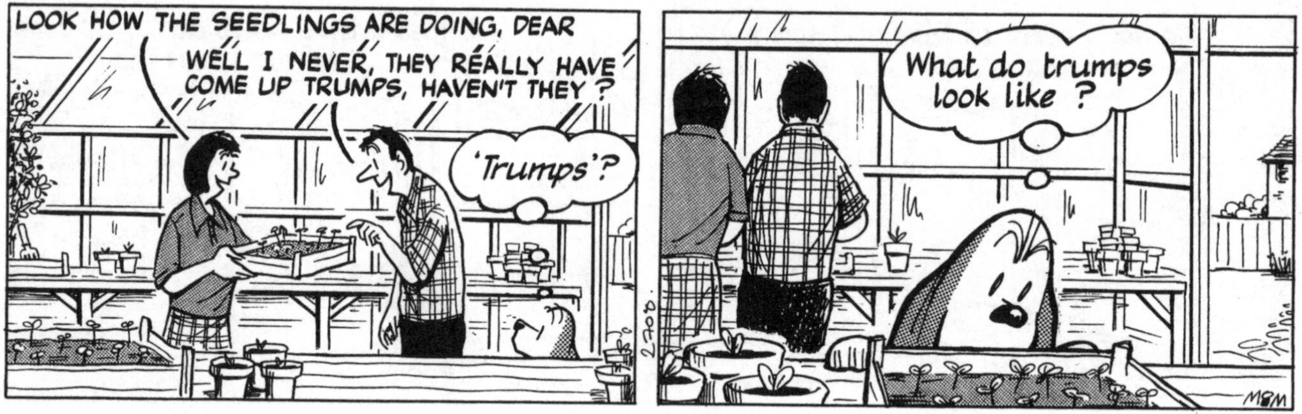
LOOK HOW THE SEEDLINGS ARE DOING, DEAR
WELL I NEVER, THEY REALLY HAVE COME UP TRUMPS, HAVEN'T THEY ?
'Trumps'?
What do trumps look like ?

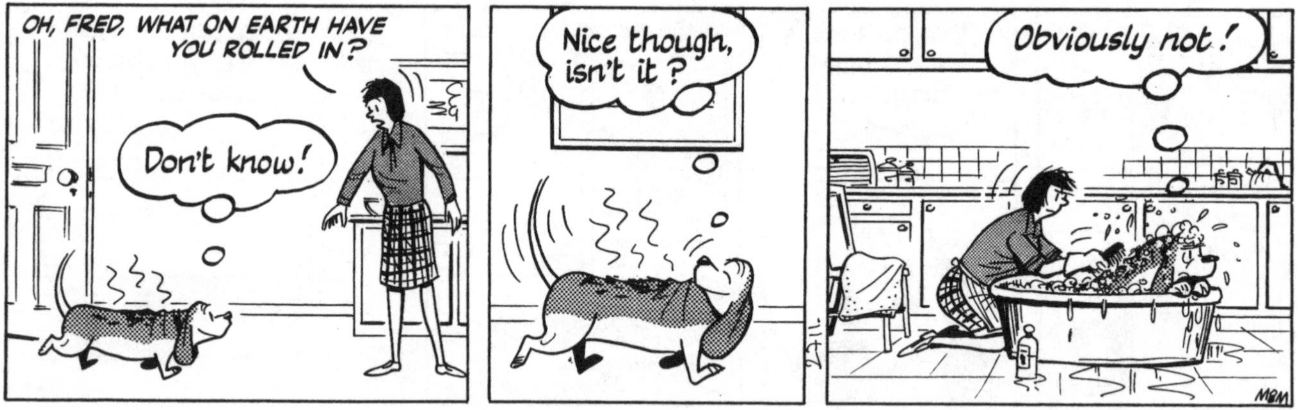
OH, FRED, WHAT ON EARTH HAVE YOU ROLLED IN?
Don't know!
Nice though, isn't it ?
Obviously not!

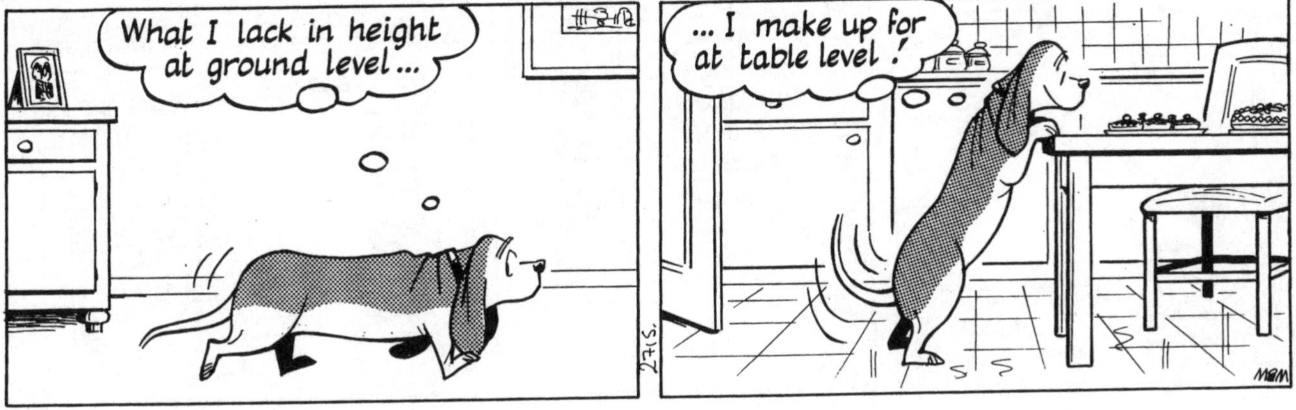
What I lack in height at ground level...
... I make up for at table level!

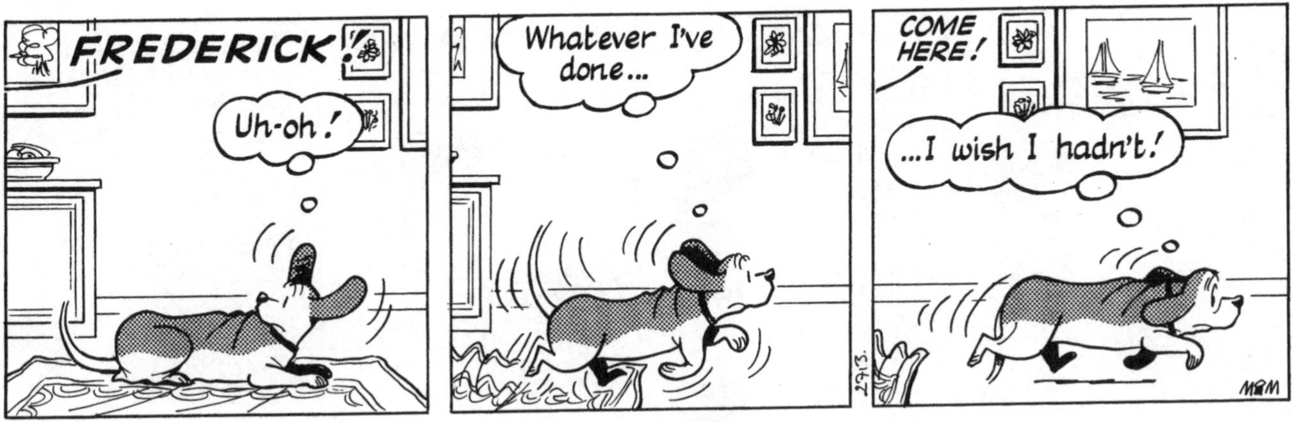
FREDERICK!
Uh-oh!
Whatever I've done...
COME HERE!
...I wish I hadn't!

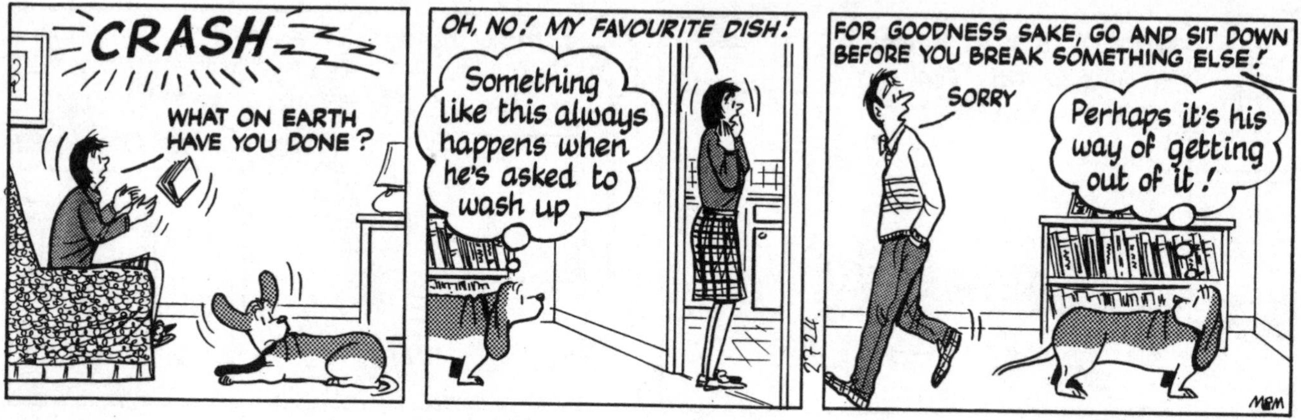
CRASH
WHAT ON EARTH HAVE YOU DONE?
OH, NO! MY FAVOURITE DISH!
Something like this always happens when he's asked to wash up
FOR GOODNESS SAKE, GO AND SIT DOWN BEFORE YOU BREAK SOMETHING ELSE!
SORRY
Perhaps it's his way of getting out of it!

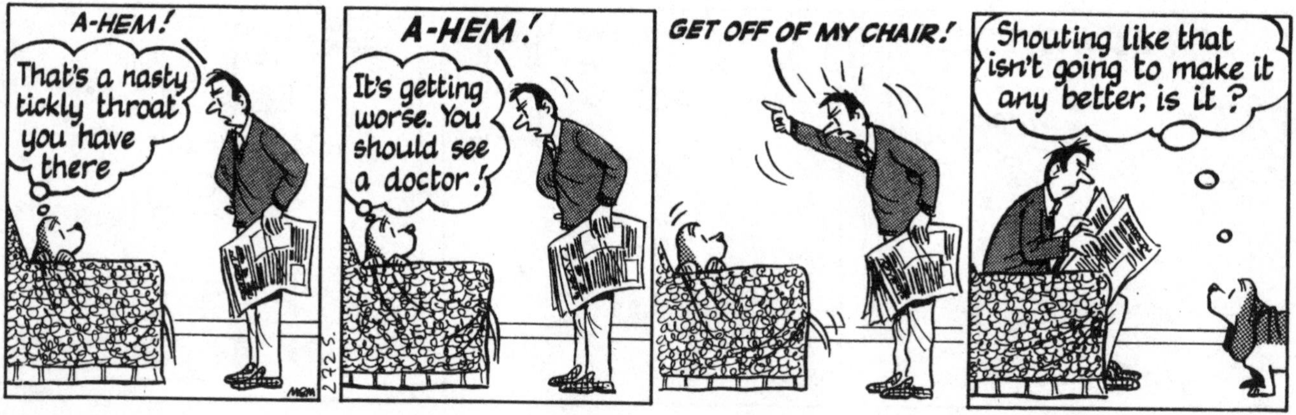
A-HEM!
That's a nasty tickly throat you have there
A-HEM!
It's getting worse. You should see a doctor!
GET OFF OF MY CHAIR!
Shouting like that isn't going to make it any better, is it?

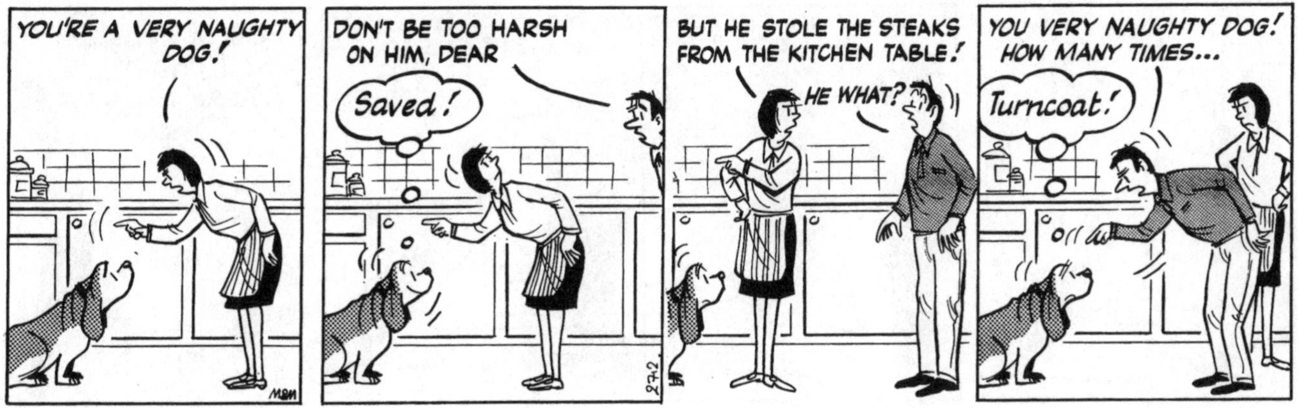
YOU'RE A VERY NAUGHTY DOG!
MSM
DON'T BE TOO HARSH ON HIM, DEAR
Saved!
BUT HE STOLE THE STEAKS FROM THE KITCHEN TABLE!
HE WHAT?
YOU VERY NAUGHTY DOG! HOW MANY TIMES...
Turncoat!

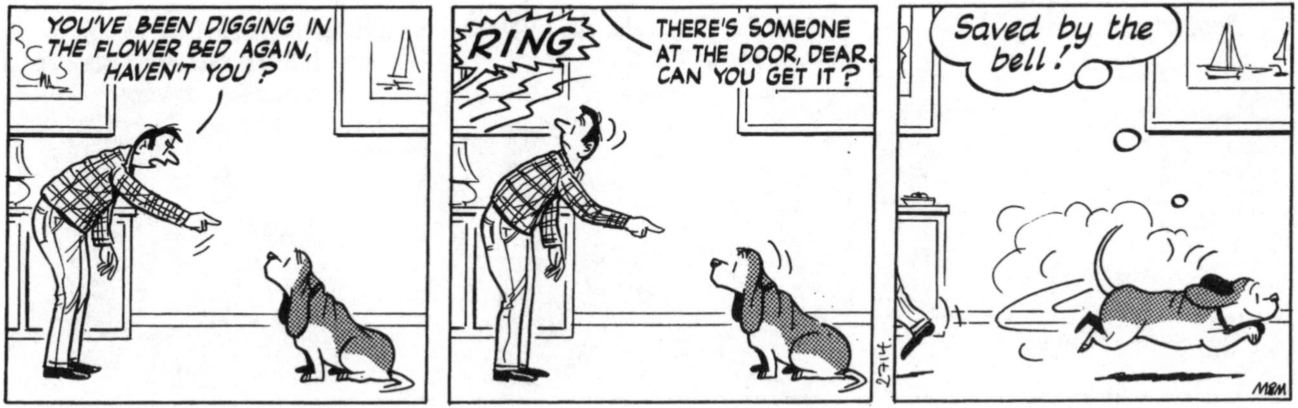
YOU'VE BEEN DIGGING IN THE FLOWER BED AGAIN, HAVEN'T YOU?
RING
THERE'S SOMEONE AT THE DOOR, DEAR. CAN YOU GET IT?
Saved by the bell!
MSM

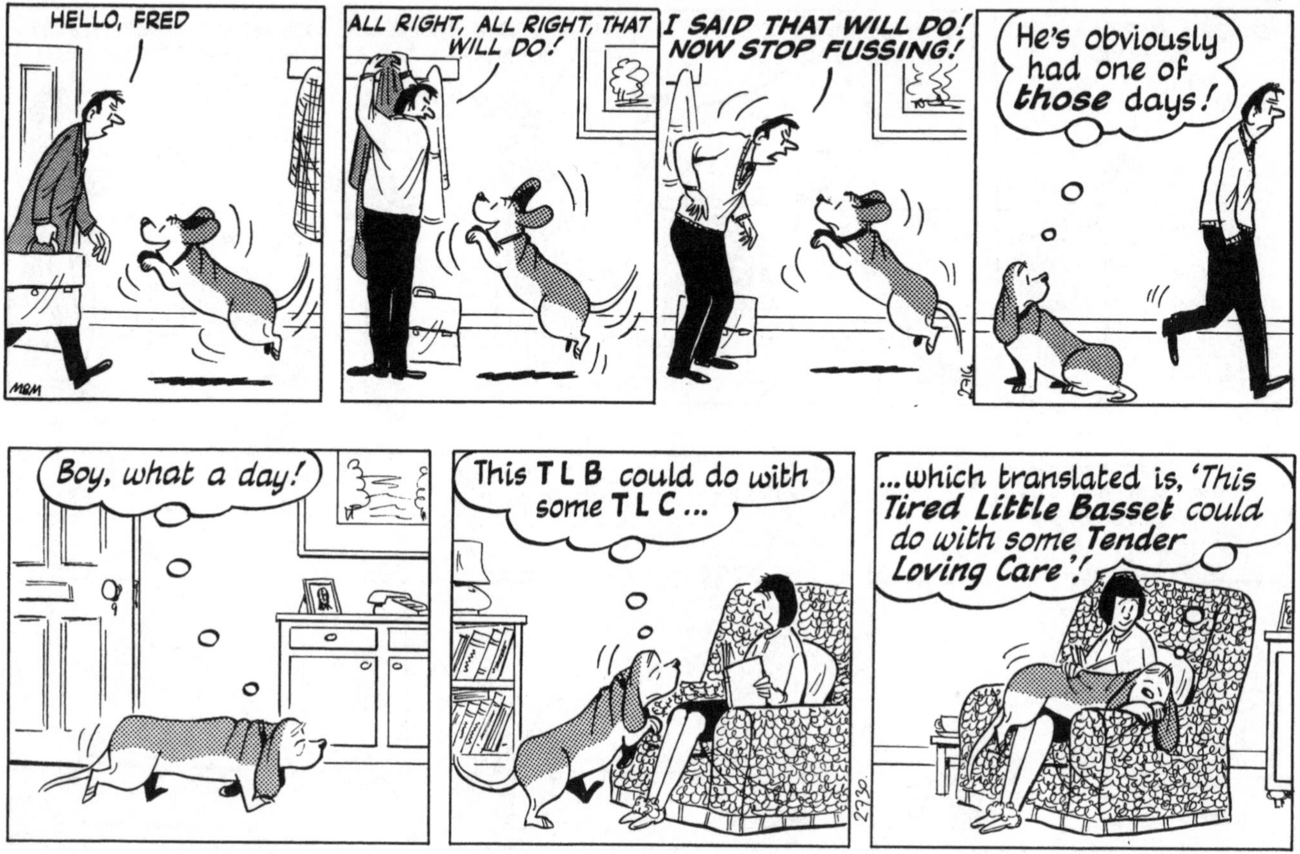
HELLO, FRED
ALL RIGHT, ALL RIGHT, THAT WILL DO!
I SAID THAT WILL DO! NOW STOP FUSSING!
He's obviously had one of *those* days!
Boy, what a day!
This **T L B** could do with some **T L C** ...
...which translated is, '*This **Tired Little Basset** could do with some **Tender Loving Care***'!

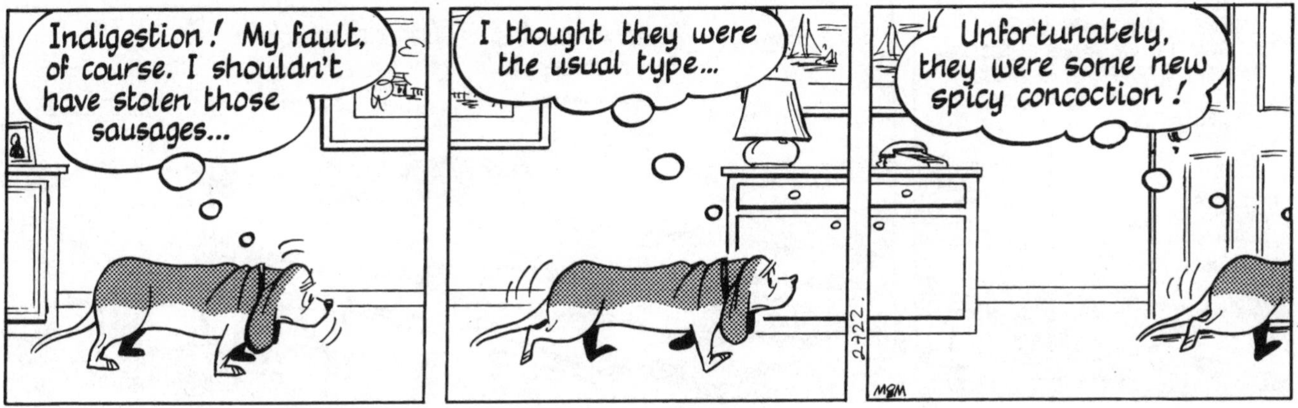
Indigestion! My fault, of course. I shouldn't have stolen those sausages...
I thought they were the usual type...
2722.
Unfortunately, they were some new spicy concoction!
M&M

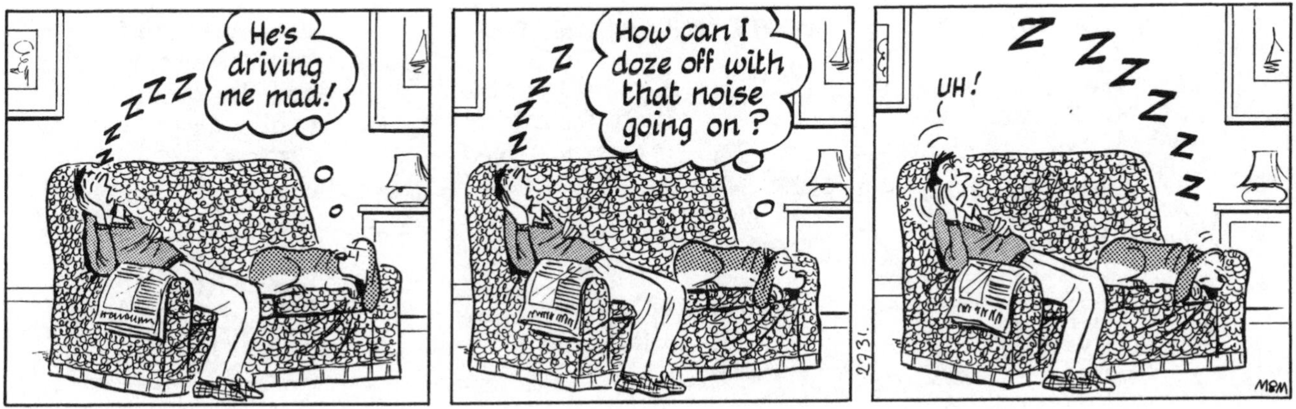
ZZZZZZ
He's driving me mad!
ZZZZZ
How can I doze off with that noise going on?
2731.
UH!
ZZZZZZ
M&M

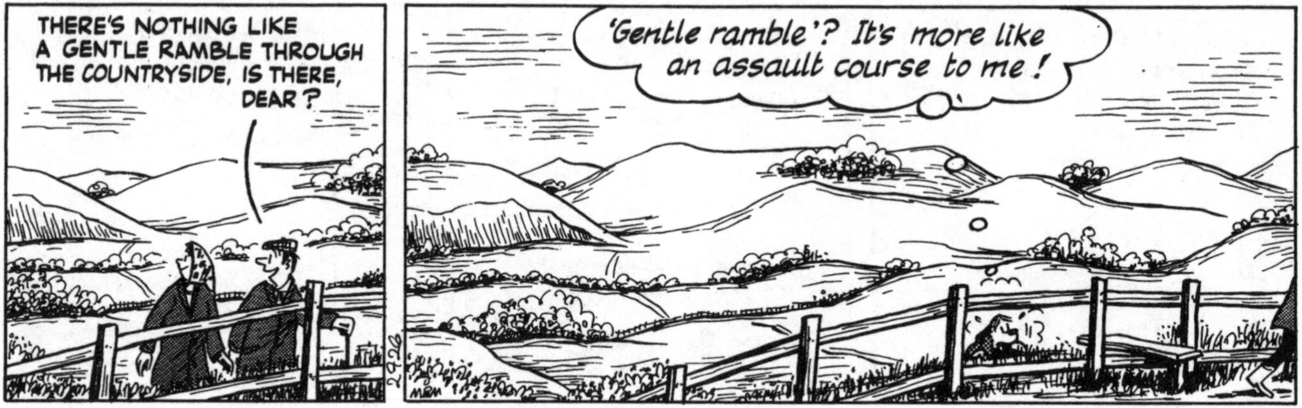
THERE'S NOTHING LIKE A GENTLE RAMBLE THROUGH THE COUNTRYSIDE, IS THERE, DEAR?
'Gentle ramble'? It's more like an assault course to me!
2926
MBM

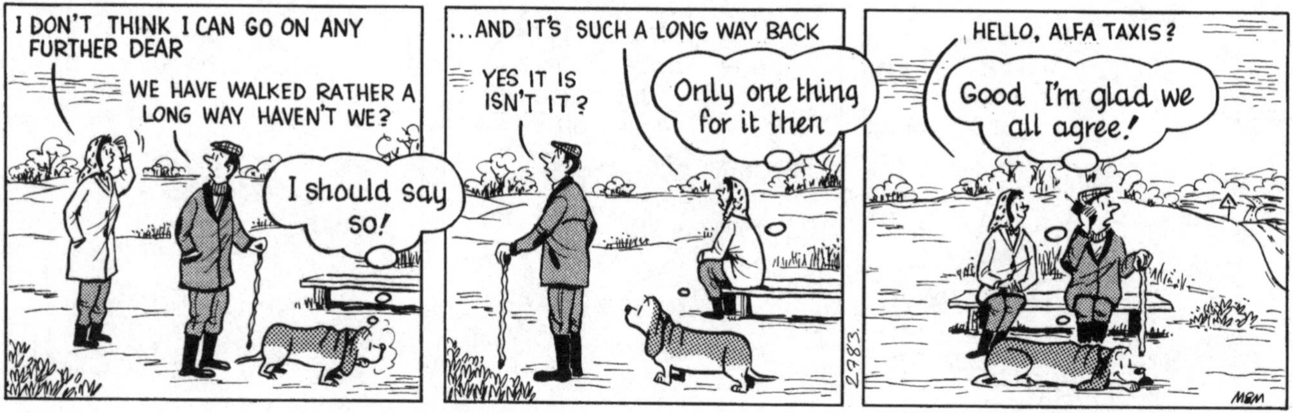
I DON'T THINK I CAN GO ON ANY FURTHER DEAR
WE HAVE WALKED RATHER A LONG WAY HAVEN'T WE?
I should say so!
...AND IT'S SUCH A LONG WAY BACK
YES IT IS ISN'T IT?
Only one thing for it then
2783
HELLO, ALFA TAXIS?
Good I'm glad we all agree!
MBM

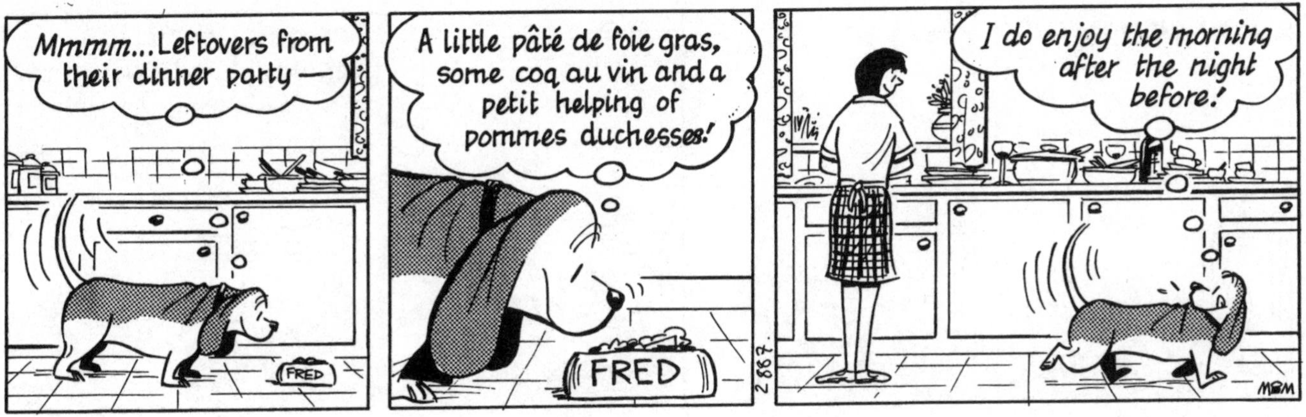
Mmmm...Leftovers from their dinner party —
A little pâté de foie gras, some coq au vin and a petit helping of pommes duchesses!
FRED
2887.
I do enjoy the morning after the night before!

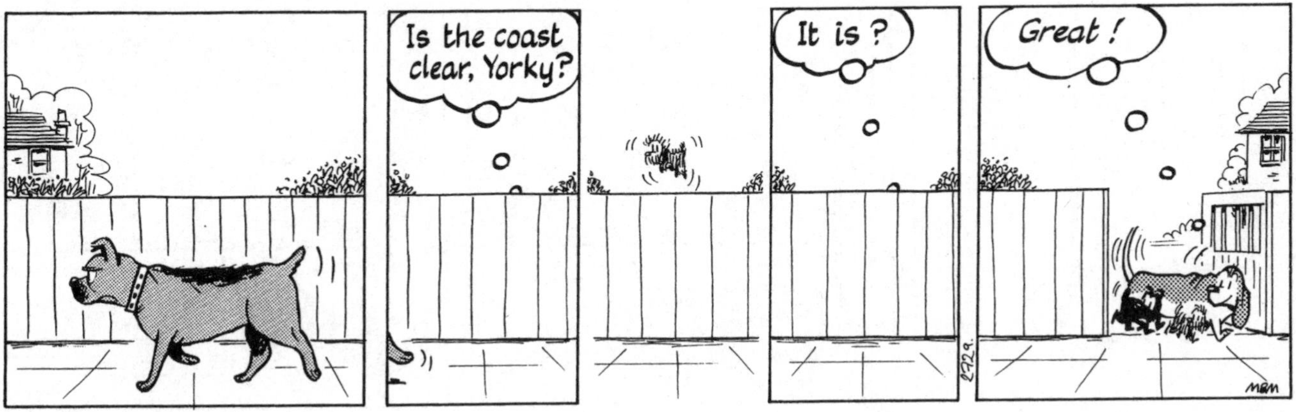
Is the coast clear, Yorky?
It is?
Great!
2929.

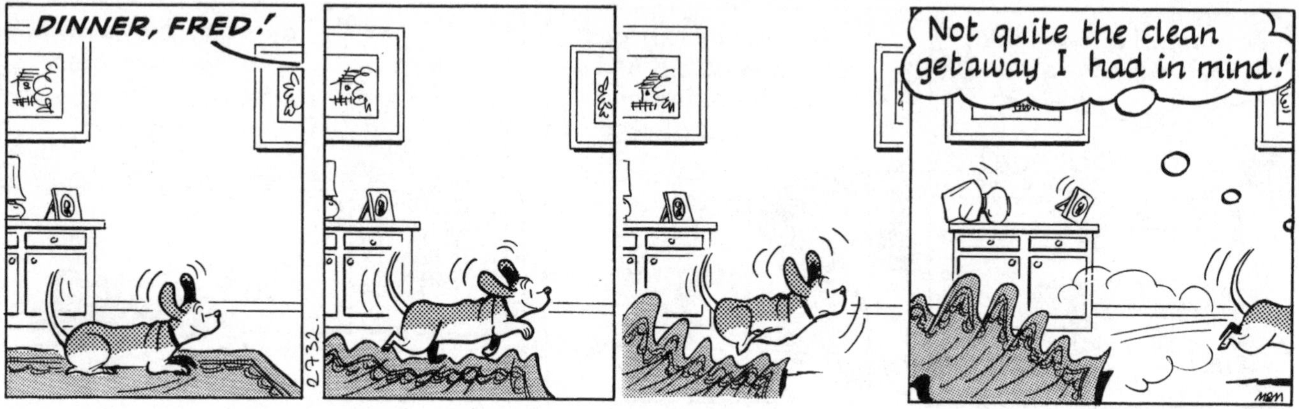
DINNER, FRED!
Not quite the clean getaway I had in mind!

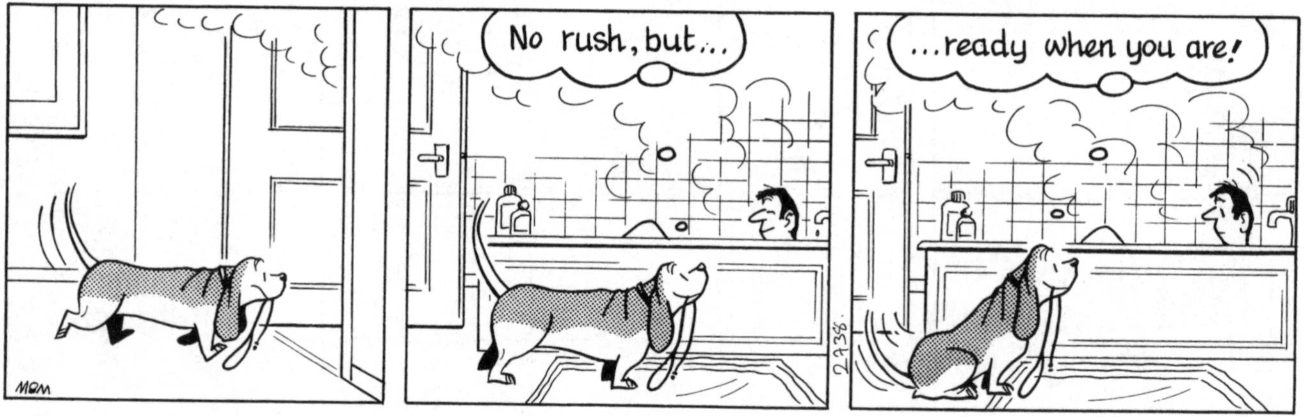
No rush, but...
...ready when you are!

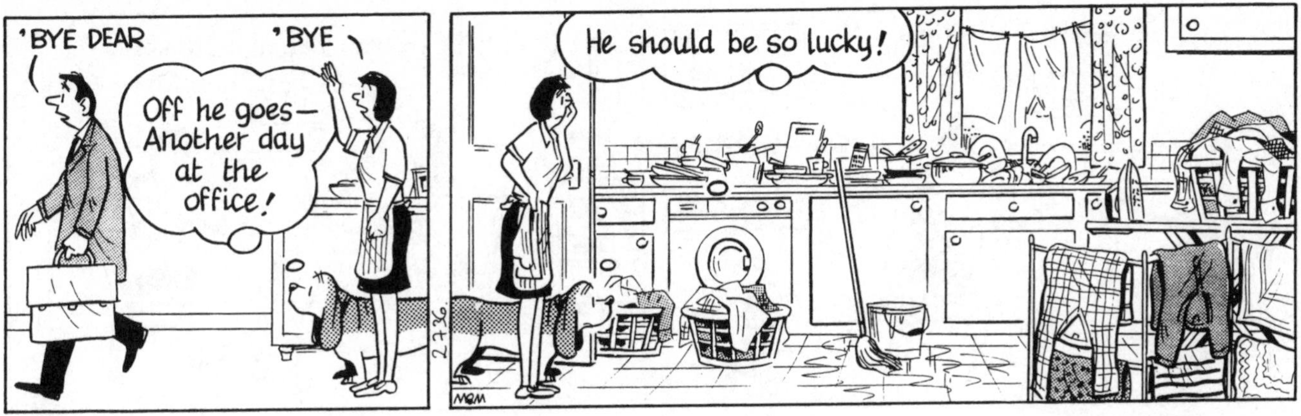
'BYE DEAR
'BYE
Off he goes— Another day at the office!
He should be so lucky!
2736.
M&M

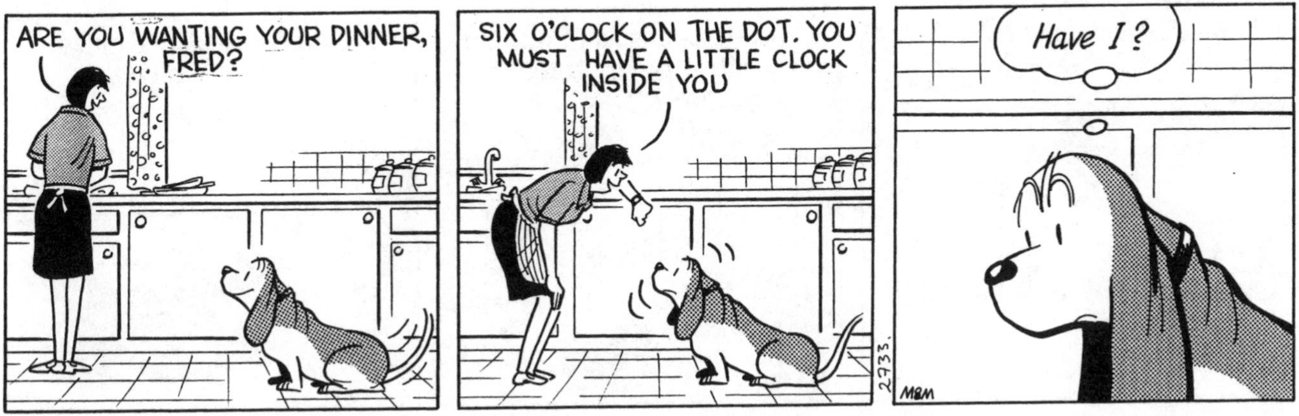
ARE YOU WANTING YOUR DINNER, FRED?
SIX O'CLOCK ON THE DOT. YOU MUST HAVE A LITTLE CLOCK INSIDE YOU
Have I?
2733.
M&M

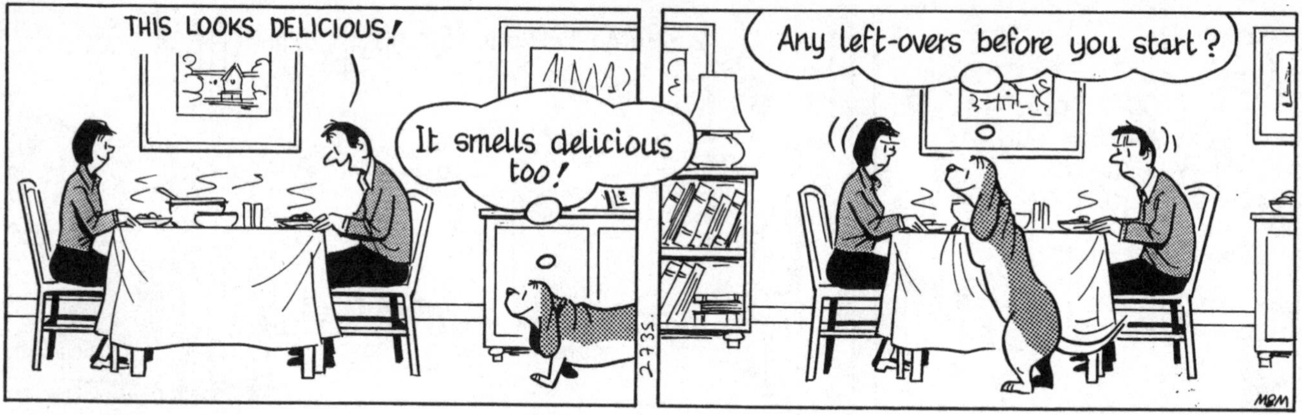
THIS LOOKS DELICIOUS!
It smells delicious too!
Any left-overs before you start?

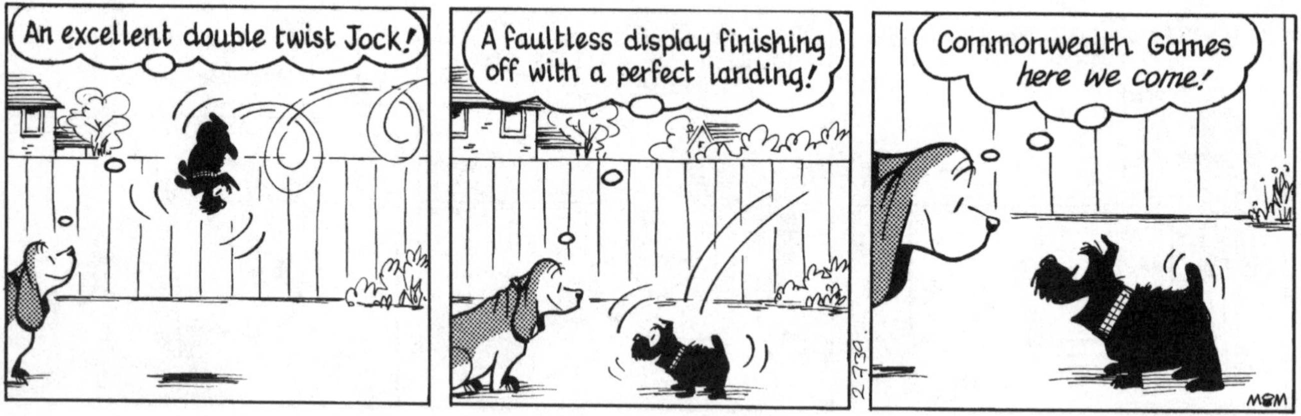
An excellent double twist Jock!
A faultless display finishing off with a perfect landing!
Commonwealth Games here we come!

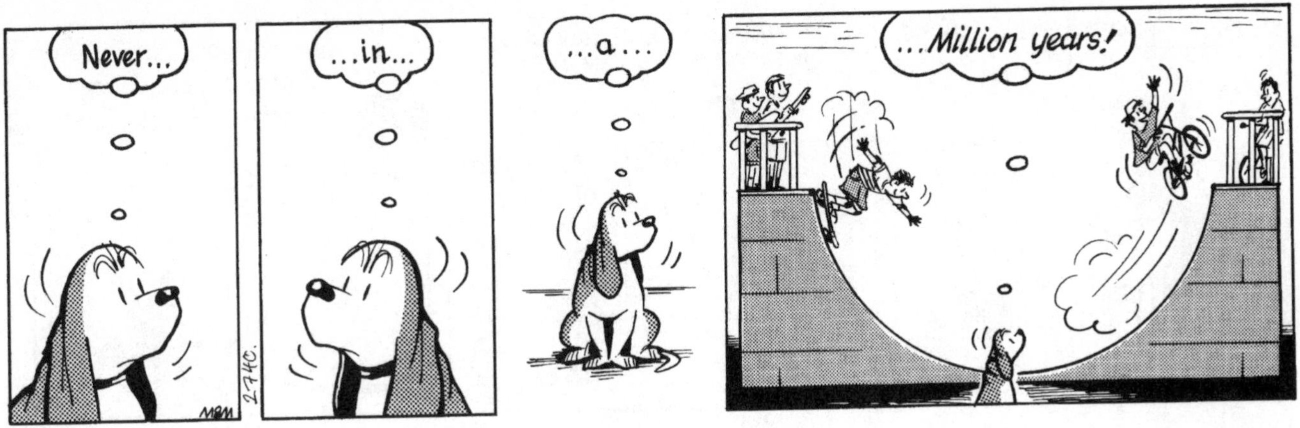
Never...
...in...
...a...
...Million years!

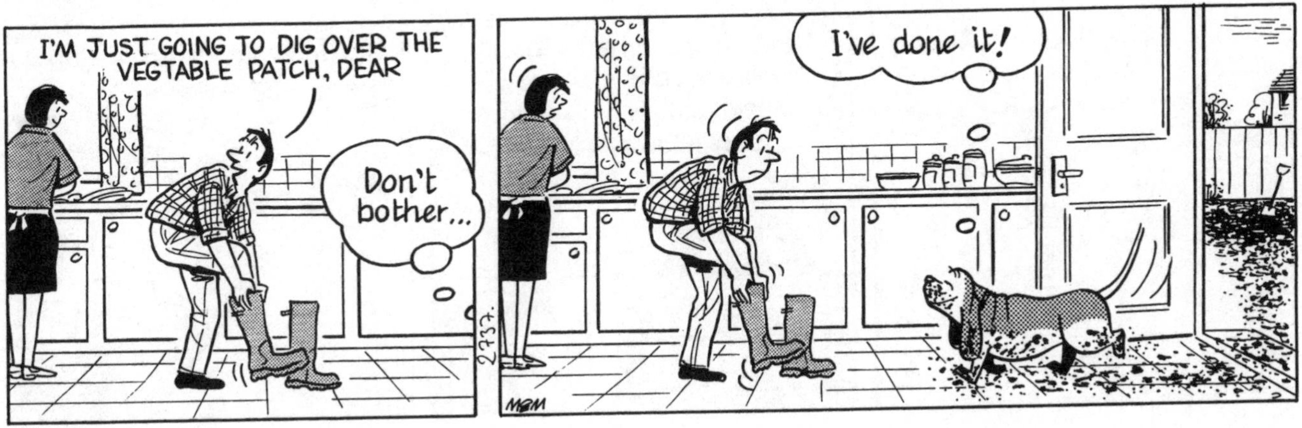
I'M JUST GOING TO DIG OVER THE VEGTABLE PATCH, DEAR
Don't bother...
I've done it!

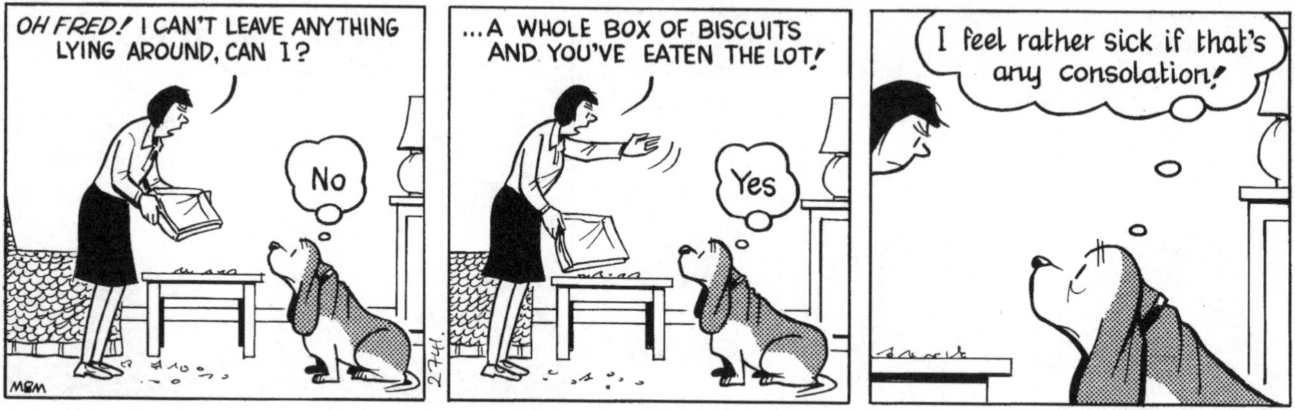
OH FRED! I CAN'T LEAVE ANYTHING LYING AROUND, CAN I?
No
...A WHOLE BOX OF BISCUITS AND YOU'VE EATEN THE LOT!
Yes
I feel rather sick if that's any consolation!

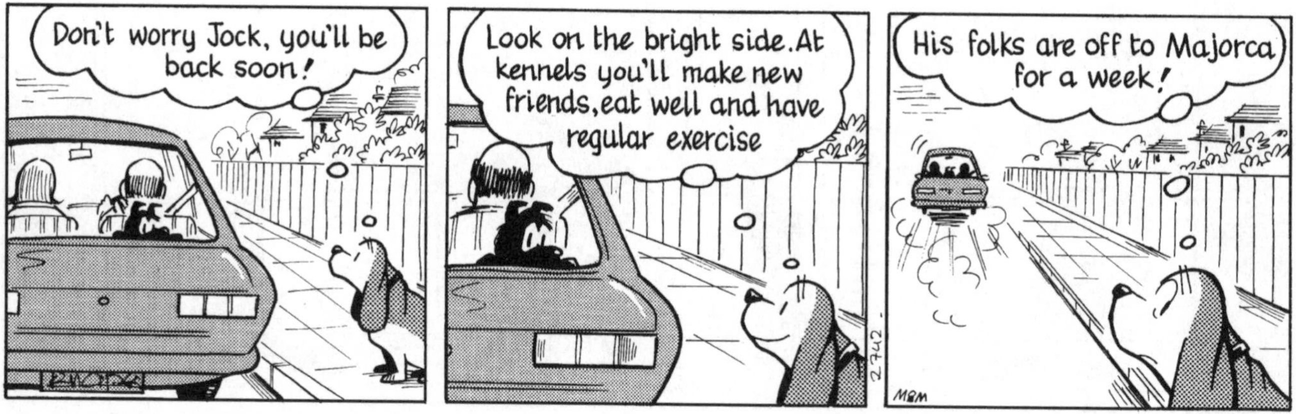
Don't worry Jock, you'll be back soon!
Look on the bright side. At kennels you'll make new friends, eat well and have regular exercise
His folks are off to Majorca for a week!

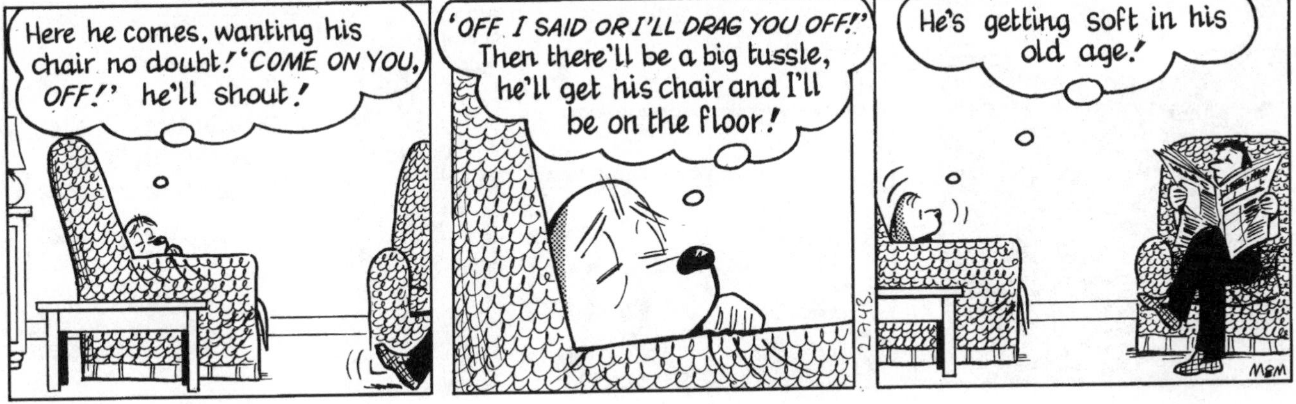
Here he comes, wanting his chair no doubt! 'COME ON YOU, OFF!' he'll shout!
'OFF I SAID OR I'LL DRAG YOU OFF!' Then there'll be a big tussle, he'll get his chair and I'll be on the floor!
He's getting soft in his old age!
2743.

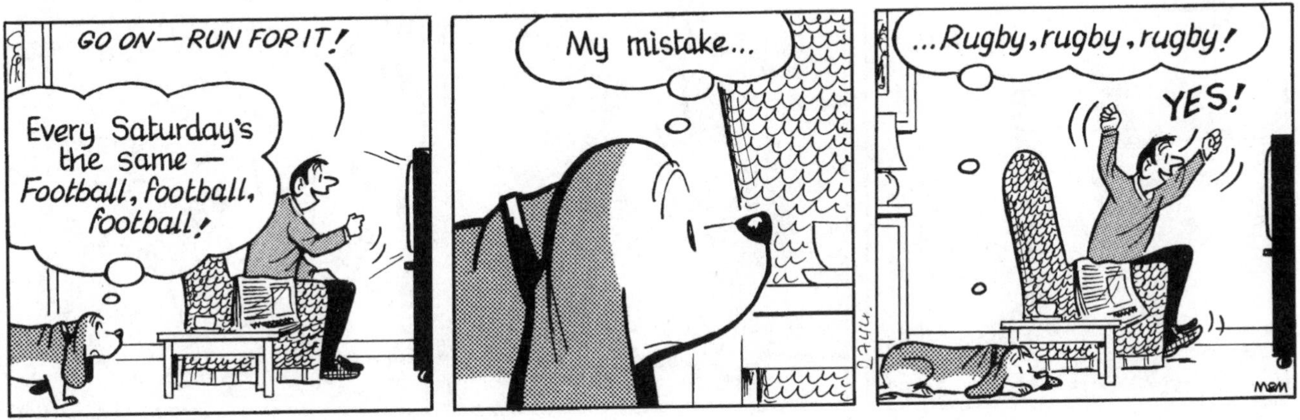
GO ON — RUN FOR IT!
Every Saturday's the same — Football, football, football!
My mistake...
...Rugby, rugby, rugby!
YES!
2744.

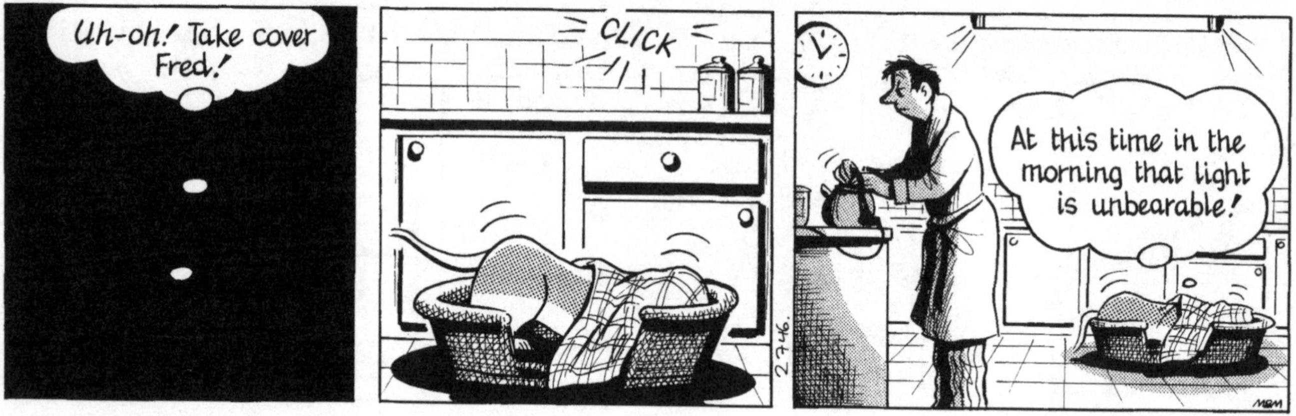
Uh-oh! Take cover Fred!
CLICK
At this time in the morning that light is unbearable!

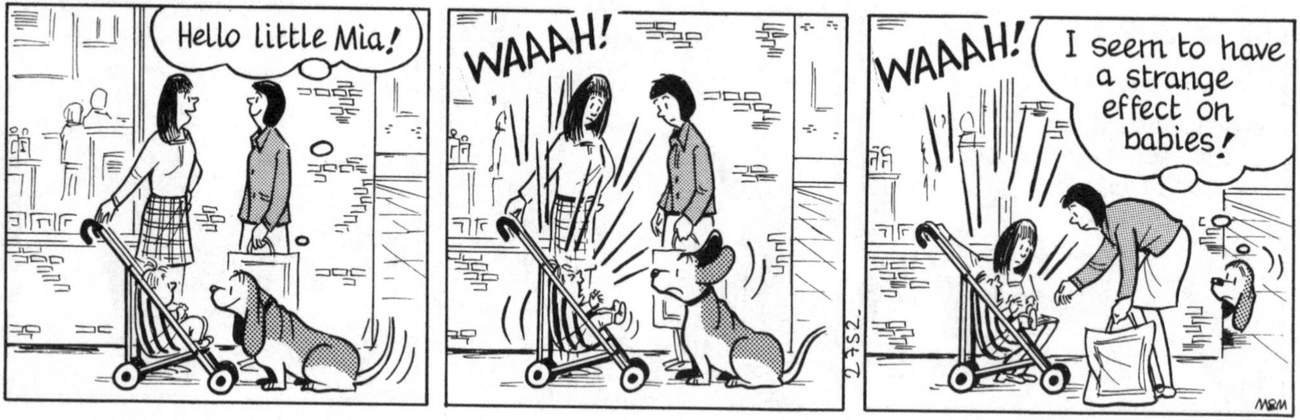
Hello little Mia!
WAAAH!
WAAAH!
I seem to have a strange effect on babies!

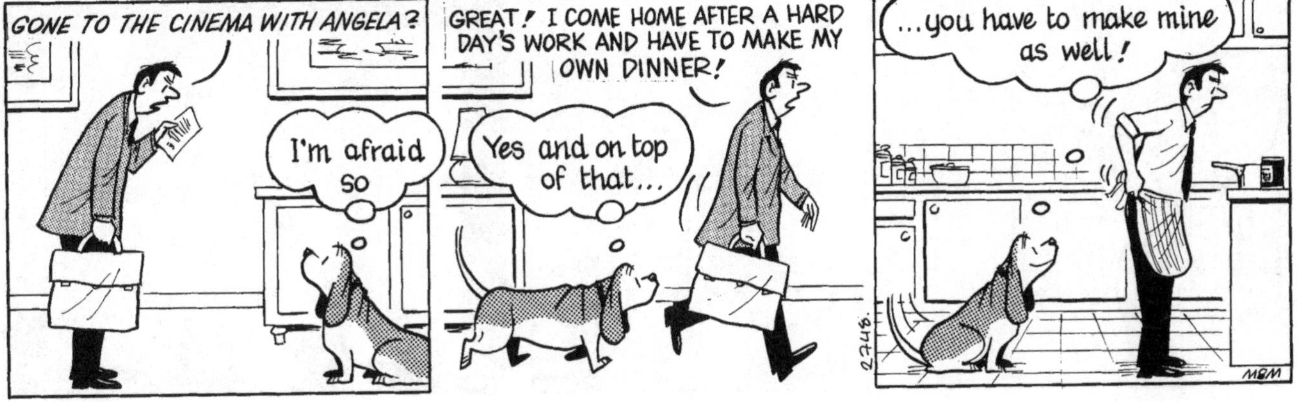
GONE TO THE CINEMA WITH ANGELA?
I'm afraid so
GREAT! I COME HOME AFTER A HARD DAY'S WORK AND HAVE TO MAKE MY OWN DINNER!
Yes and on top of that...
...you have to make mine as well!

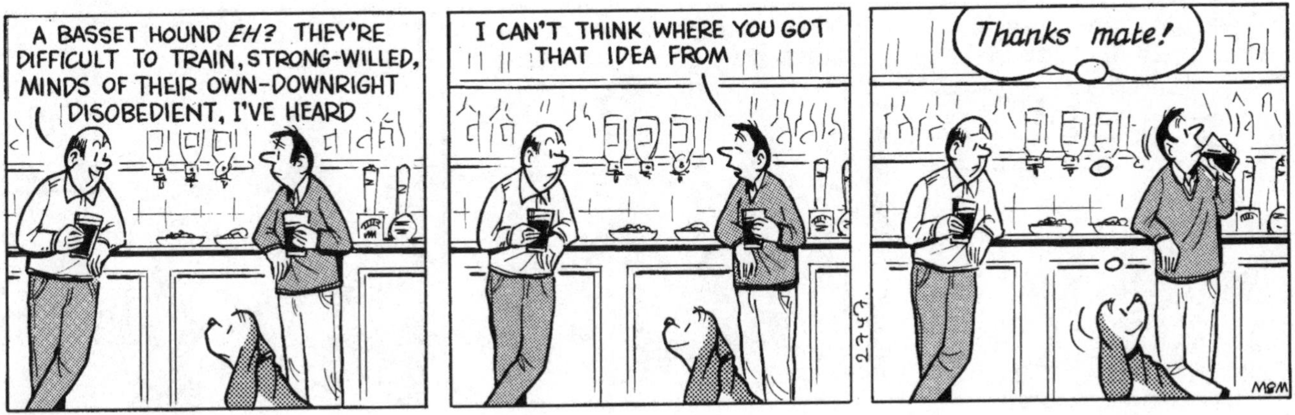
A BASSET HOUND EH? THEY'RE DIFFICULT TO TRAIN, STRONG-WILLED, MINDS OF THEIR OWN-DOWNRIGHT DISOBEDIENT, I'VE HEARD
I CAN'T THINK WHERE YOU GOT THAT IDEA FROM
Thanks mate!

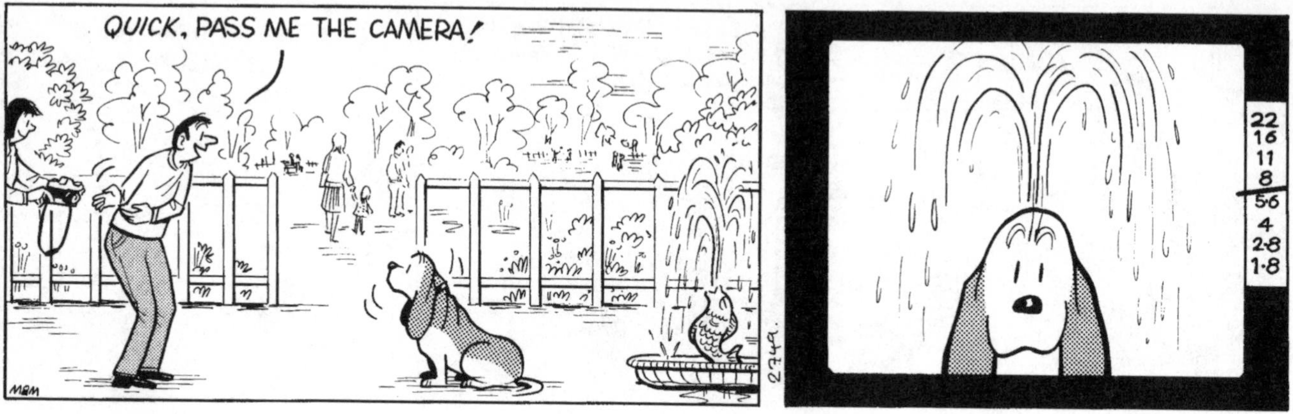
QUICK, PASS ME THE CAMERA!
M&M
2749.
22
16
11
8
5·6
4
2·8
1·8

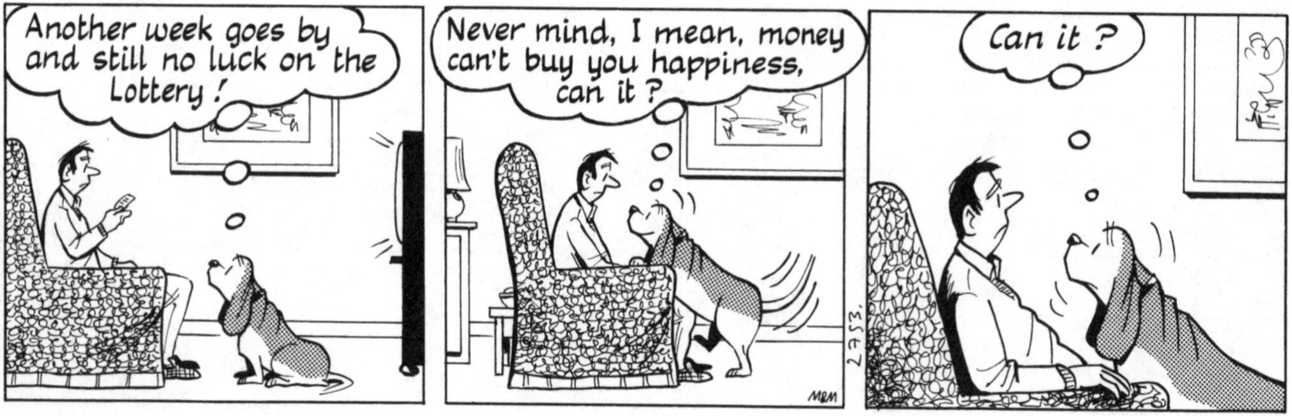
Another week goes by and still no luck on the Lottery!
Never mind, I mean, money can't buy you happiness, can it?
2753.
M&M
Can it?

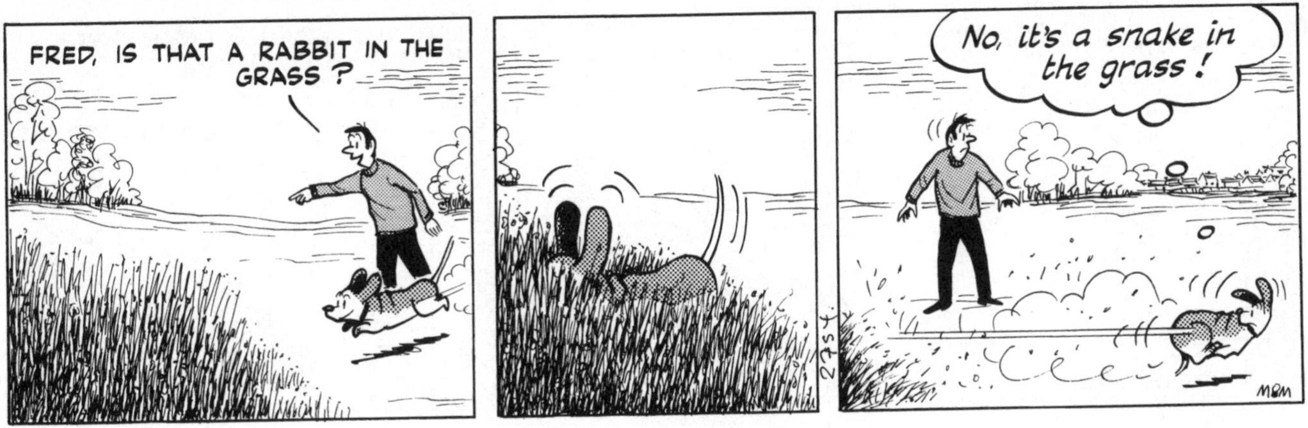
FRED, IS THAT A RABBIT IN THE GRASS ?
No, it's a snake in the grass !
2754
M&M

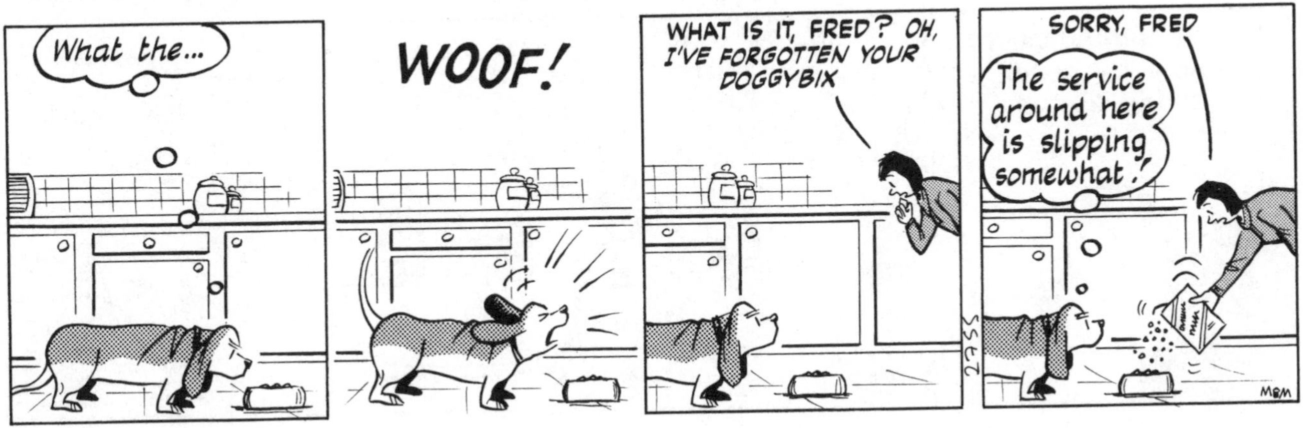
What the...
WOOF!
WHAT IS IT, FRED? OH, I'VE FORGOTTEN YOUR DOGGYBIX
SORRY, FRED
The service around here is slipping somewhat.
2755
M&M

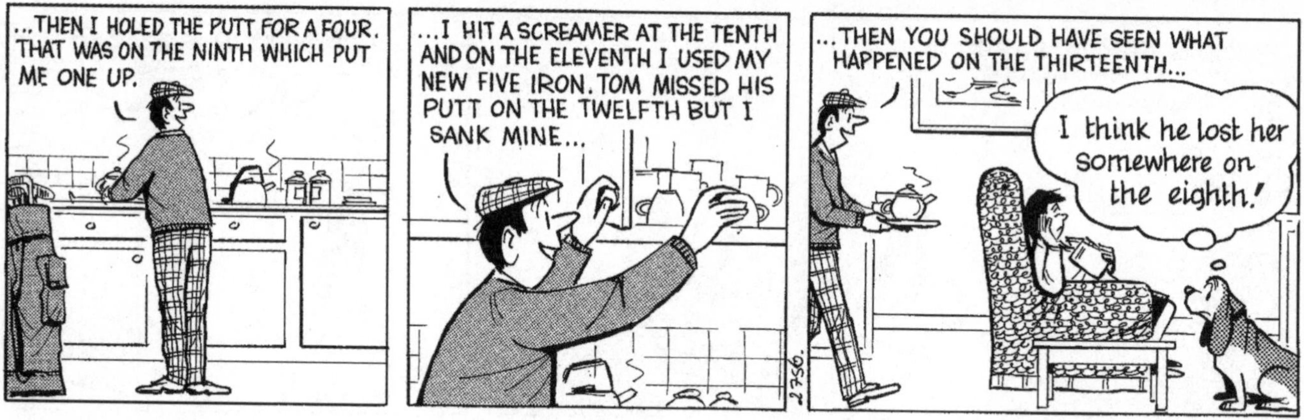
...THEN I HOLED THE PUTT FOR A FOUR. THAT WAS ON THE NINTH WHICH PUT ME ONE UP.
...I HIT A SCREAMER AT THE TENTH AND ON THE ELEVENTH I USED MY NEW FIVE IRON. TOM MISSED HIS PUTT ON THE TWELFTH BUT I SANK MINE...
2756.
...THEN YOU SHOULD HAVE SEEN WHAT HAPPENED ON THE THIRTEENTH...
I think he lost her somewhere on the eighth!

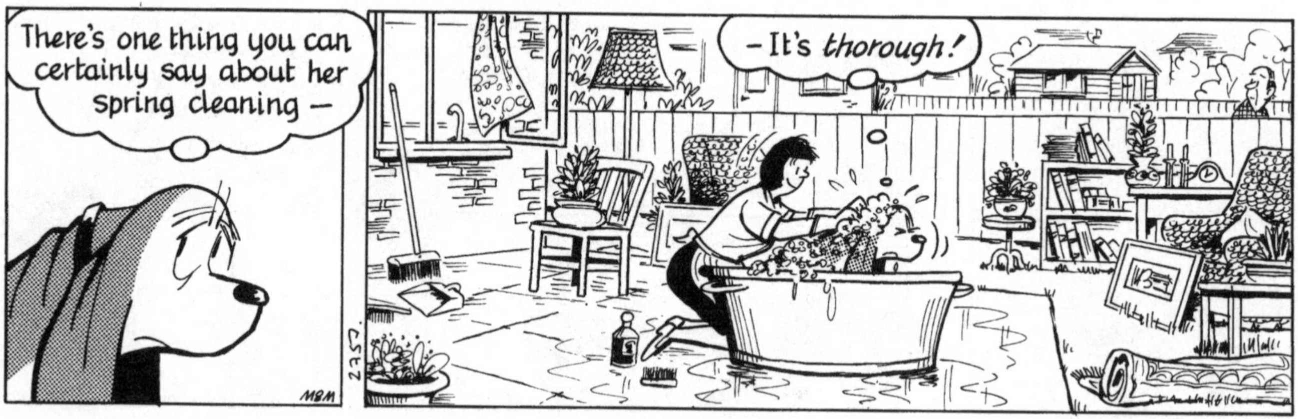
There's one thing you can certainly say about her spring cleaning —
MBM
2757.
– It's *thorough*!

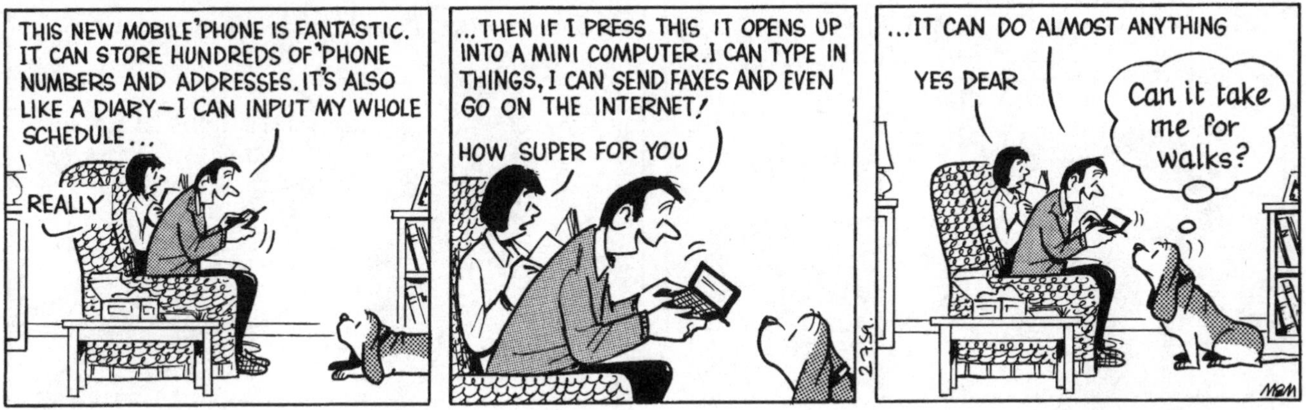

THIS NEW MOBILE'PHONE IS FANTASTIC. IT CAN STORE HUNDREDS OF 'PHONE NUMBERS AND ADDRESSES. IT'S ALSO LIKE A DIARY—I CAN INPUT MY WHOLE SCHEDULE...
REALLY
...THEN IF I PRESS THIS IT OPENS UP INTO A MINI COMPUTER. I CAN TYPE IN THINGS, I CAN SEND FAXES AND EVEN GO ON THE INTERNET!
HOW SUPER FOR YOU
...IT CAN DO ALMOST ANYTHING
YES DEAR
Can it take me for walks?

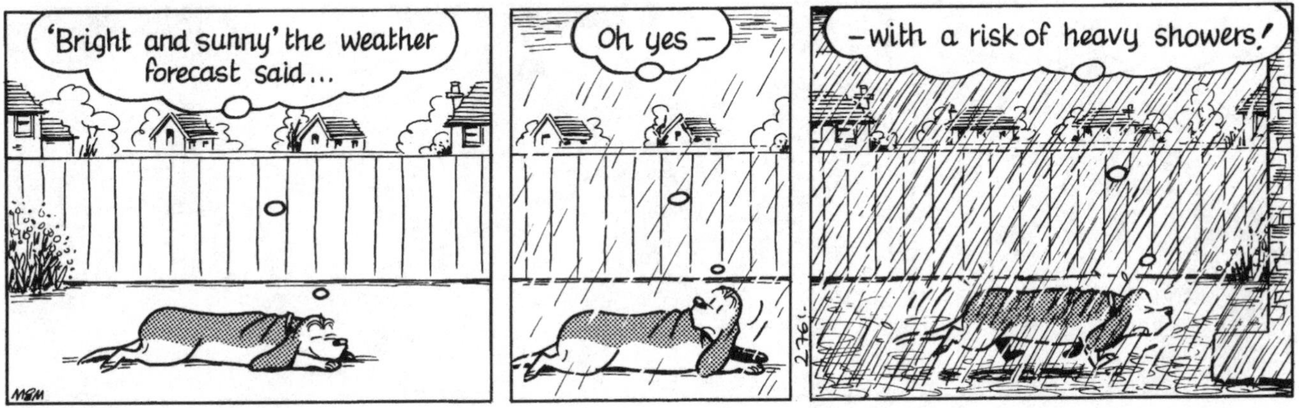

'Bright and sunny' the weather forecast said...
Oh yes –
–with a risk of heavy showers!

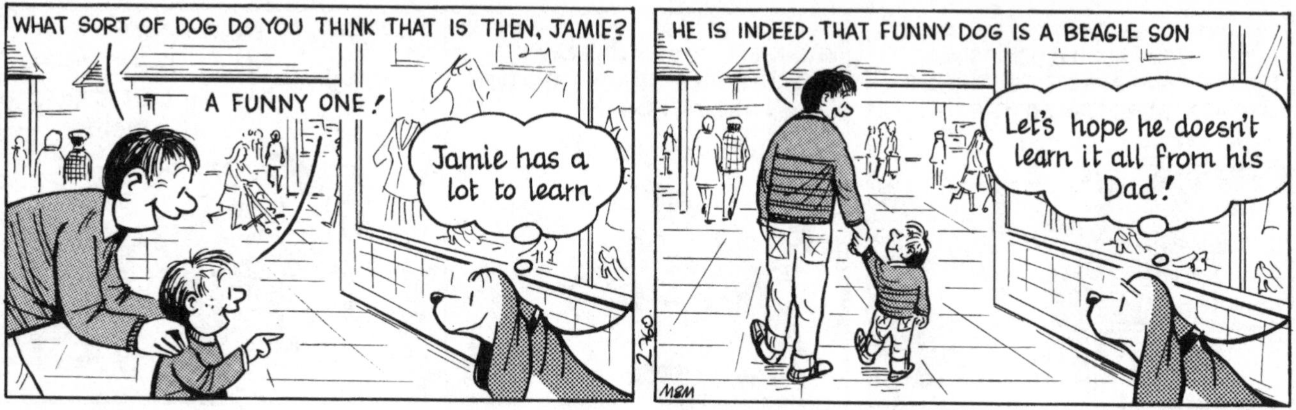
WHAT SORT OF DOG DO YOU THINK THAT IS THEN, JAMIE?
A FUNNY ONE!
Jamie has a lot to learn
2760.
HE IS INDEED. THAT FUNNY DOG IS A BEAGLE SON
Let's hope he doesn't learn it all from his Dad!
M&M

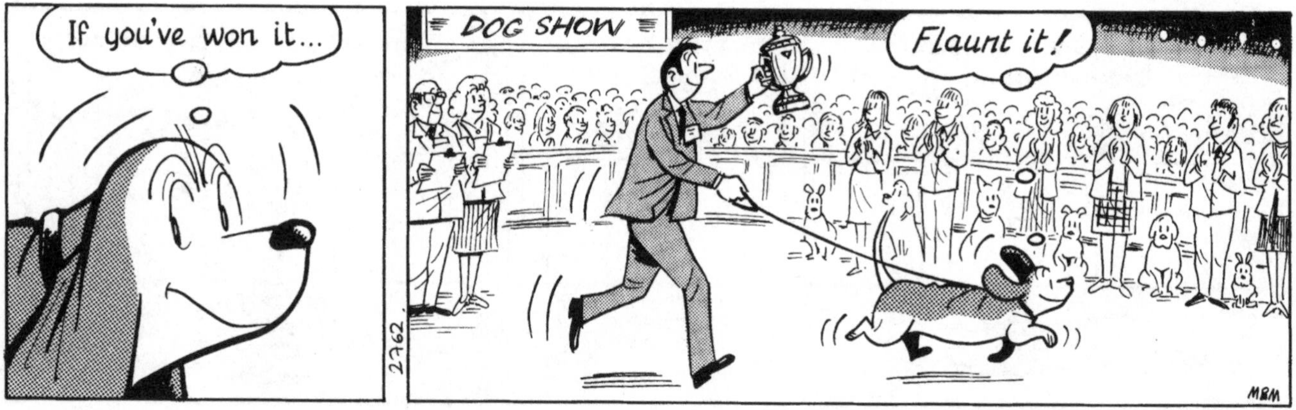
If you've won it...
2762.
DOG SHOW
Flaunt it!
M&M

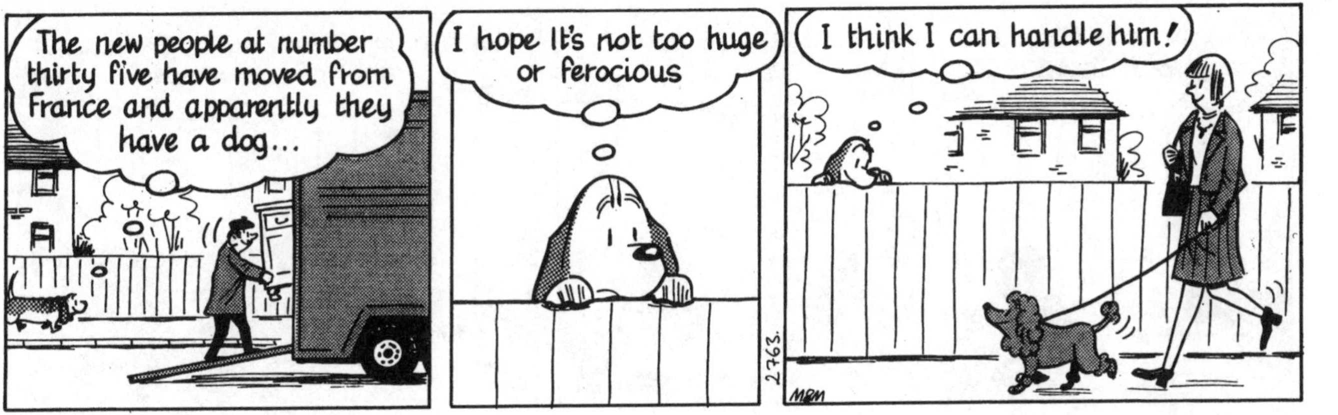
The new people at number thirty five have moved from France and apparently they have a dog...
I hope It's not too huge or ferocious
I think I can handle him!
2763.
MGM

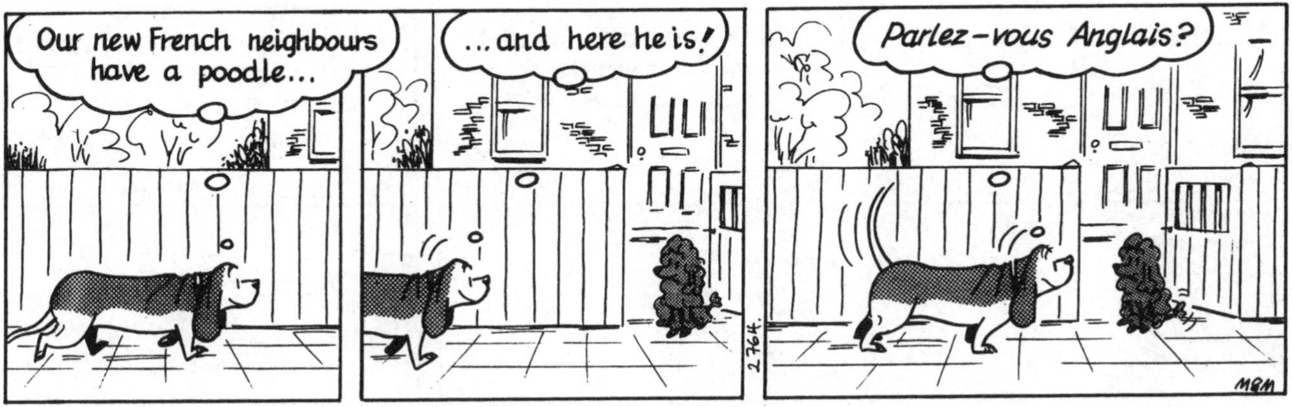
Our new French neighbours have a poodle...
...and here he is!
Parlez-vous Anglais?
2764.
MGM

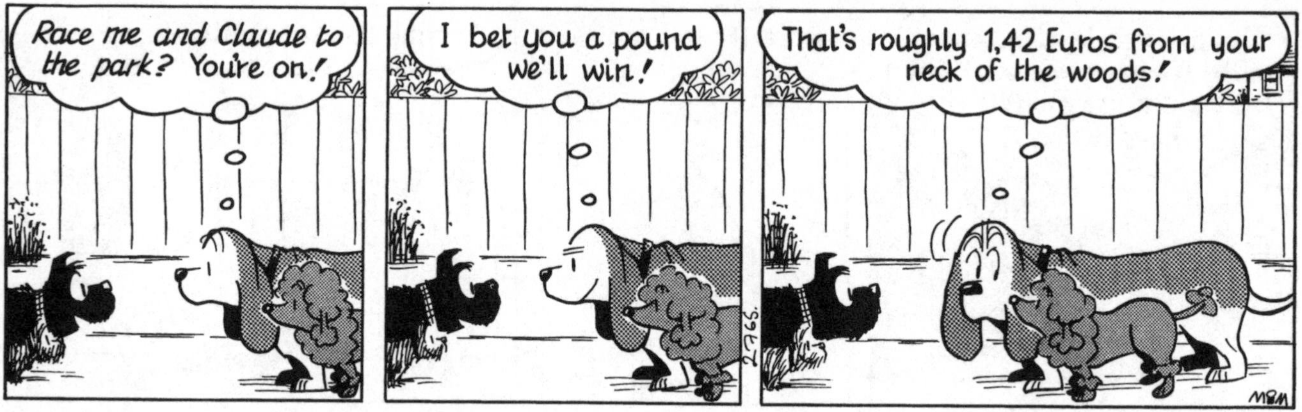
Race me and Claude to the park? You're on!
I bet you a pound we'll win!
That's roughly 1,42 Euros from your neck of the woods!

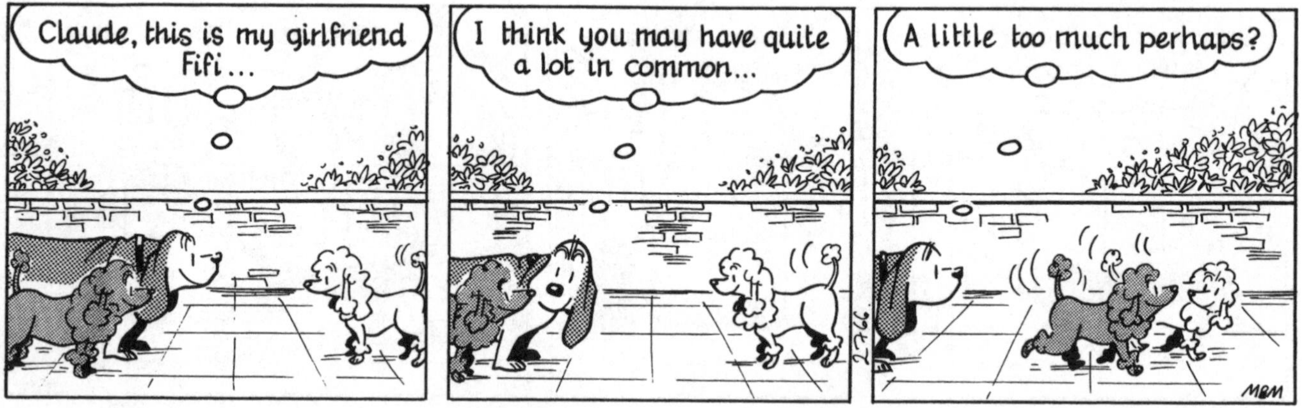
Claude, this is my girlfriend Fifi...
I think you may have quite a lot in common...
A little too much perhaps?

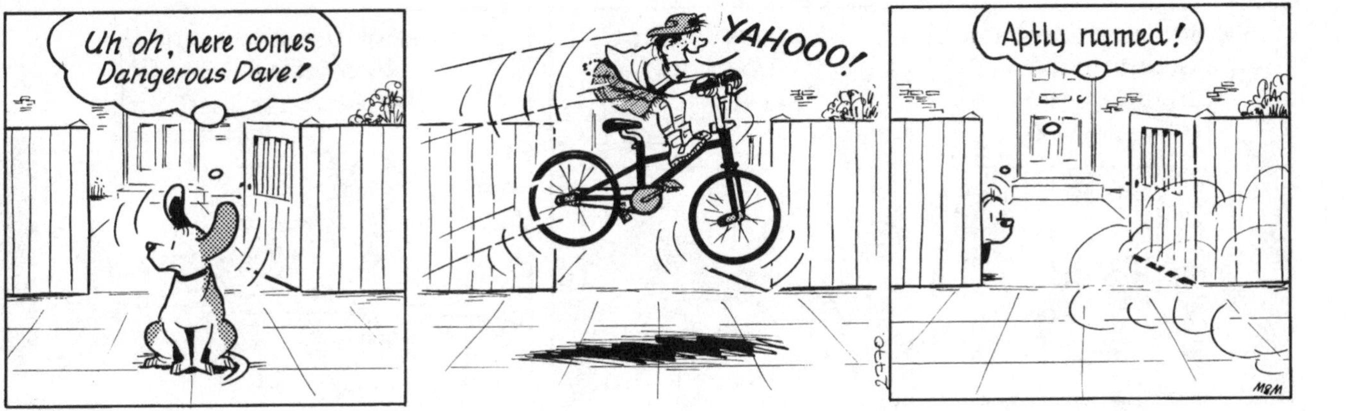
Uh oh, here comes Dangerous Dave!
YAHOOO!
Aptly named!

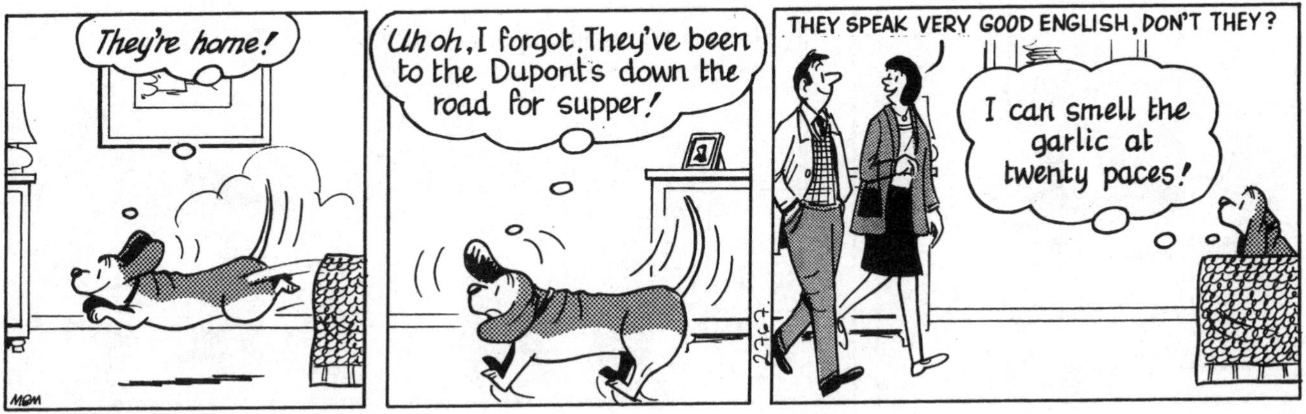
They're home!
Uh oh, I forgot. They've been to the Dupont's down the road for supper!
THEY SPEAK VERY GOOD ENGLISH, DON'T THEY?
I can smell the garlic at twenty paces!

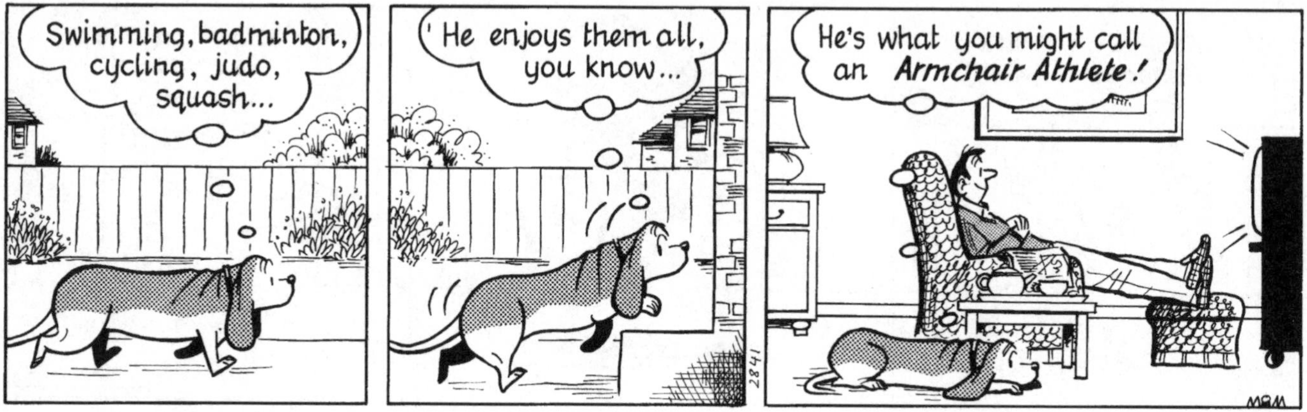
Swimming, badminton, cycling, judo, squash...
He enjoys them all, you know...
He's what you might call an *Armchair Athlete!*

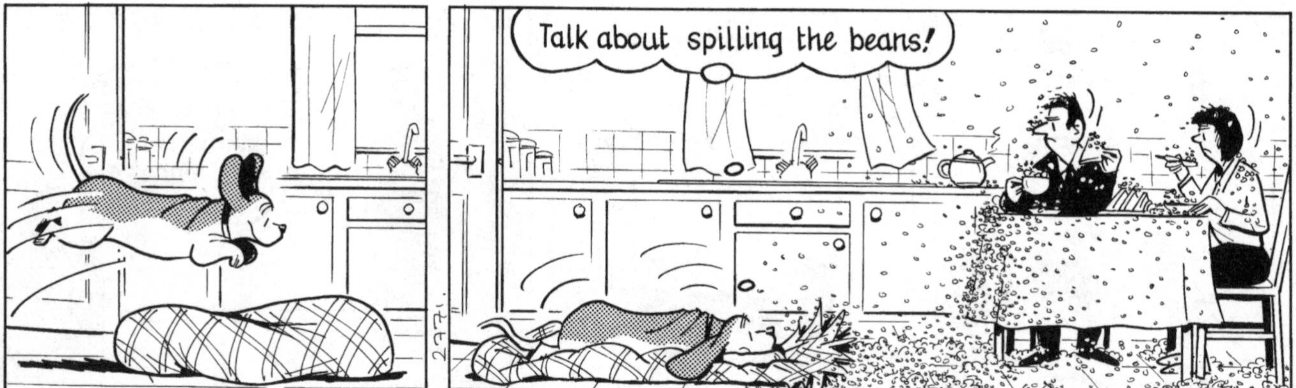
Talk about spilling the beans!

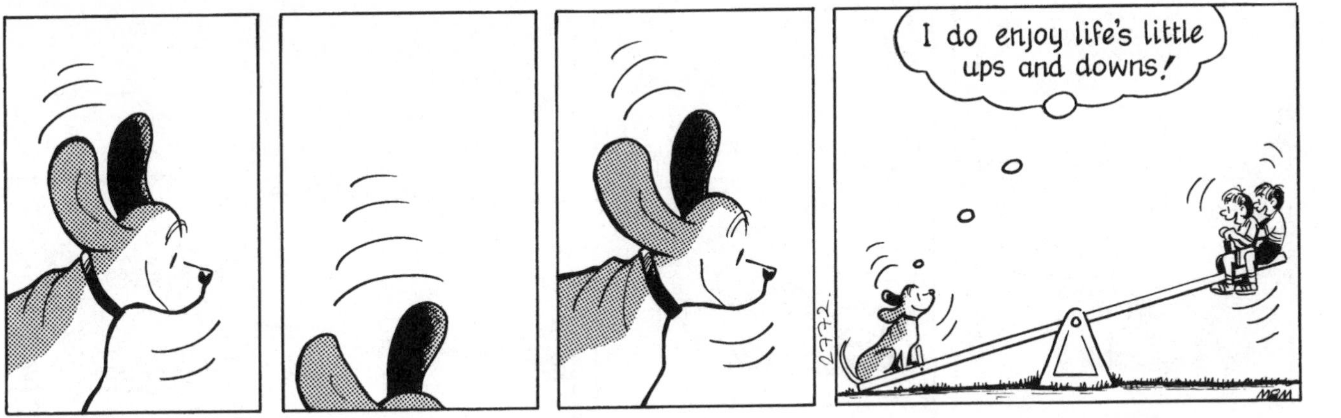
I do enjoy life's little ups and downs!
2772.
MBM

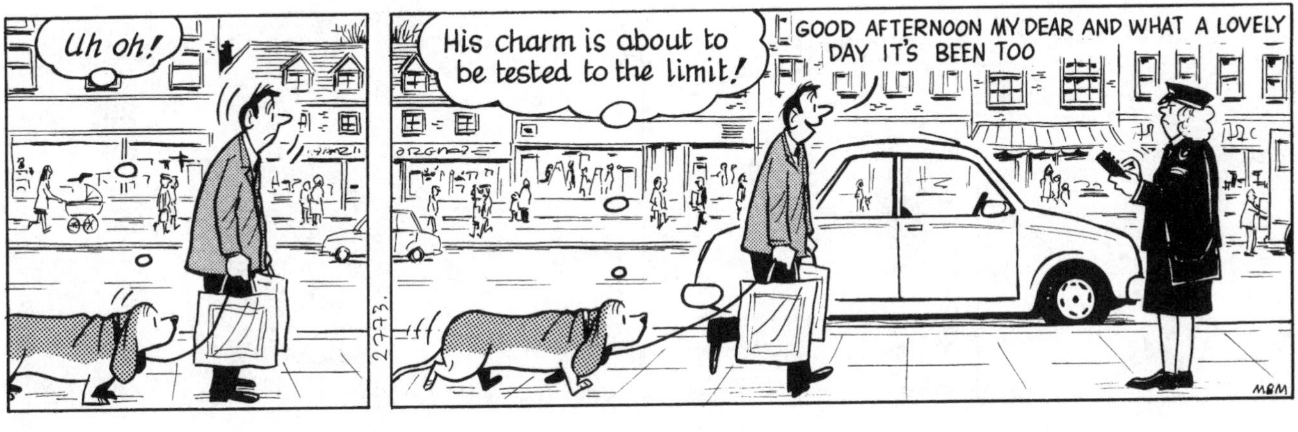
Uh oh!
2773.
His charm is about to be tested to the limit!
GOOD AFTERNOON MY DEAR AND WHAT A LOVELY DAY IT'S BEEN TOO
MBM

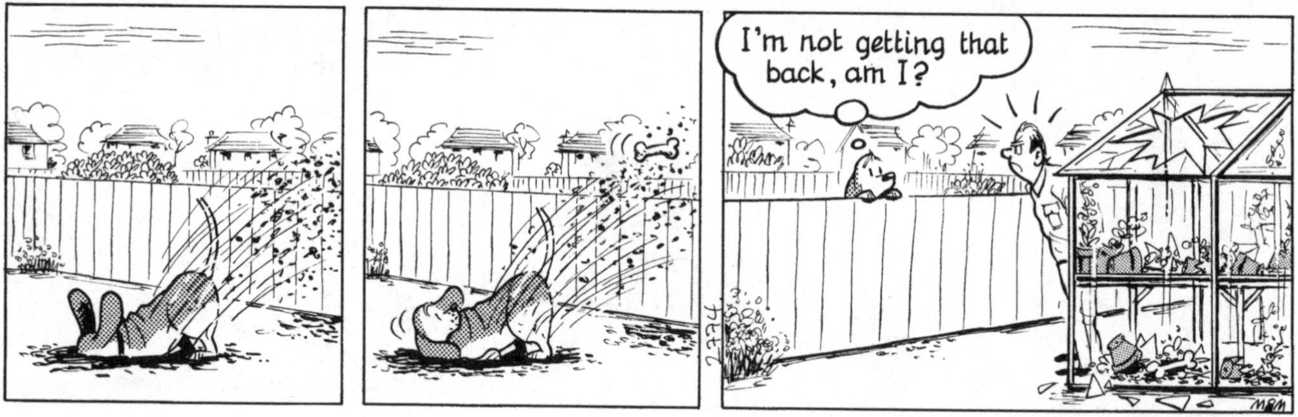
I'm not getting that back, am I?

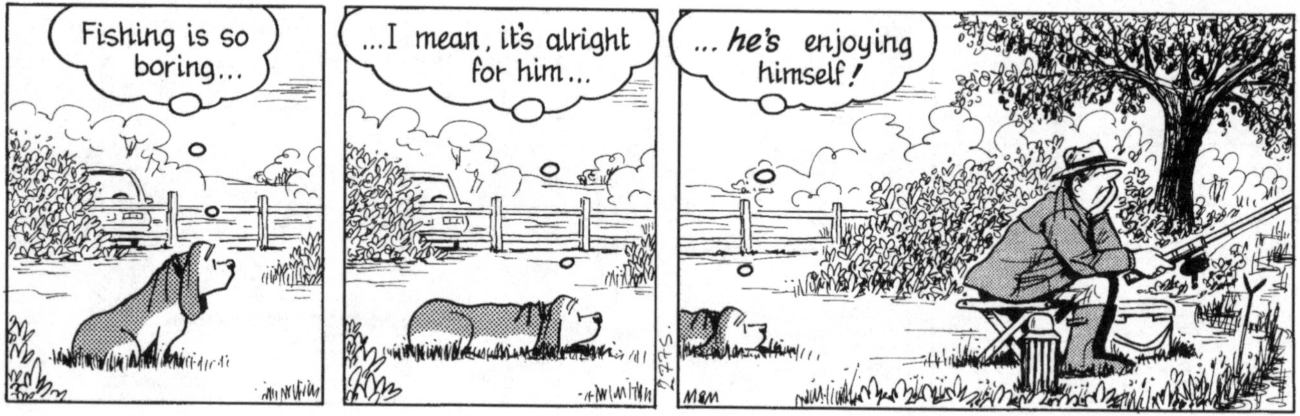
Fishing is so boring...
...I mean, it's alright for him...
... he's enjoying himself!

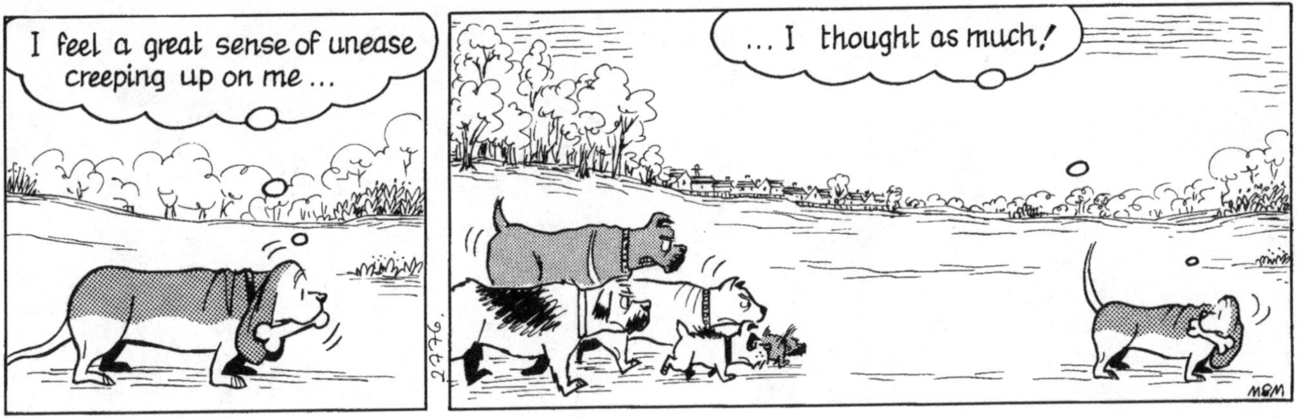
I feel a great sense of unease creeping up on me ...
... I thought as much!

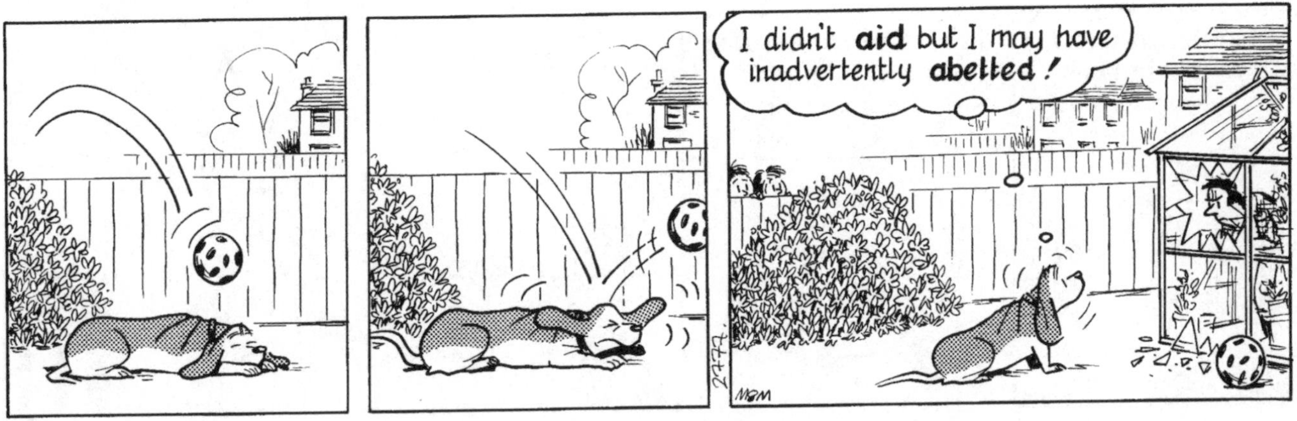
I didn't **aid** but I may have inadvertently **abetted**!

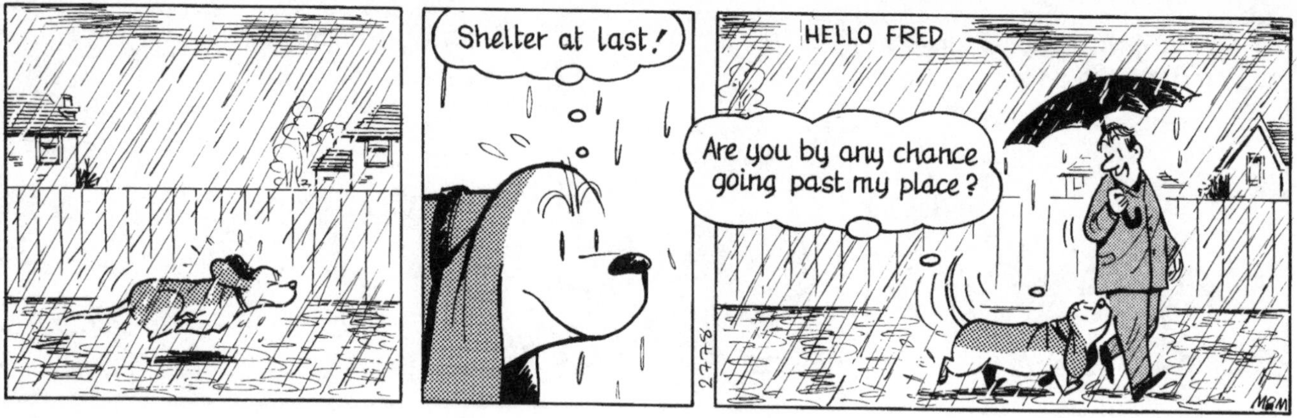
Shelter at last!
HELLO FRED
Are you by any chance going past my place?
2778.

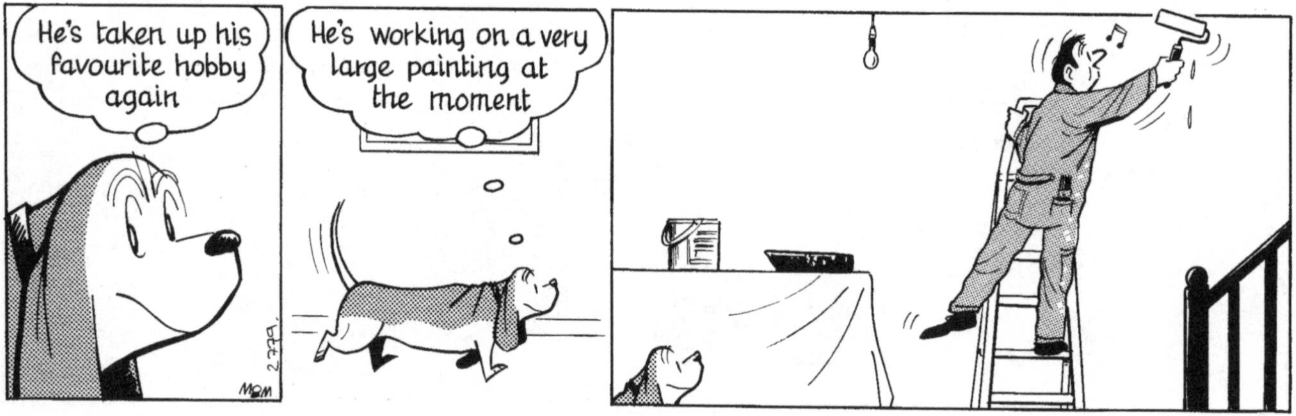
He's taken up his favourite hobby again
2779.
He's working on a very large painting at the moment

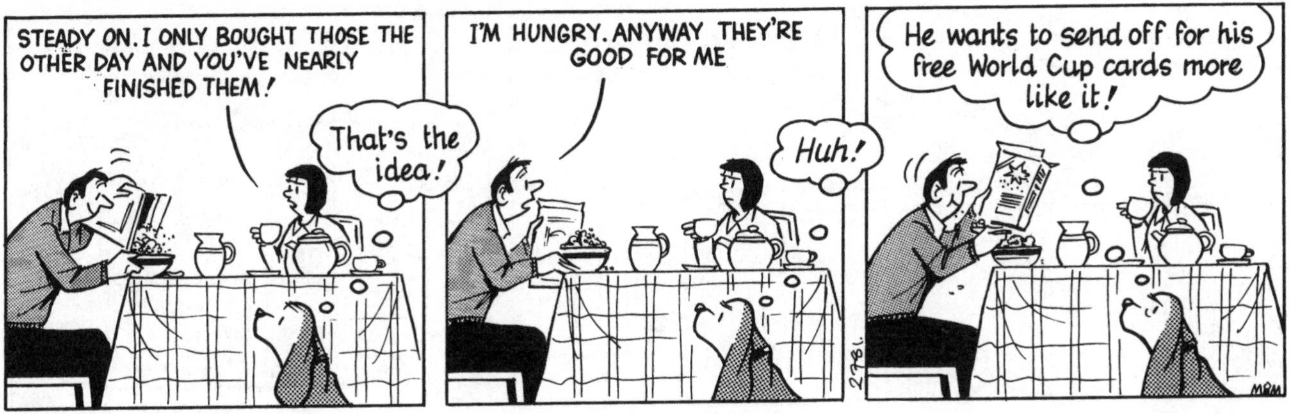
STEADY ON. I ONLY BOUGHT THOSE THE OTHER DAY AND YOU'VE NEARLY FINISHED THEM!
That's the idea!
I'M HUNGRY. ANYWAY THEY'RE GOOD FOR ME
Huh!
He wants to send off for his free World Cup cards more like it!
2781.
MGM

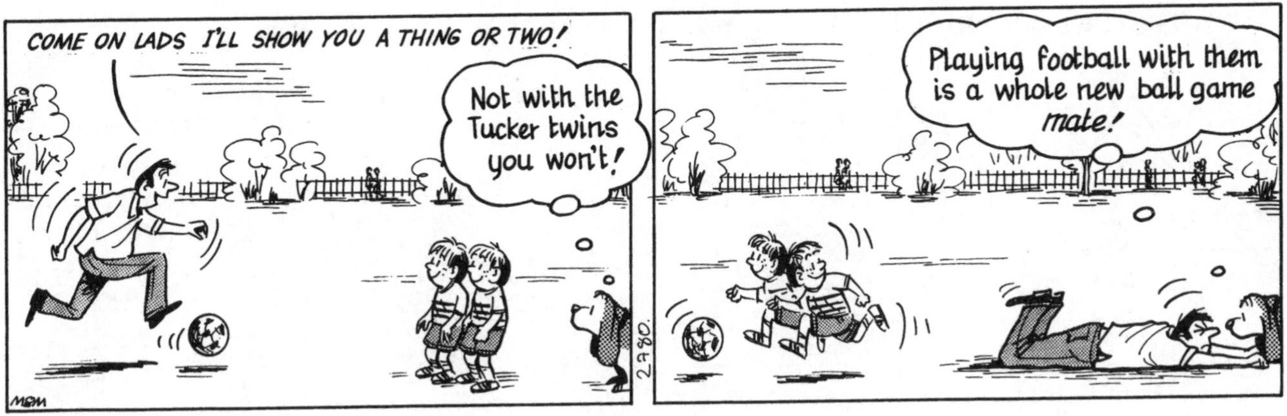
COME ON LADS I'LL SHOW YOU A THING OR TWO!
Not with the Tucker twins you won't!
Playing football with them is a whole new ball game mate!
2780.
MGM

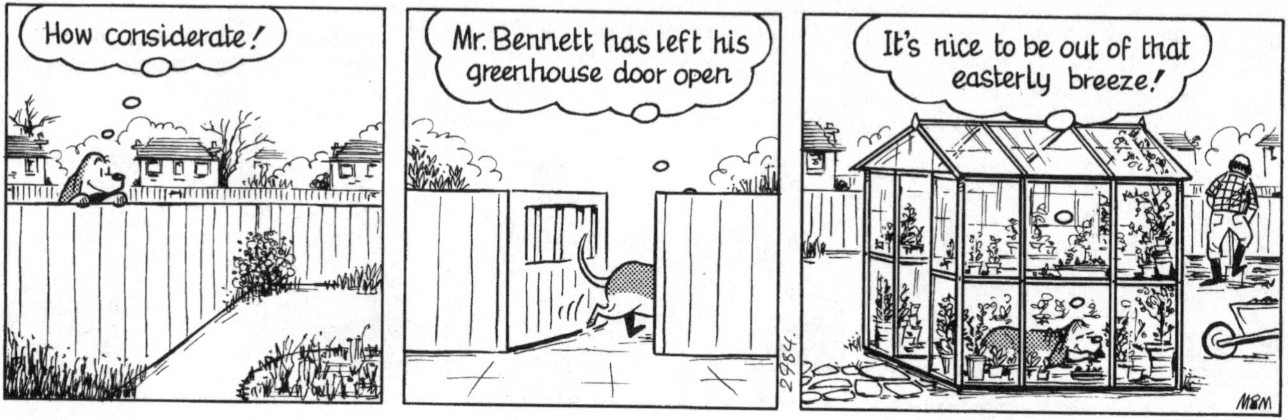
How considerate!
Mr. Bennett has left his greenhouse door open
It's nice to be out of that easterly breeze!

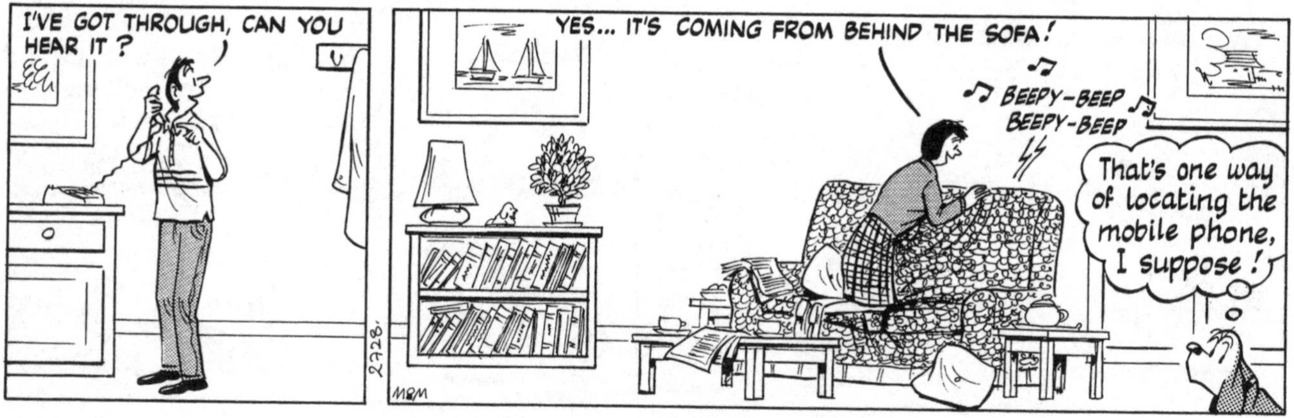
I'VE GOT THROUGH, CAN YOU HEAR IT ?
YES... IT'S COMING FROM BEHIND THE SOFA!
BEEPY-BEEP BEEPY-BEEP
That's one way of locating the mobile phone, I suppose!

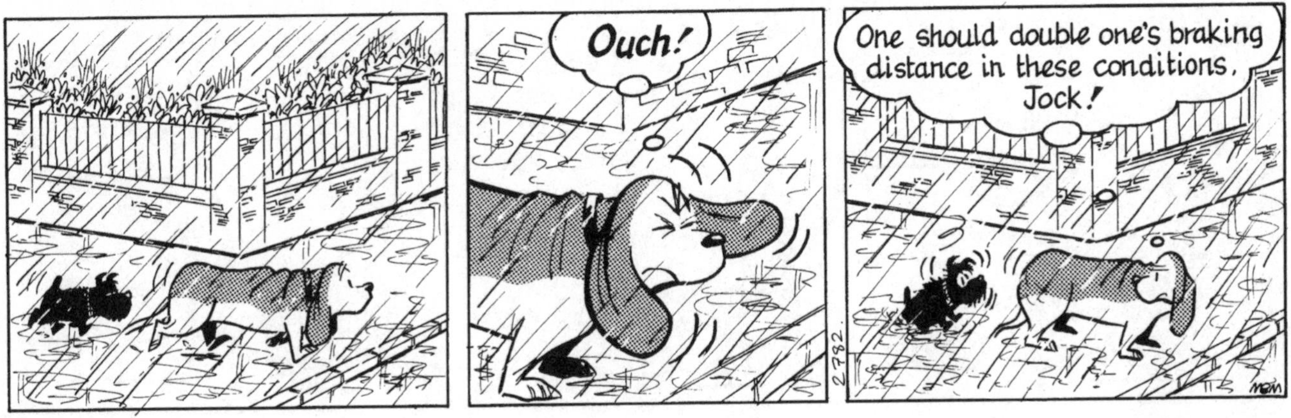
Ouch!
One should double one's braking distance in these conditions, Jock!
2782
MBM

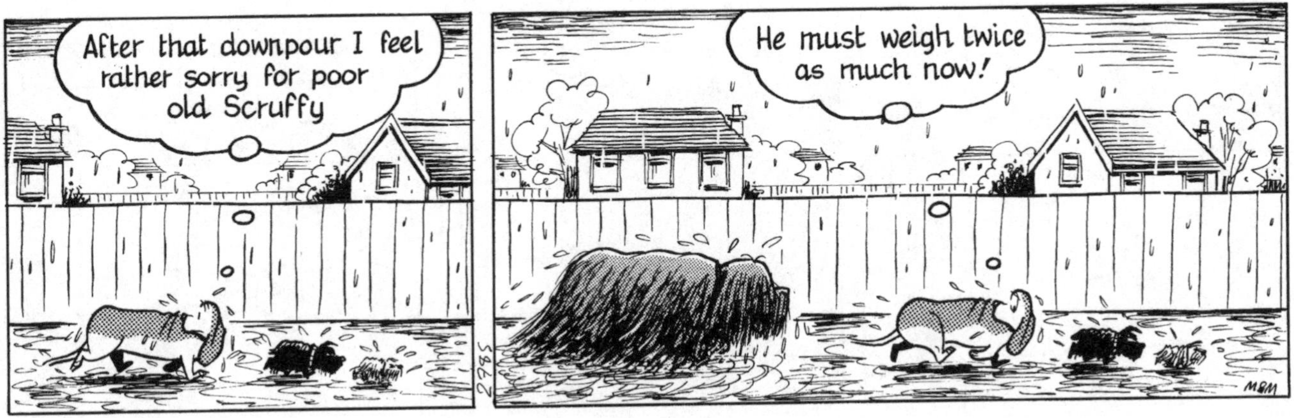
After that downpour I feel rather sorry for poor old Scruffy
He must weigh twice as much now!
2785
MBM

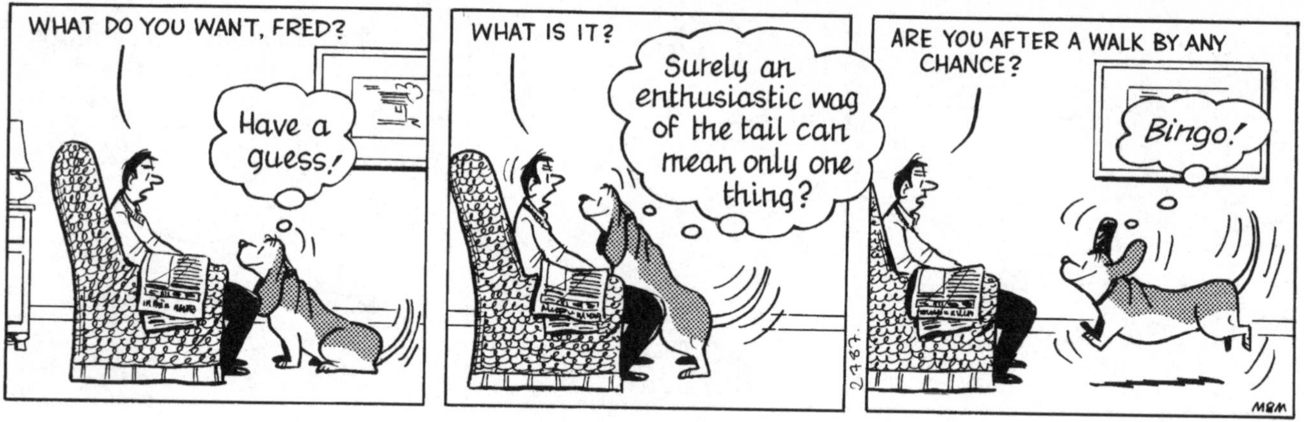
WHAT DO YOU WANT, FRED?
Have a guess!
WHAT IS IT?
Surely an enthusiastic wag of the tail can mean only one thing?
2787.
ARE YOU AFTER A WALK BY ANY CHANCE?
Bingo!
MBM

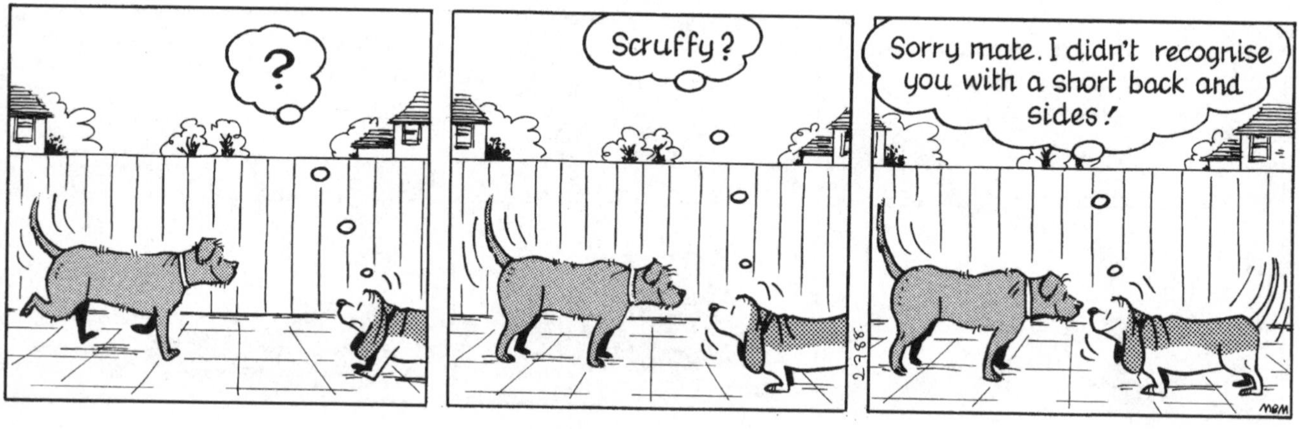
?
Scruffy?
2788.
Sorry mate. I didn't recognise you with a short back and sides!
MBM

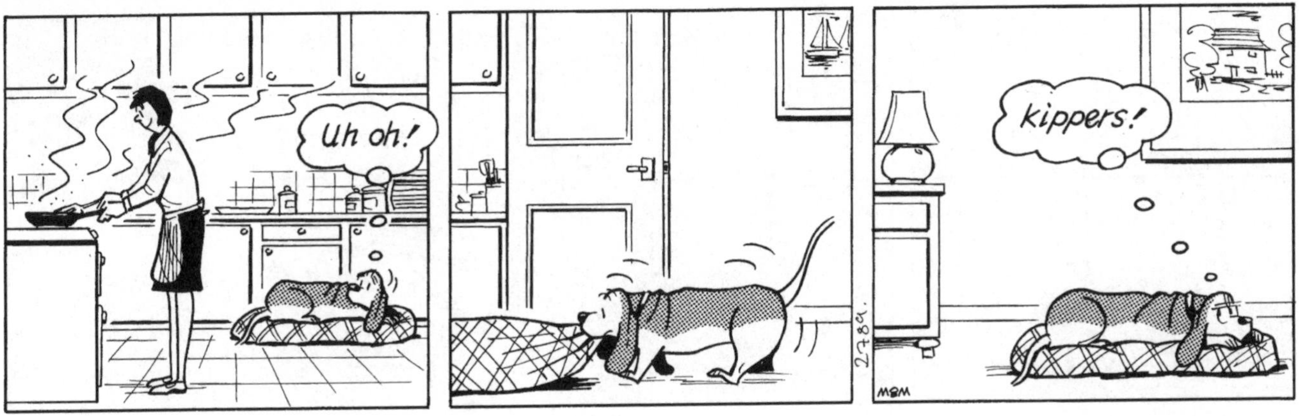
Uh oh!
kippers!
2789.

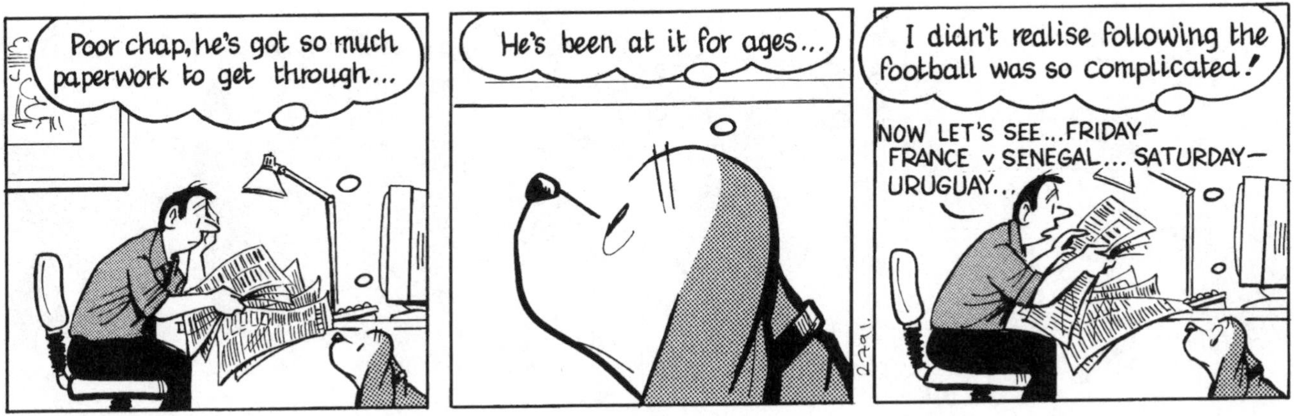
Poor chap, he's got so much paperwork to get through...
He's been at it for ages...
I didn't realise following the football was so complicated!
NOW LET'S SEE... FRIDAY– FRANCE v SENEGAL... SATURDAY– URUGUAY...
2791.

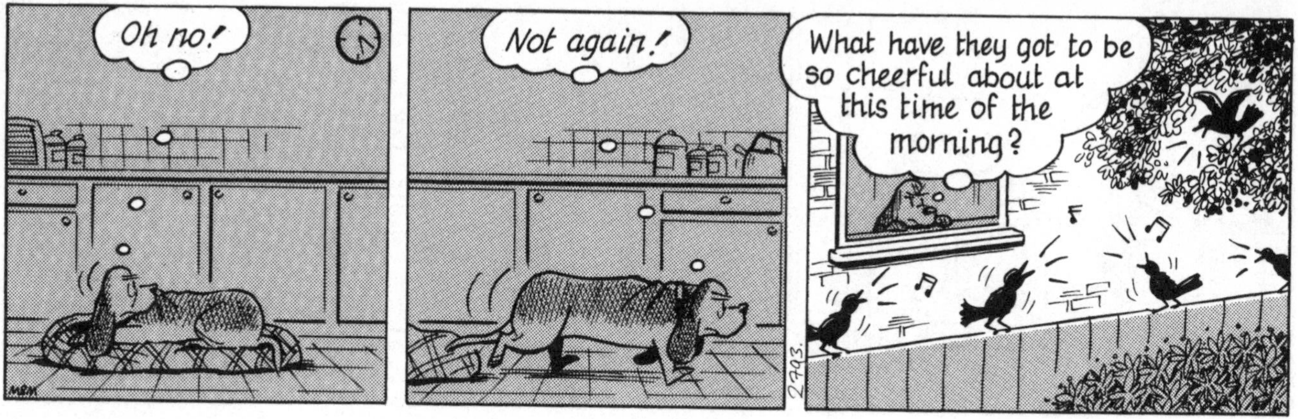
Oh no!
Not again!
What have they got to be so cheerful about at this time of the morning?
2793.
MBM

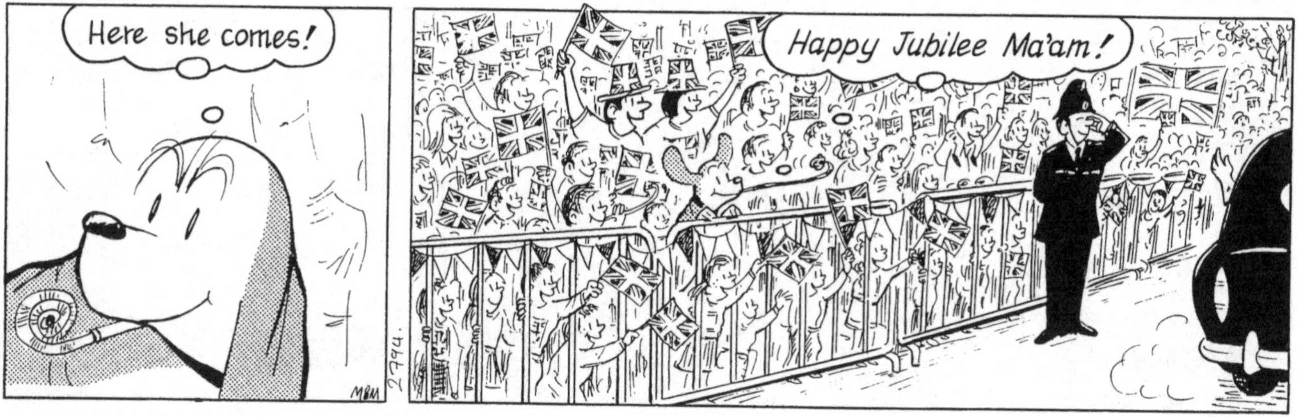
Here she comes!
Happy Jubilee Ma'am!
2794.
MBM

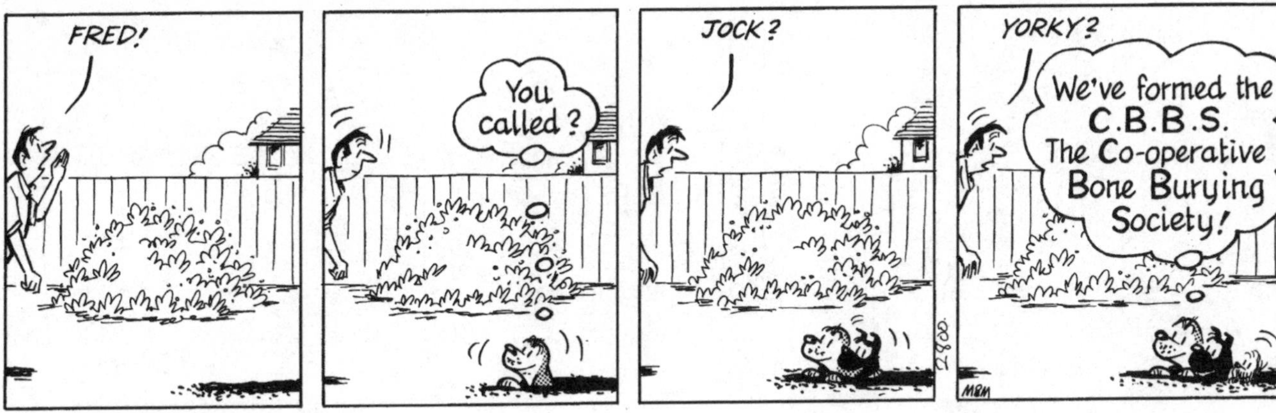
FRED!
You called?
JOCK?
YORKY?
We've formed the C.B.B.S. The Co-operative Bone Burying Society!

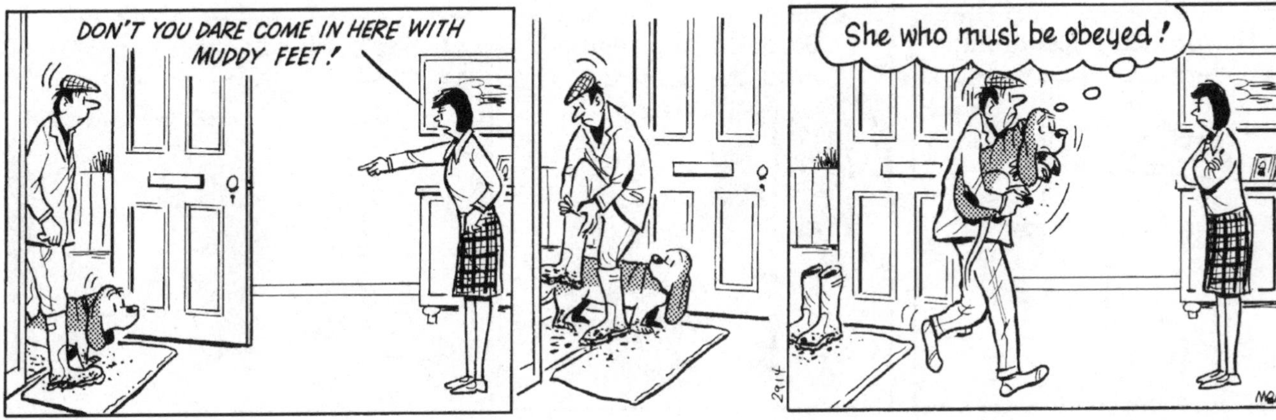
DON'T YOU DARE COME IN HERE WITH MUDDY FEET!
She who must be obeyed!

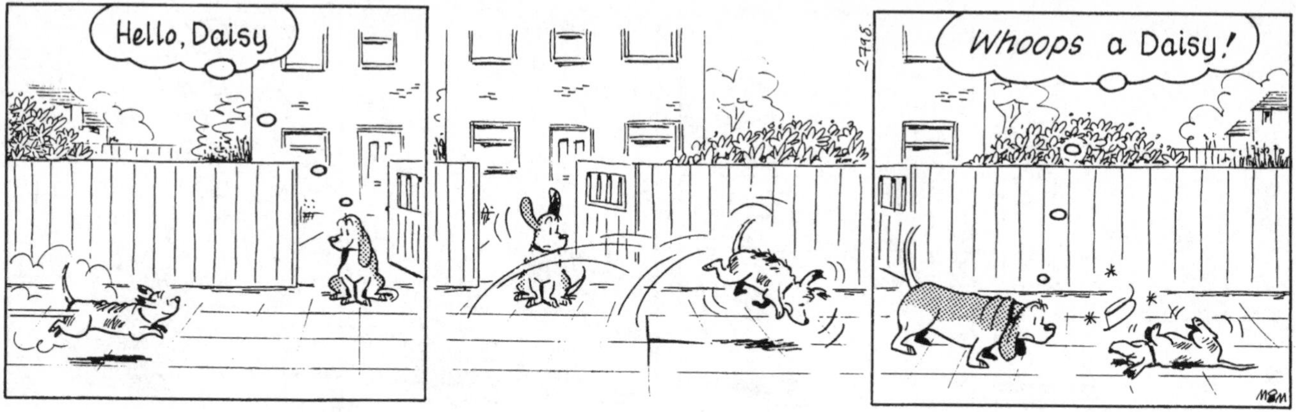
Hello, Daisy
Whoops a Daisy!

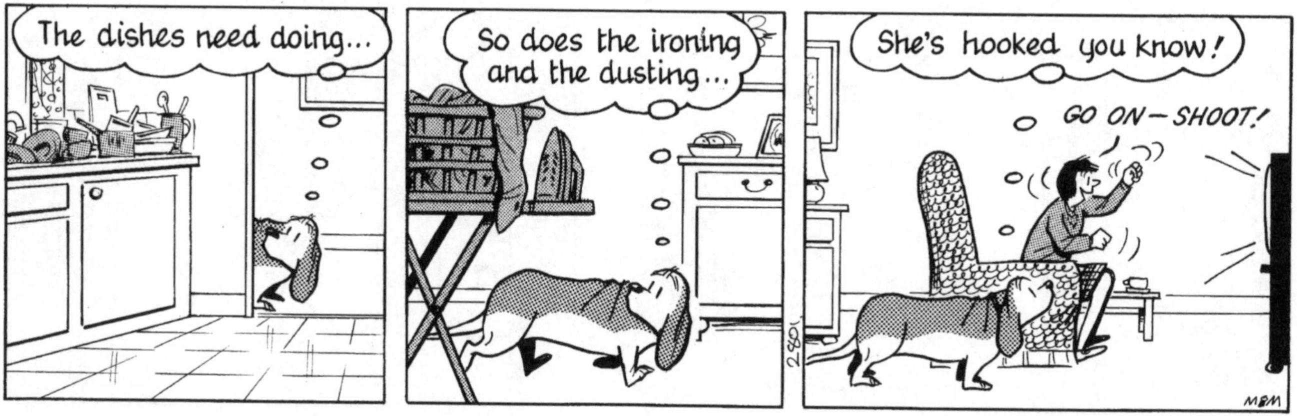
The dishes need doing...
So does the ironing and the dusting...
She's hooked you know!
GO ON—SHOOT!

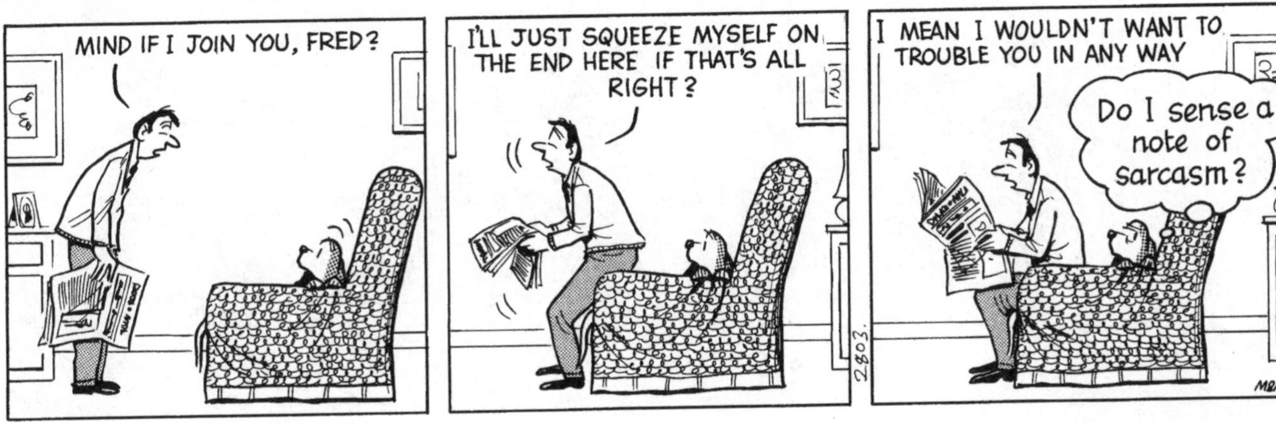
MIND IF I JOIN YOU, FRED?
I'LL JUST SQUEEZE MYSELF ON THE END HERE IF THAT'S ALL RIGHT?
I MEAN I WOULDN'T WANT TO TROUBLE YOU IN ANY WAY
Do I sense a note of sarcasm?
2803.
MBM

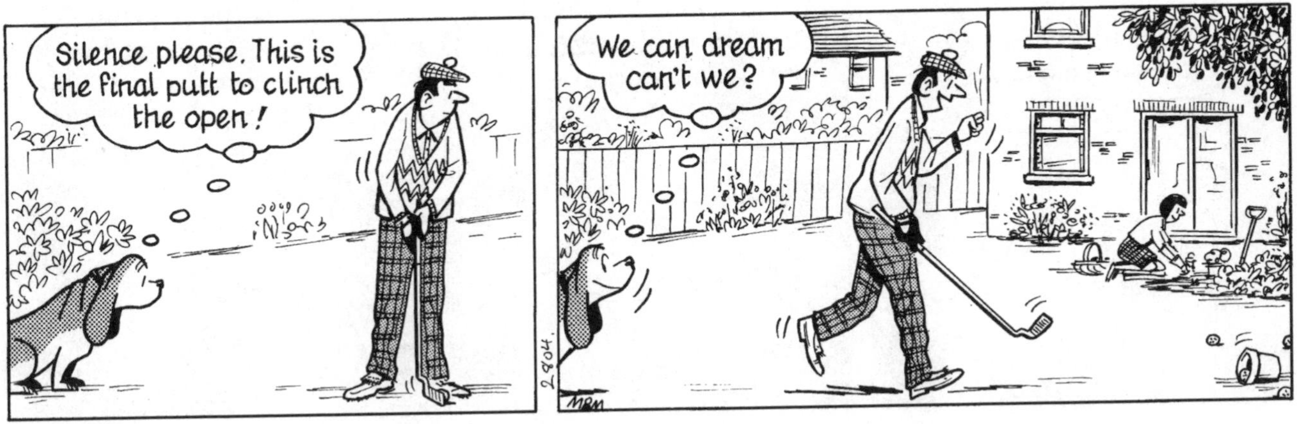
Silence please. This is the final putt to clinch the open!
We can dream can't we?
2804.
MBM

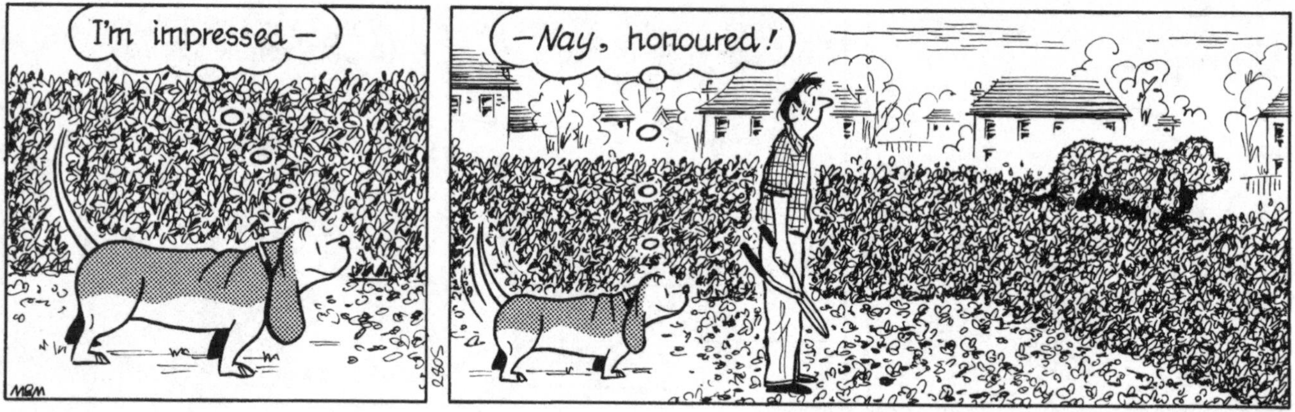
I'm impressed –
–Nay, honoured!
MGM
2805

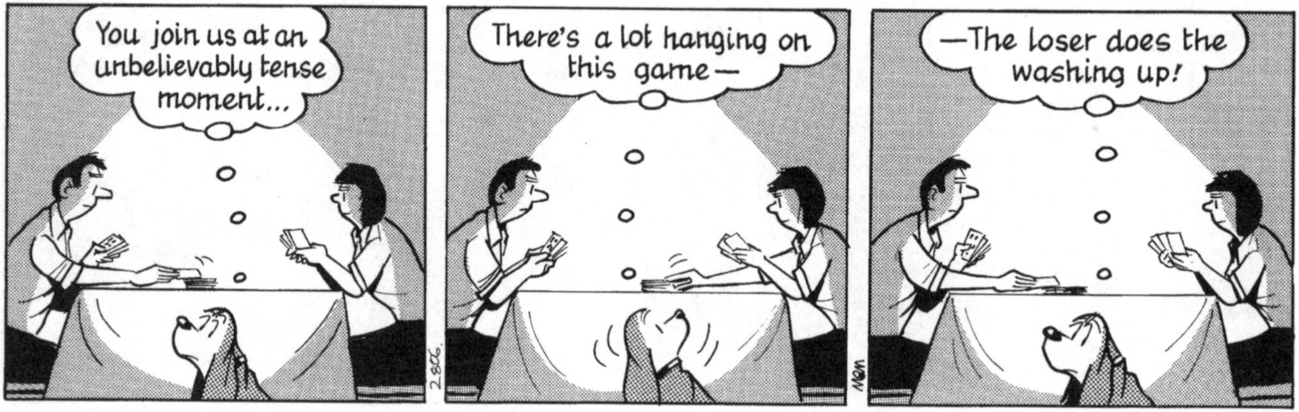
You join us at an unbelievably tense moment...
There's a lot hanging on this game –
–The loser does the washing up!
2806
MGM

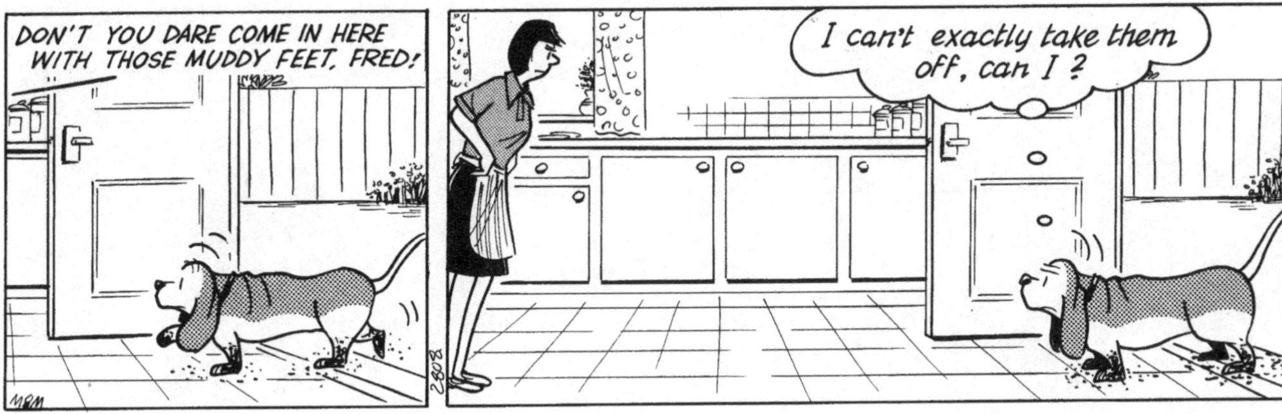
DON'T YOU DARE COME IN HERE WITH THOSE MUDDY FEET, FRED!
I can't exactly take them off, can I ?
2808
MGM

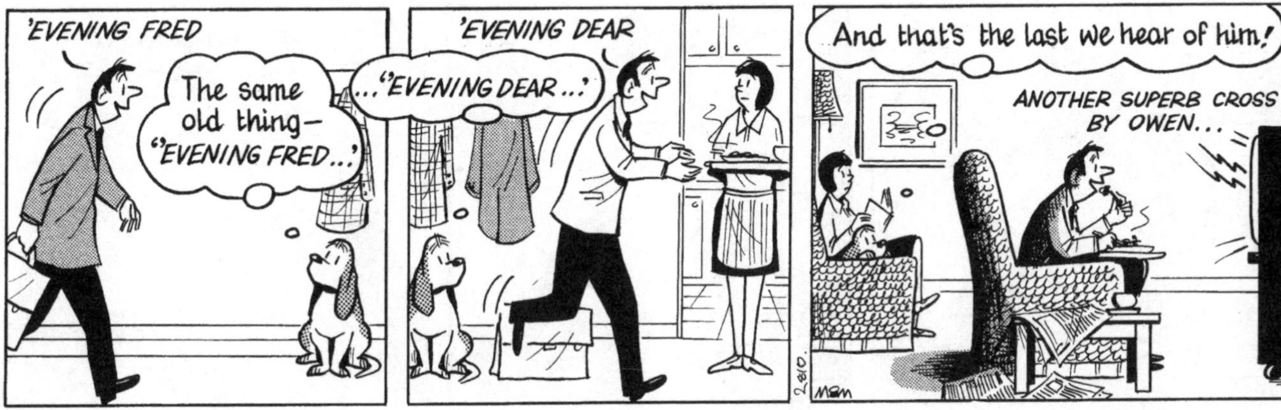
'EVENING FRED
The same old thing— "EVENING FRED..."
'EVENING DEAR
..."EVENING DEAR..."
And that's the last we hear of him!
ANOTHER SUPERB CROSS BY OWEN...
2810.
MGM

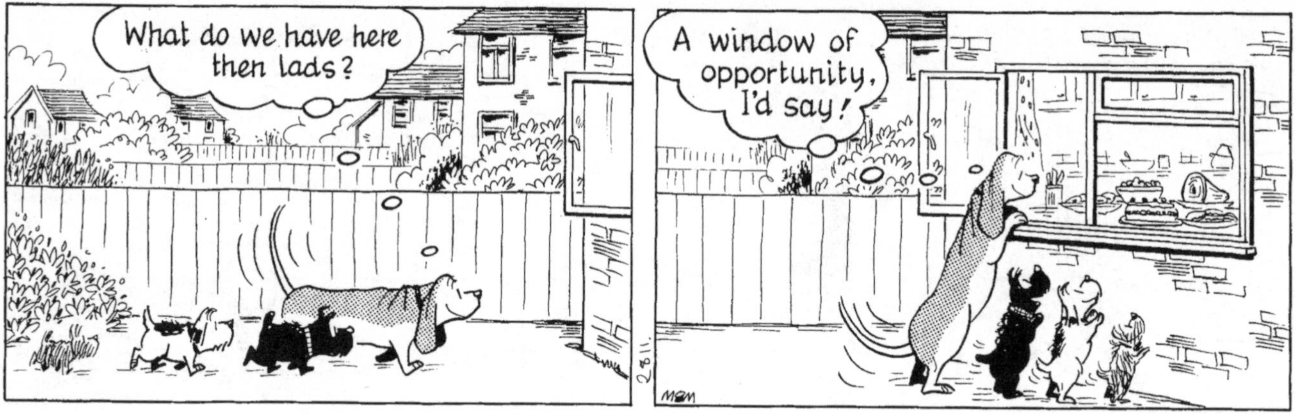
What do we have here then lads?
A window of opportunity, I'd say!

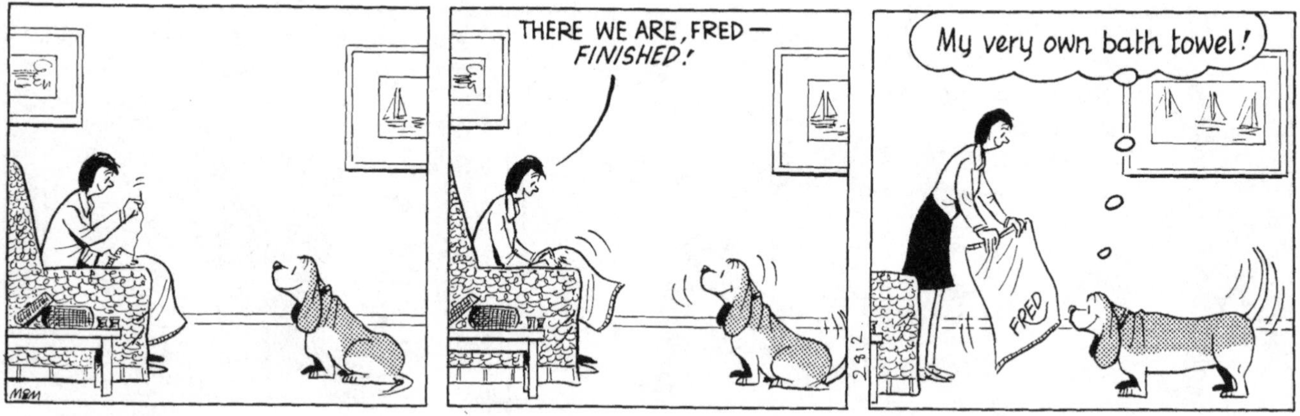
THERE WE ARE, FRED — *FINISHED!*
My very own bath towel!
FRED

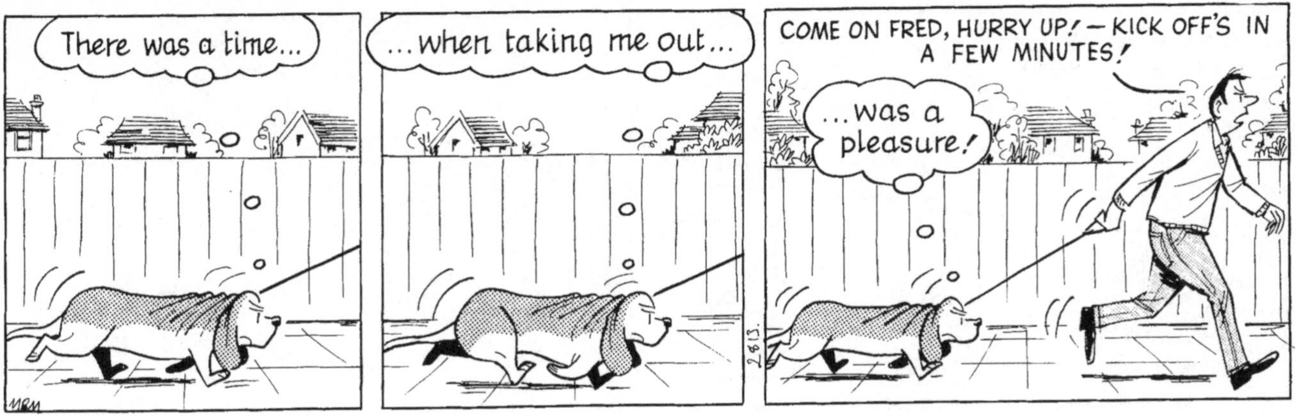
There was a time...
...when taking me out...
COME ON FRED, HURRY UP! — KICK OFF'S IN A FEW MINUTES!
...was a pleasure!
MBM
2813.

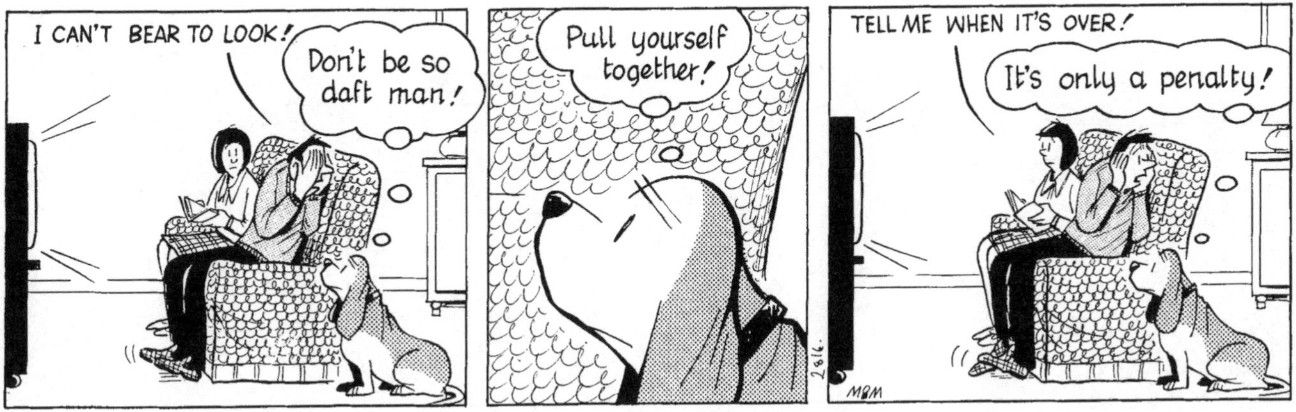
I CAN'T BEAR TO LOOK!
Don't be so daft man!
Pull yourself together!
TELL ME WHEN IT'S OVER!
It's only a penalty!
2816.
MBM

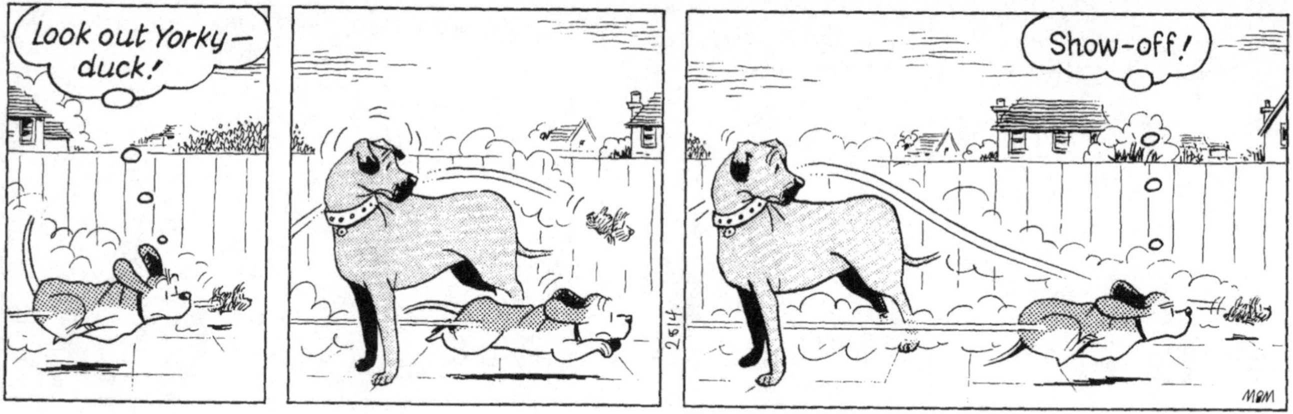
Look out Yorky—duck!
Show-off!

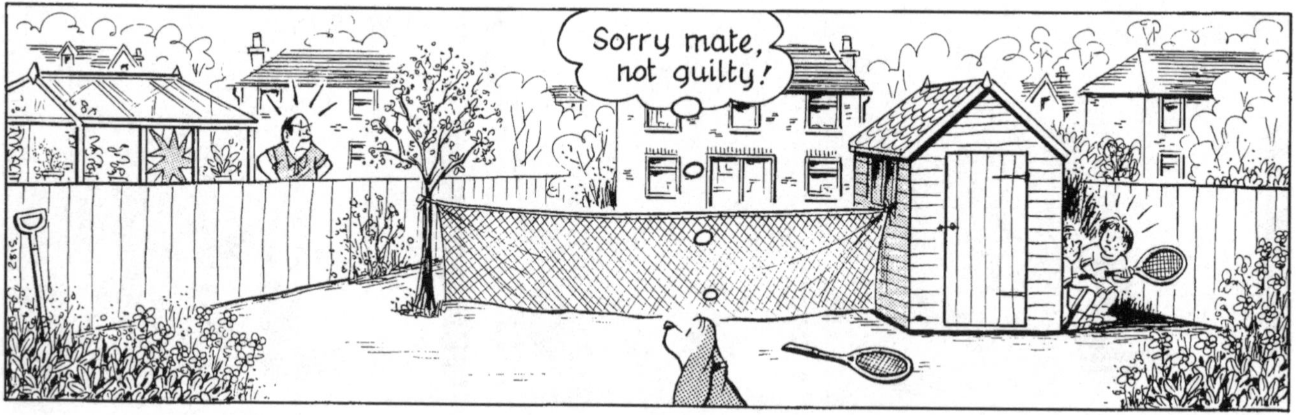
Sorry mate, not guilty!

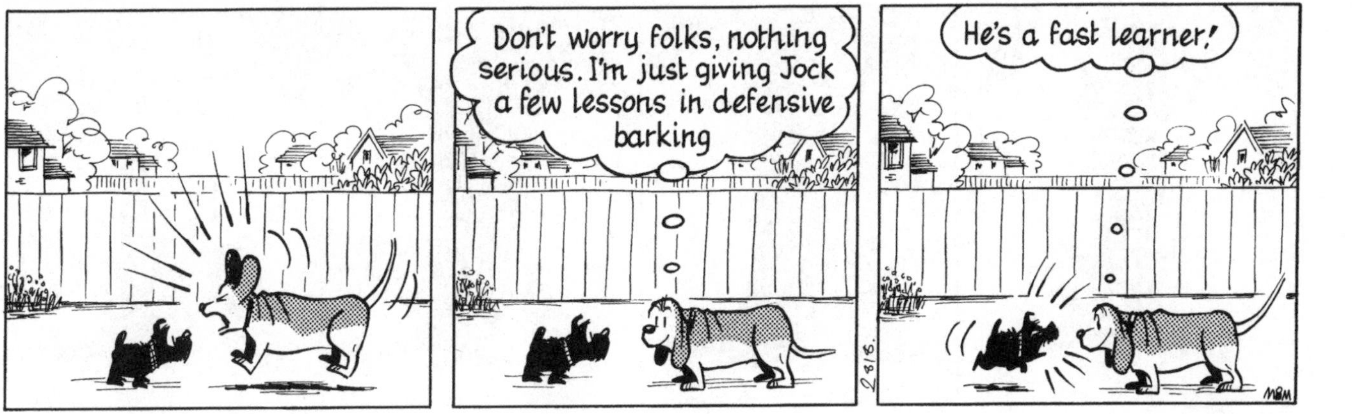
Don't worry folks, nothing serious. I'm just giving Jock a few lessons in defensive barking
He's a fast learner!
MBM

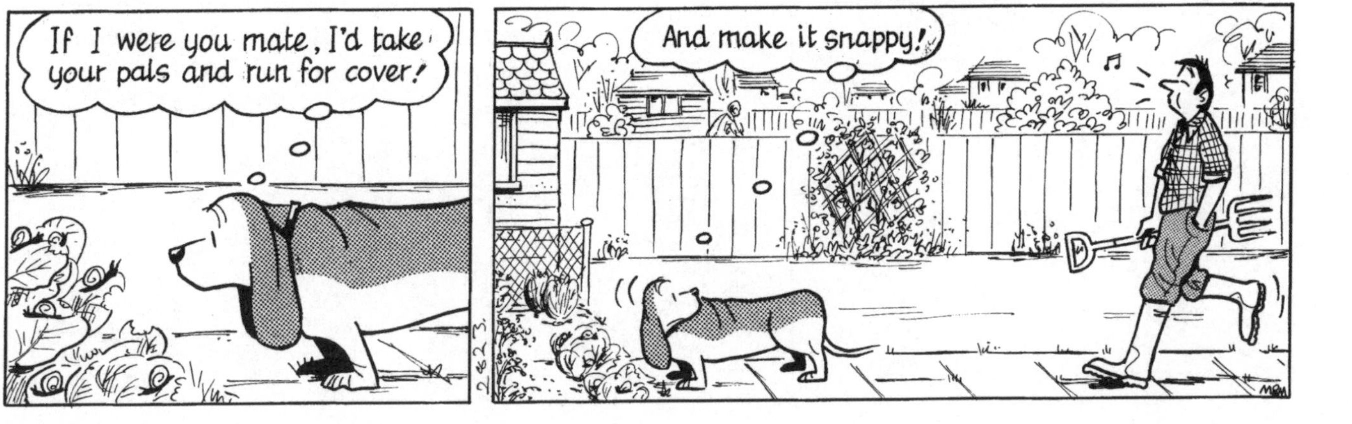
If I were you mate, I'd take your pals and run for cover!
And make it snappy!
MBM

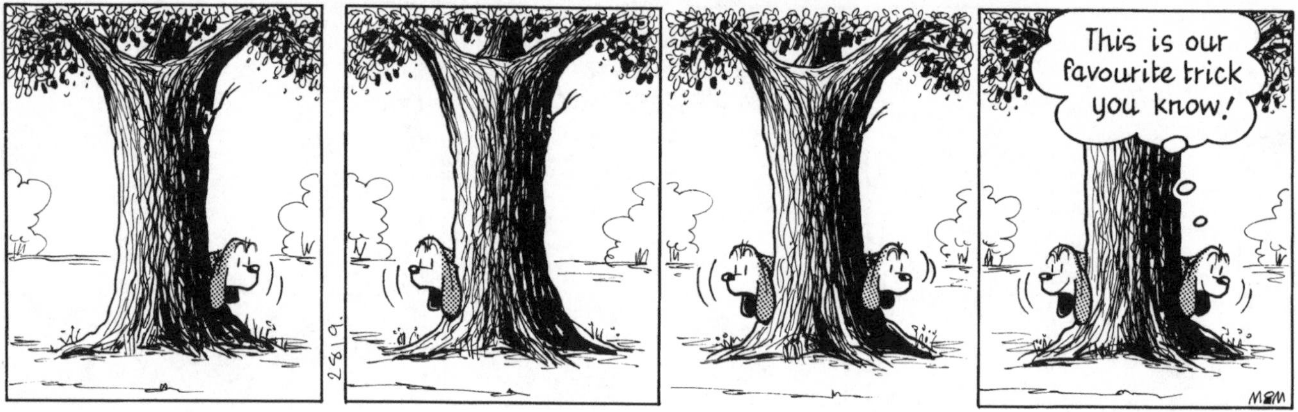
This is our favourite trick you know!

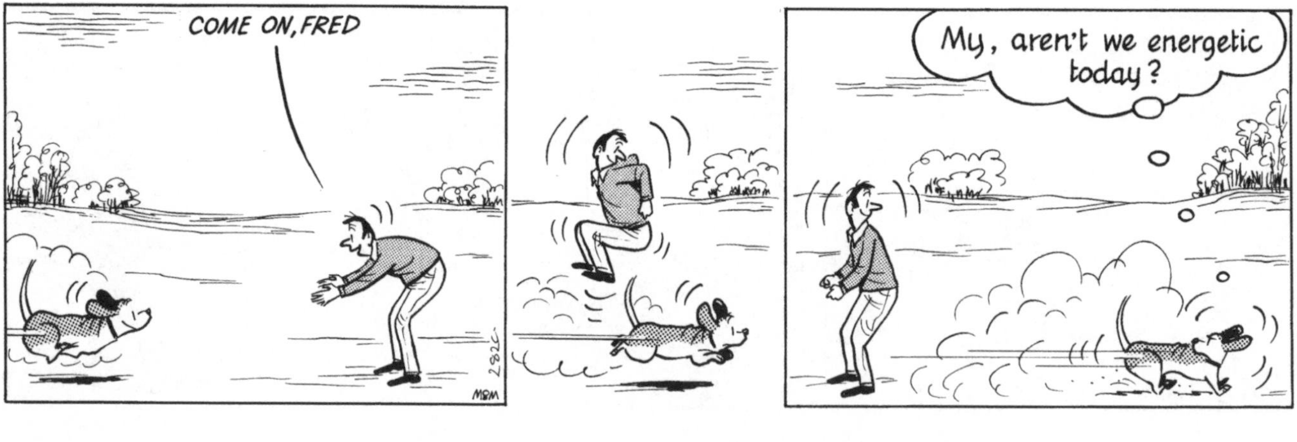
COME ON, FRED
My, aren't we energetic today?

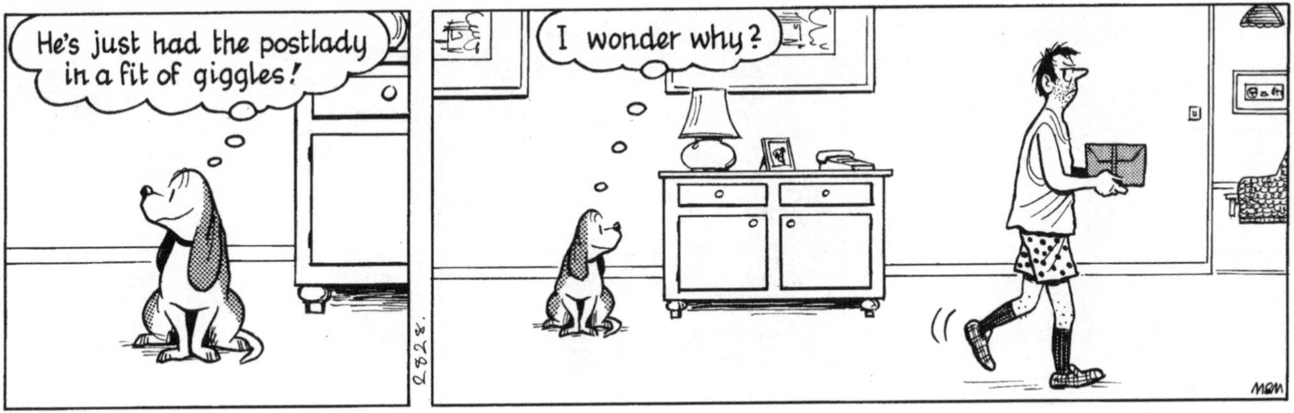
He's just had the postlady in a fit of giggles!
I wonder why?

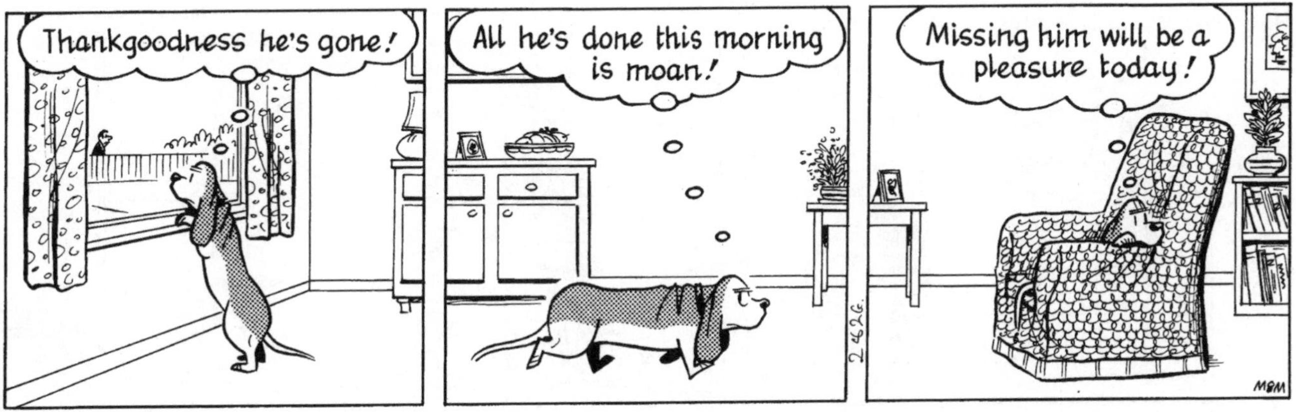
Thankgoodness he's gone!
All he's done this morning is moan!
Missing him will be a pleasure today!

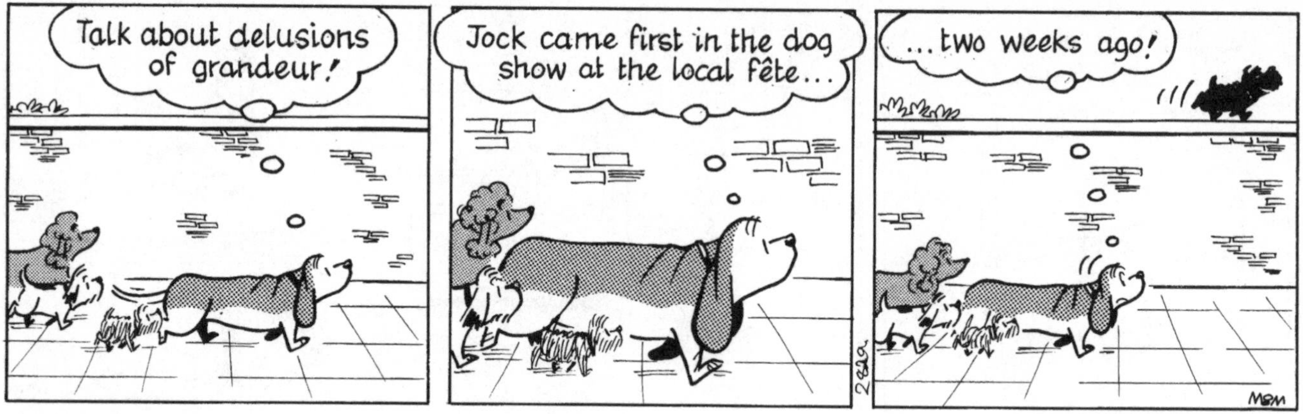
Talk about delusions of grandeur!
Jock came first in the dog show at the local fête...
...two weeks ago!

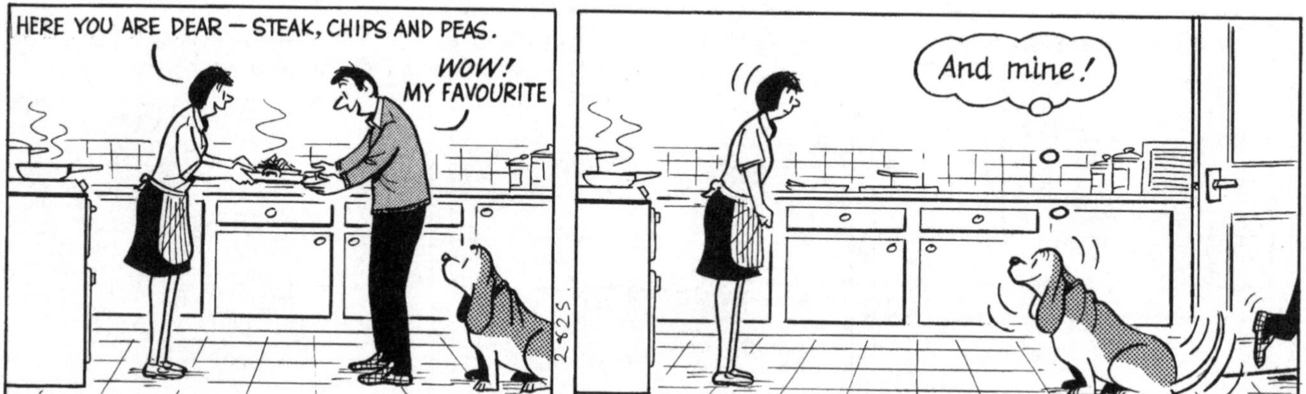
HERE YOU ARE DEAR — STEAK, CHIPS AND PEAS.
WOW! MY FAVOURITE
And mine!

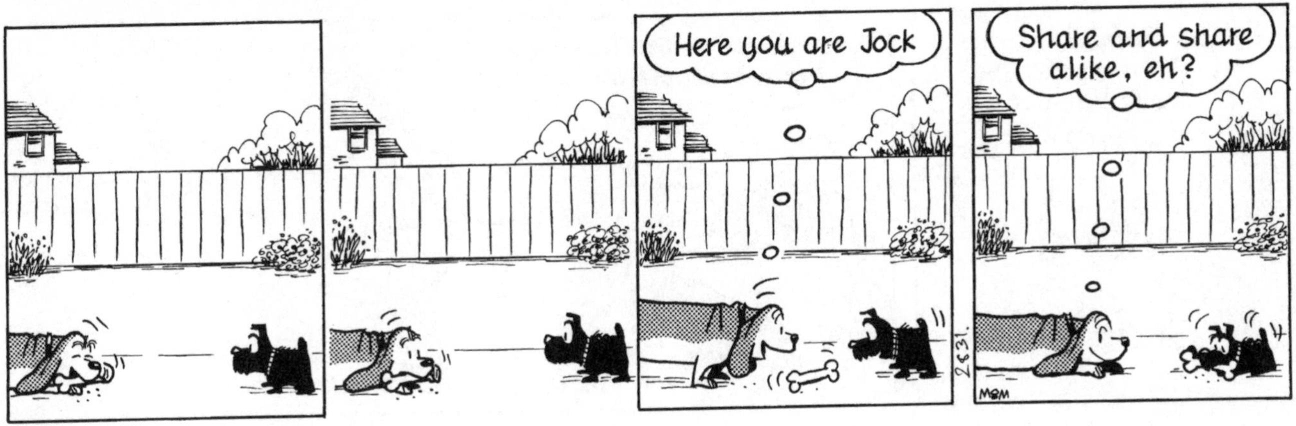
Here you are Jock
Share and share alike, eh?
2631.
M&M

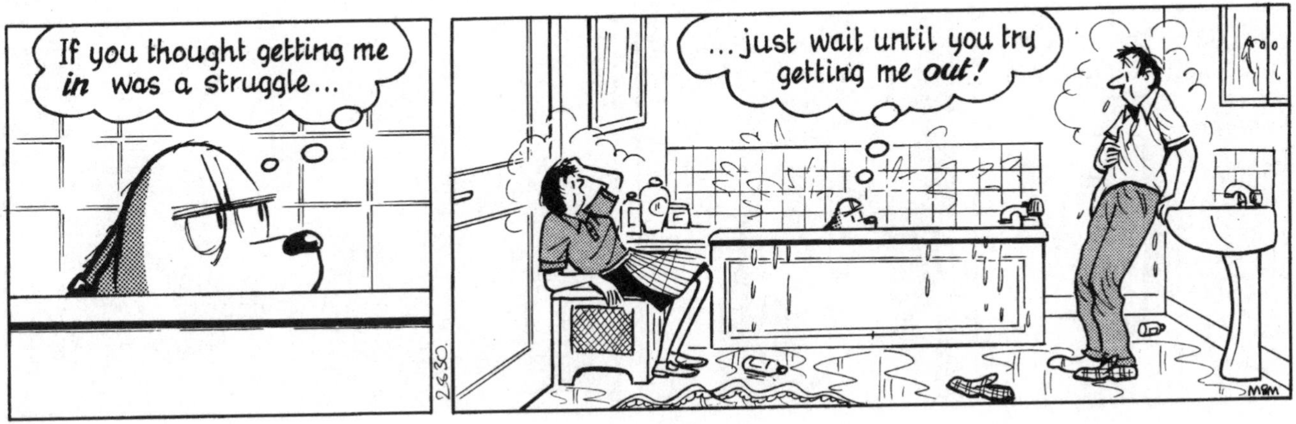
If you thought getting me *in* was a struggle...
...just wait until you try getting me *out*!
2630.
M&M

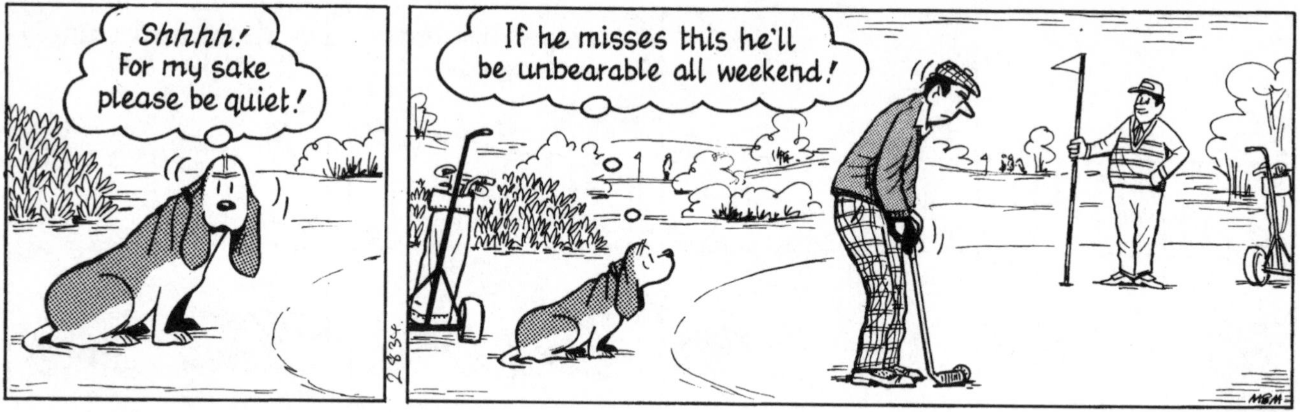
Shhhh! For my sake please be quiet!
If he misses this he'll be unbearable all weekend!

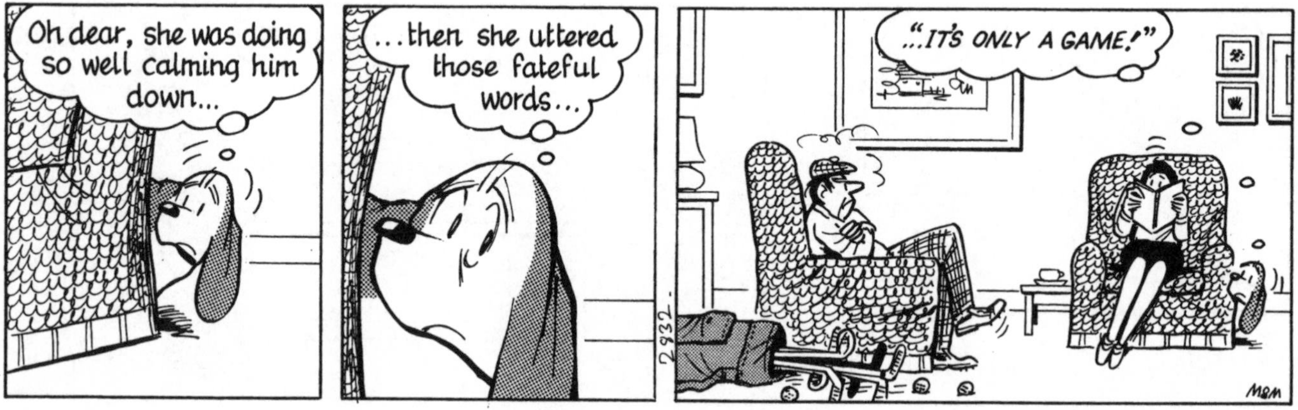
Oh dear, she was doing so well calming him down...
...then she uttered those fateful words...
..."IT'S ONLY A GAME!"

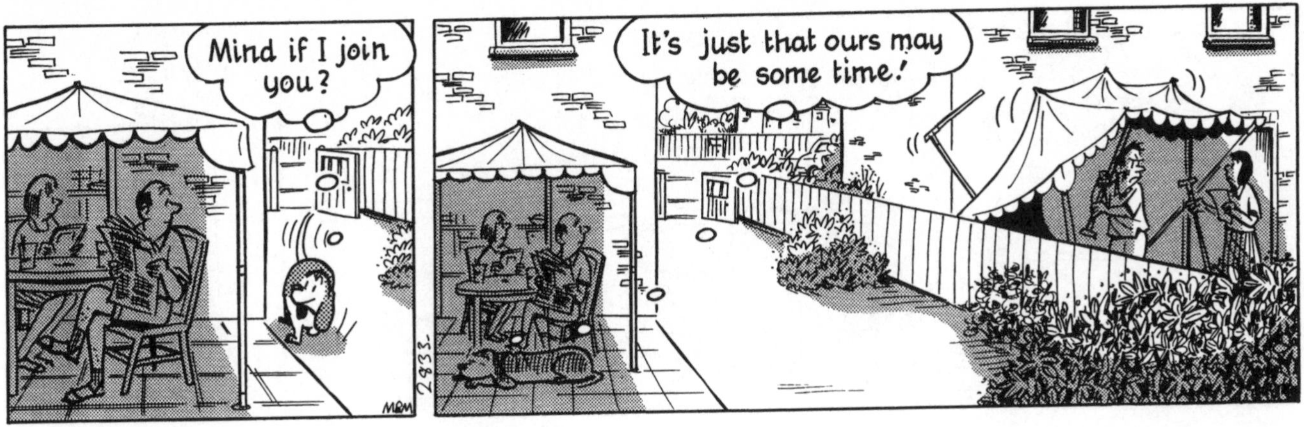
Mind if I join you?
It's just that ours may be some time!

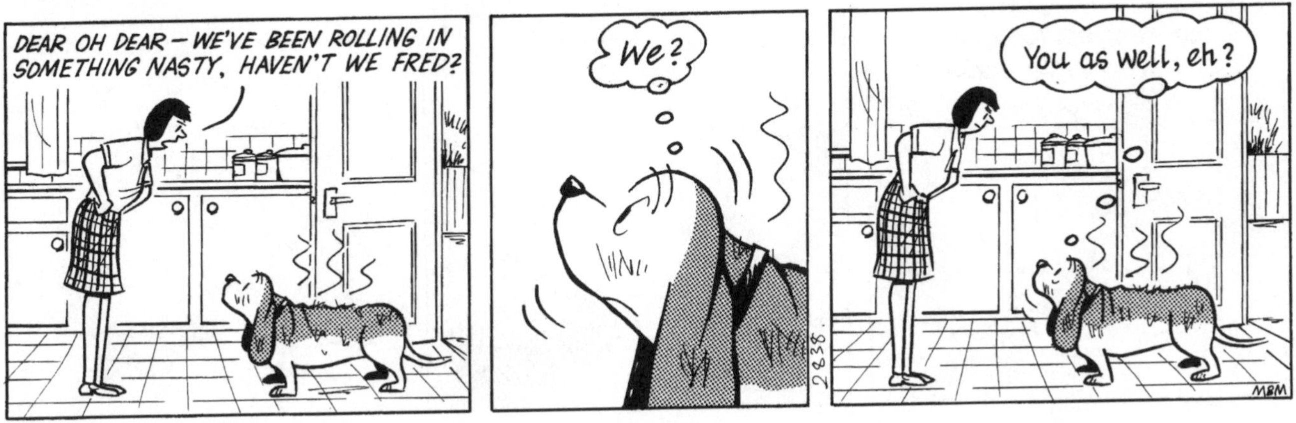
DEAR OH DEAR – WE'VE BEEN ROLLING IN SOMETHING NASTY, HAVEN'T WE FRED?
We?
You as well, eh?

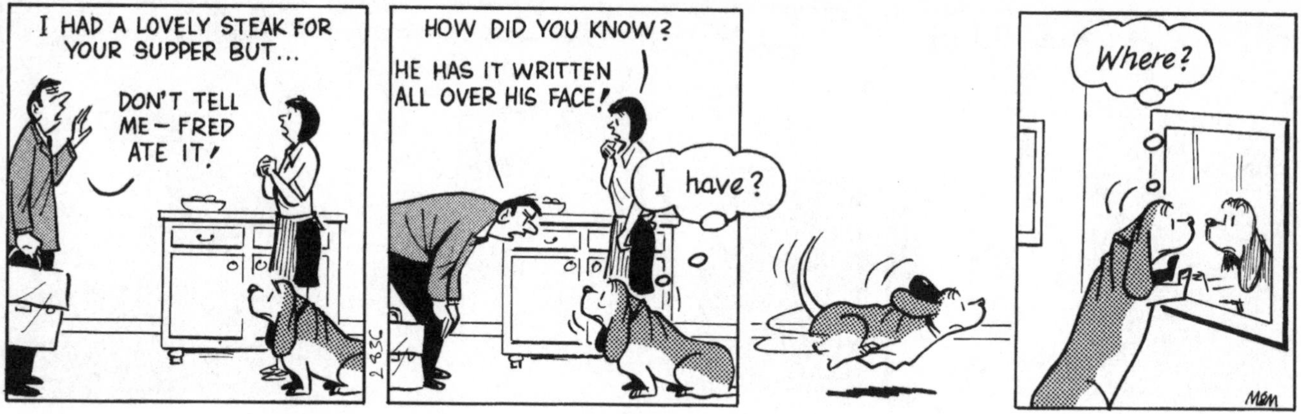
I HAD A LOVELY STEAK FOR YOUR SUPPER BUT...
DON'T TELL ME – FRED ATE IT!
HOW DID YOU KNOW?
HE HAS IT WRITTEN ALL OVER HIS FACE!
I have?
Where?

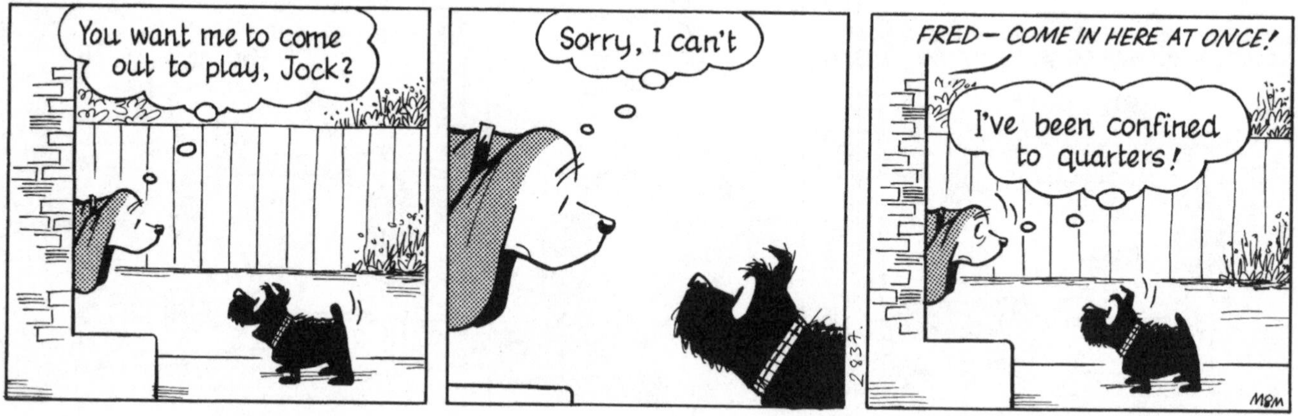
You want me to come out to play, Jock?
Sorry, I can't
FRED – COME IN HERE AT ONCE!
I've been confined to quarters!

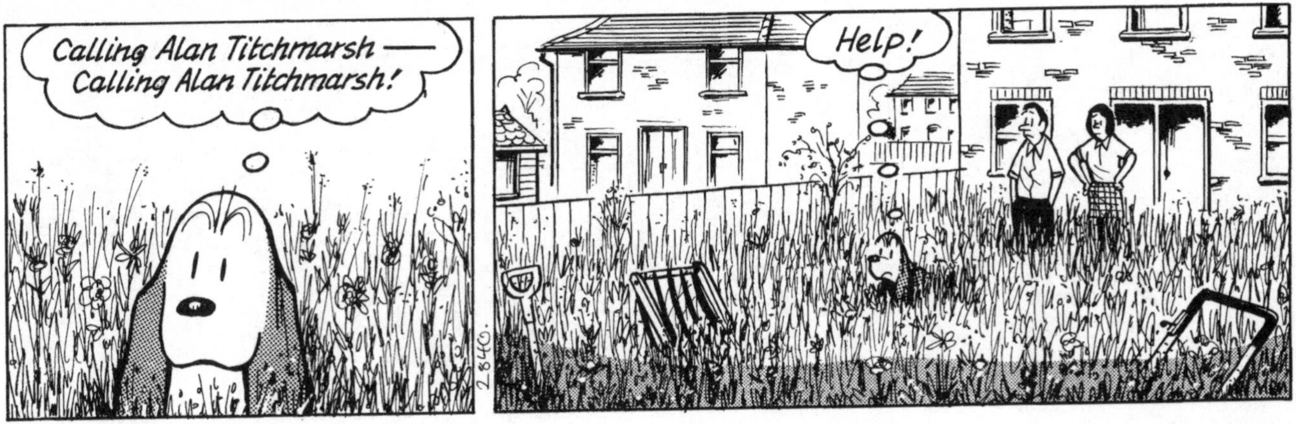
Calling Alan Titchmarsh — Calling Alan Titchmarsh!
2840.
Help!

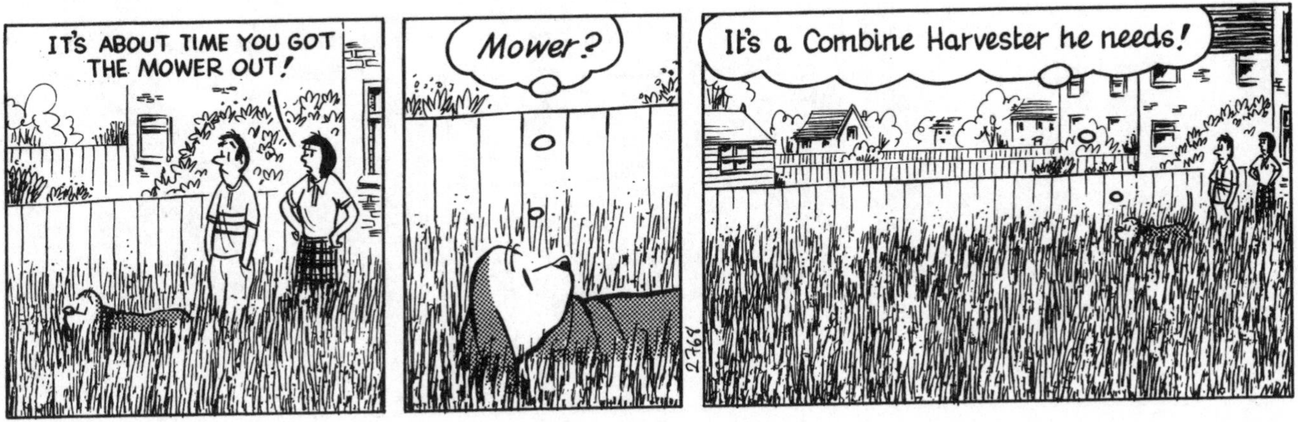
IT'S ABOUT TIME YOU GOT THE MOWER OUT!
Mower?
2769
It's a Combine Harvester he needs!

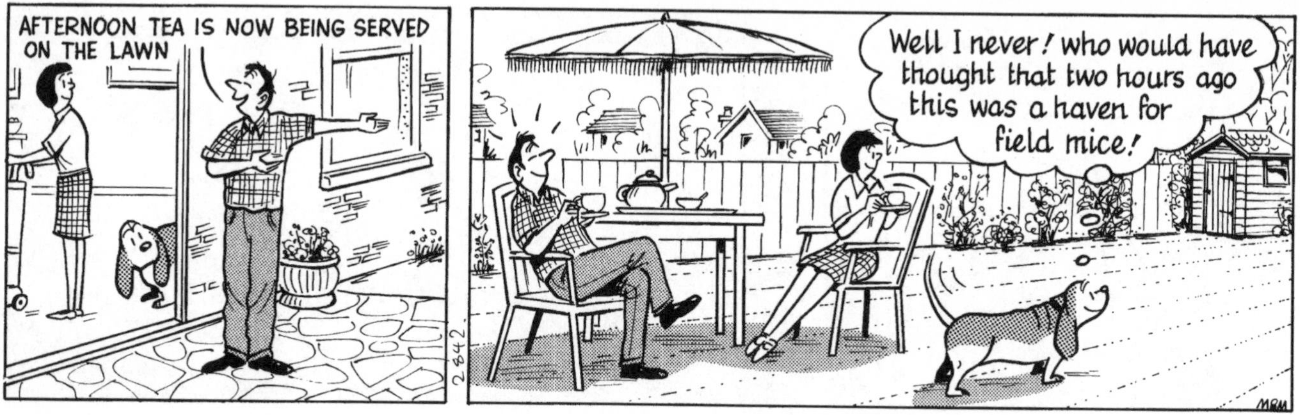
AFTERNOON TEA IS NOW BEING SERVED ON THE LAWN
Well I never! who would have thought that two hours ago this was a haven for field mice!

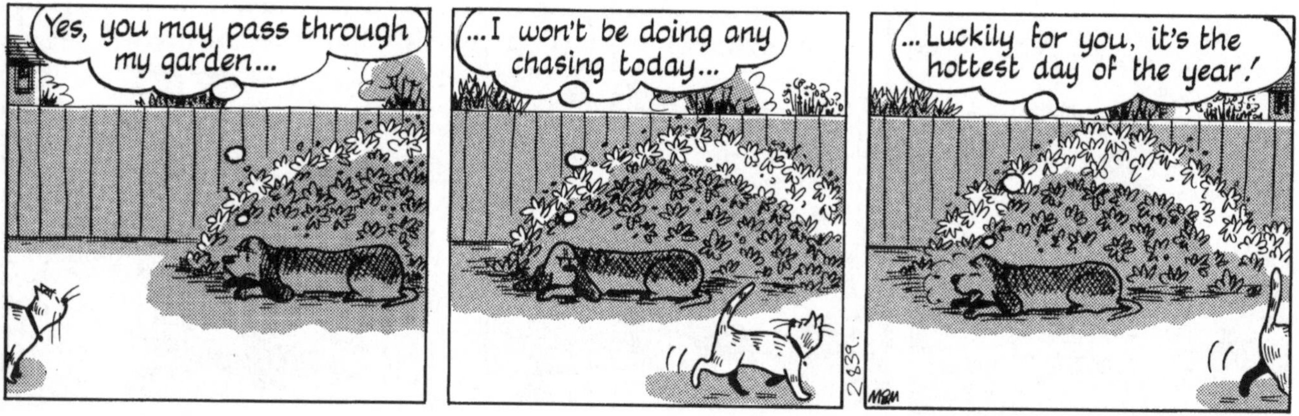
Yes, you may pass through my garden...
...I won't be doing any chasing today...
...Luckily for you, it's the hottest day of the year!

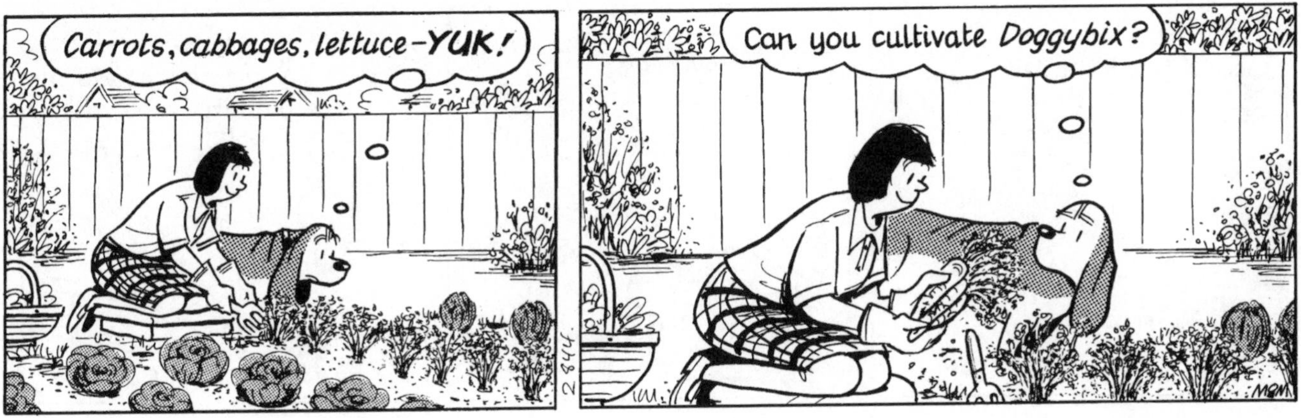
Carrots, cabbages, lettuce–YUK!
Can you cultivate Doggybix?
2844.

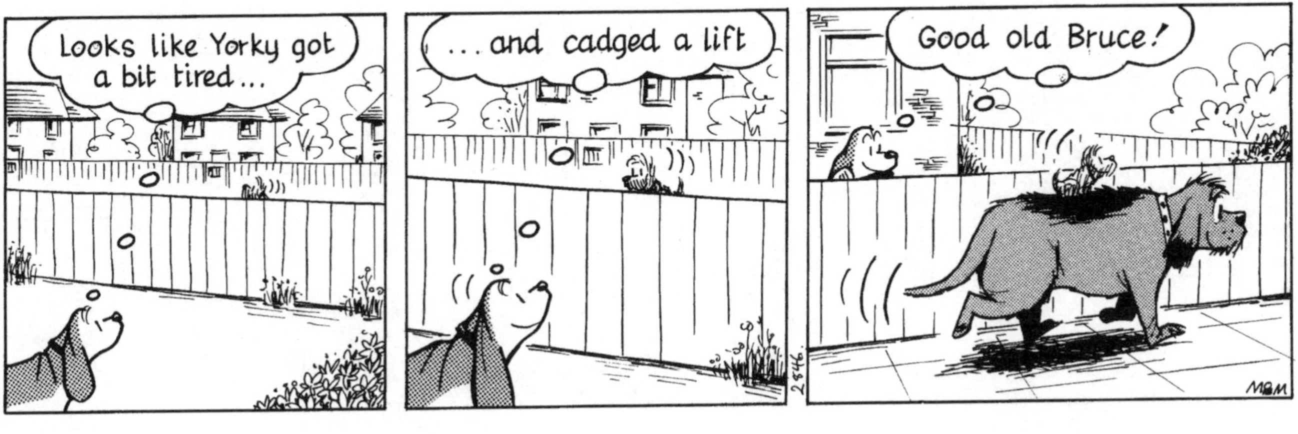
Looks like Yorky got a bit tired...
...and cadged a lift
Good old Bruce!
2846.

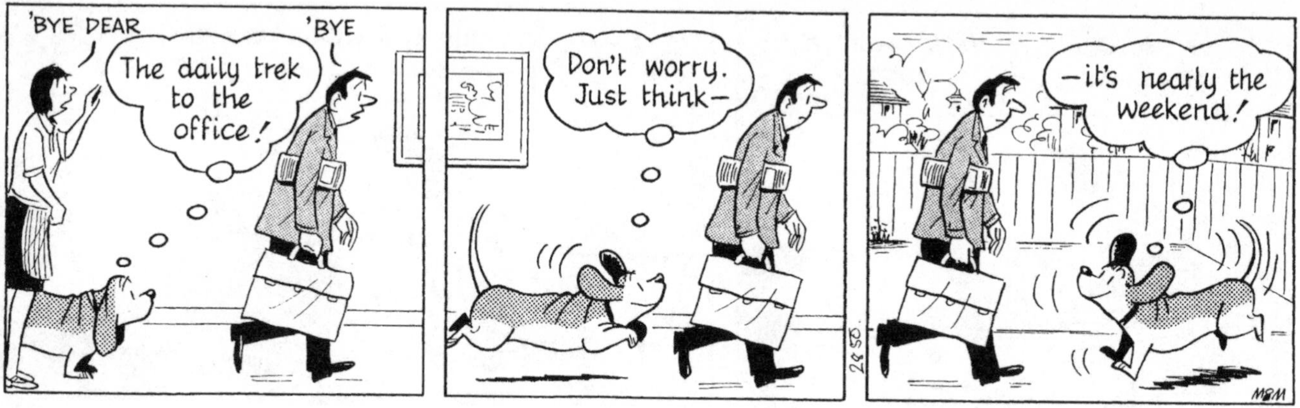
'BYE DEAR
The daily trek to the office!
'BYE
Don't worry. Just think—
—it's nearly the weekend!

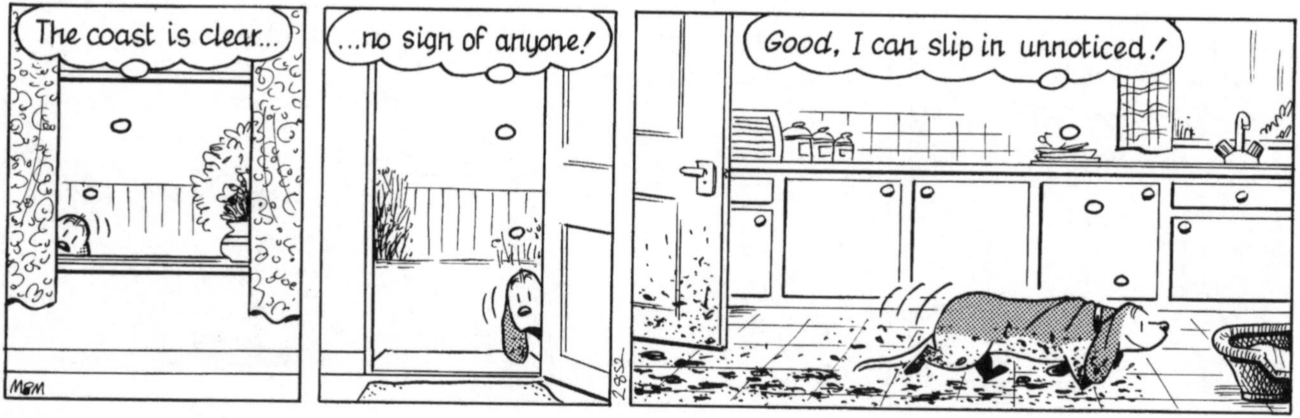
The coast is clear...
...no sign of anyone!
Good, I can slip in unnoticed!

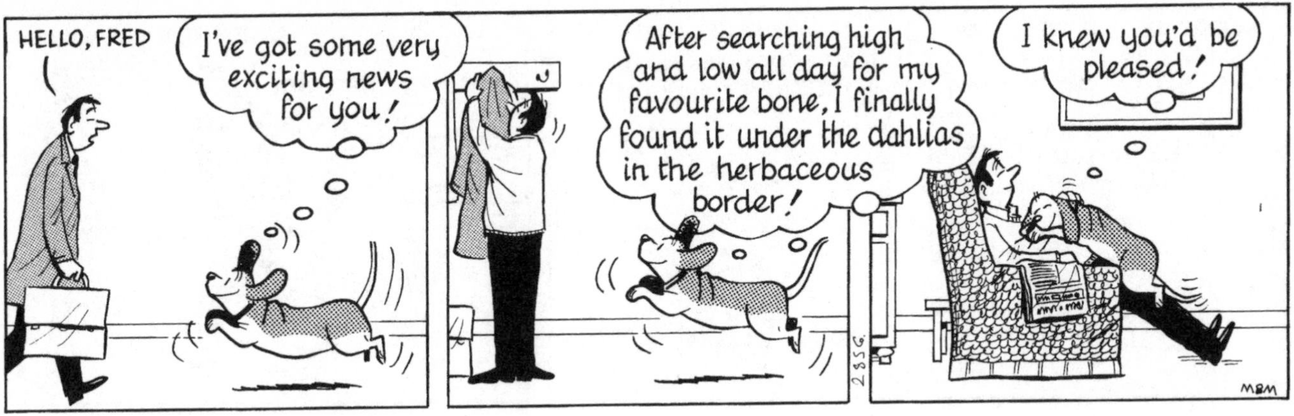
HELLO, FRED
I've got some very exciting news for you!
After searching high and low all day for my favourite bone, I finally found it under the dahlias in the herbaceous border!
I knew you'd be pleased!
MBM

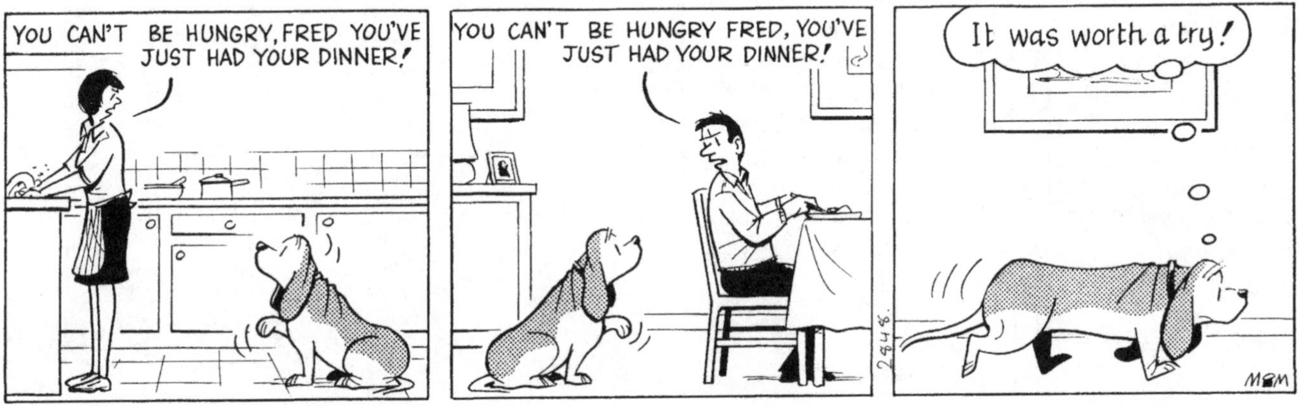
YOU CAN'T BE HUNGRY, FRED YOU'VE JUST HAD YOUR DINNER!
YOU CAN'T BE HUNGRY FRED, YOU'VE JUST HAD YOUR DINNER!
It was worth a try!
MBM

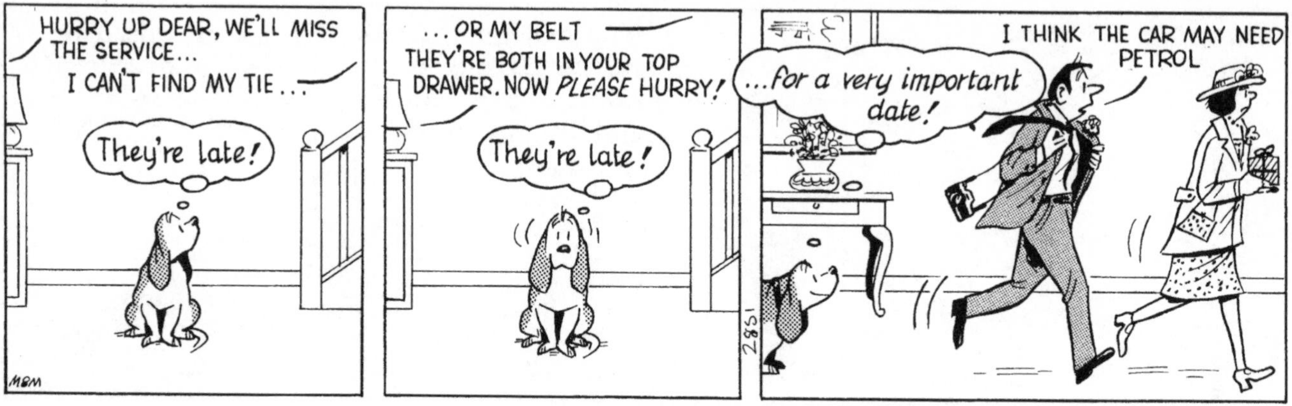
HURRY UP DEAR, WE'LL MISS THE SERVICE...
I CAN'T FIND MY TIE...
They're late!
MBM
...OR MY BELT
THEY'RE BOTH IN YOUR TOP DRAWER. NOW *PLEASE* HURRY!
They're late!
2851
...for a very important date!
I THINK THE CAR MAY NEED PETROL

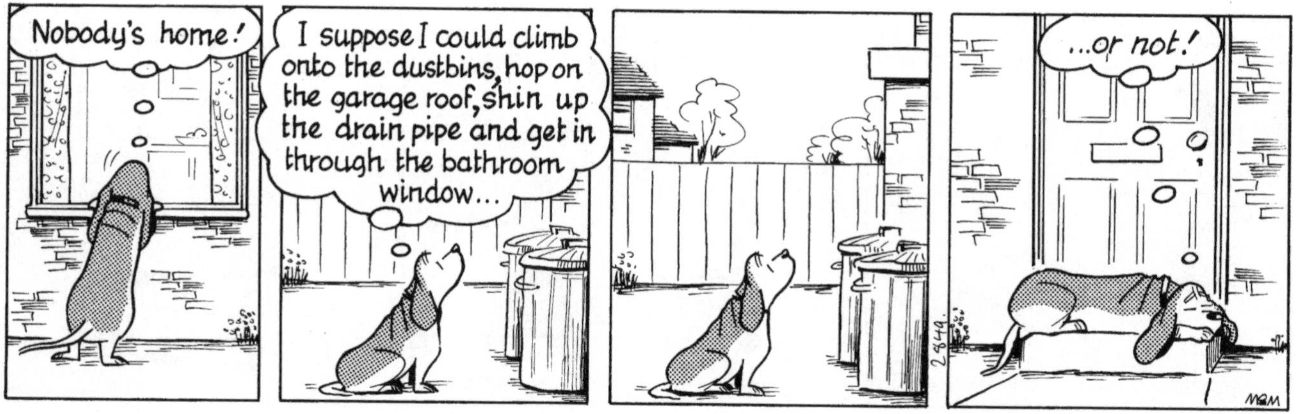
Nobody's home!
I suppose I could climb onto the dustbins, hop on the garage roof, shin up the drain pipe and get in through the bathroom window...
2449.
...or not!
MBM

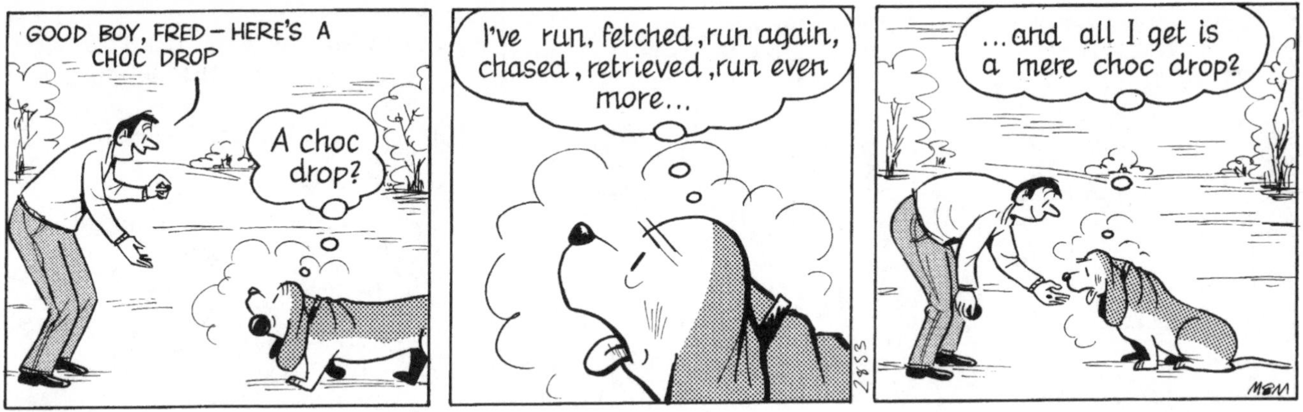
GOOD BOY, FRED – HERE'S A CHOC DROP
A choc drop?
I've run, fetched, run again, chased, retrieved, run even more...
2853
...and all I get is a mere choc drop?
M&M

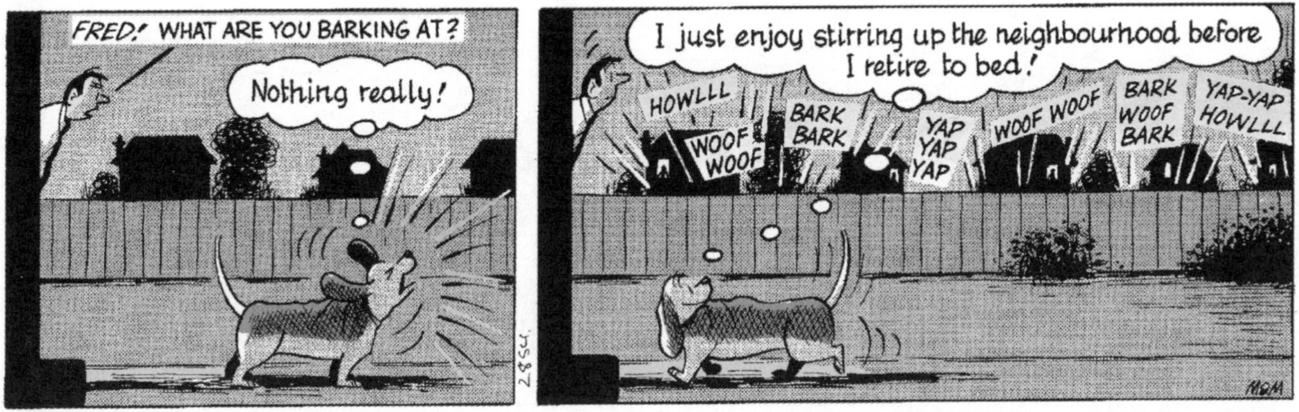
FRED! WHAT ARE YOU BARKING AT?
Nothing really!
2854
I just enjoy stirring up the neighbourhood before I retire to bed!
HOWLLL
WOOF WOOF
BARK BARK
YAP YAP YAP
WOOF WOOF
BARK WOOF BARK
YAP-YAP HOWLLL
M&M

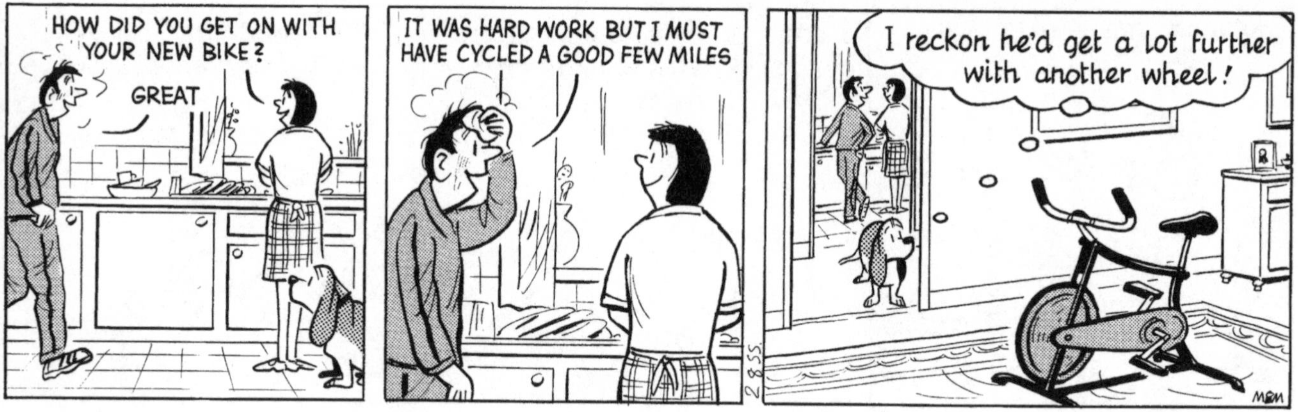
HOW DID YOU GET ON WITH YOUR NEW BIKE?
GREAT
IT WAS HARD WORK BUT I MUST HAVE CYCLED A GOOD FEW MILES
I reckon he'd get a lot further with another wheel!

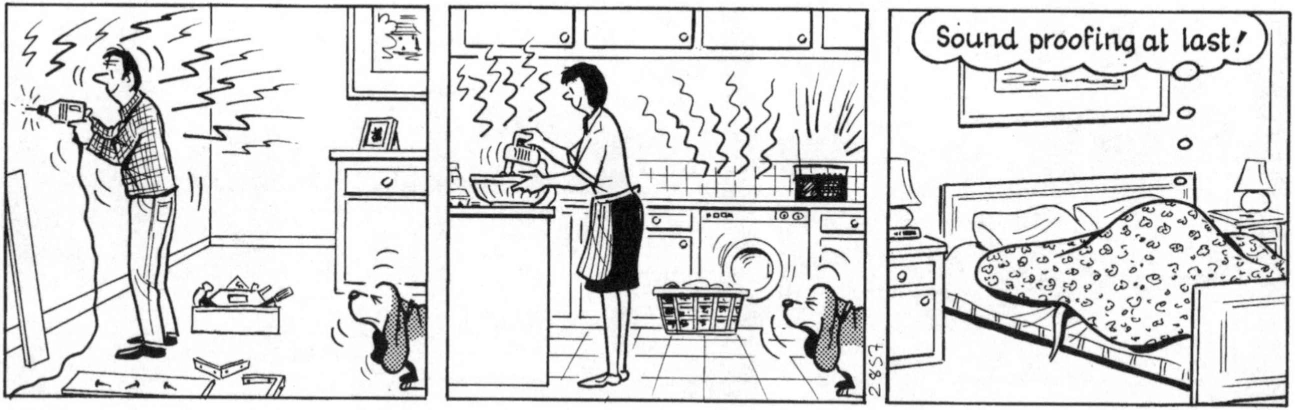
Sound proofing at last!

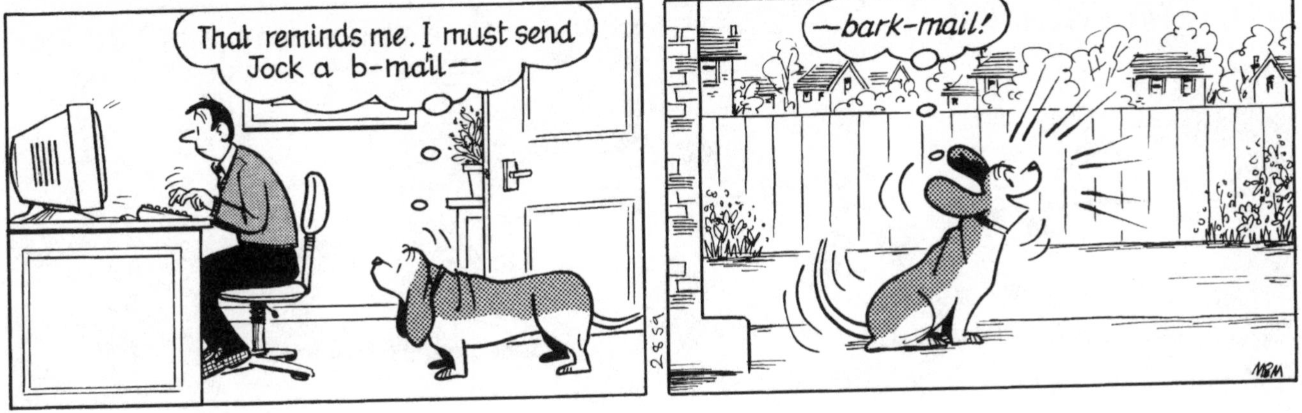
That reminds me. I must send Jock a b-mail—
—bark-mail!
2859

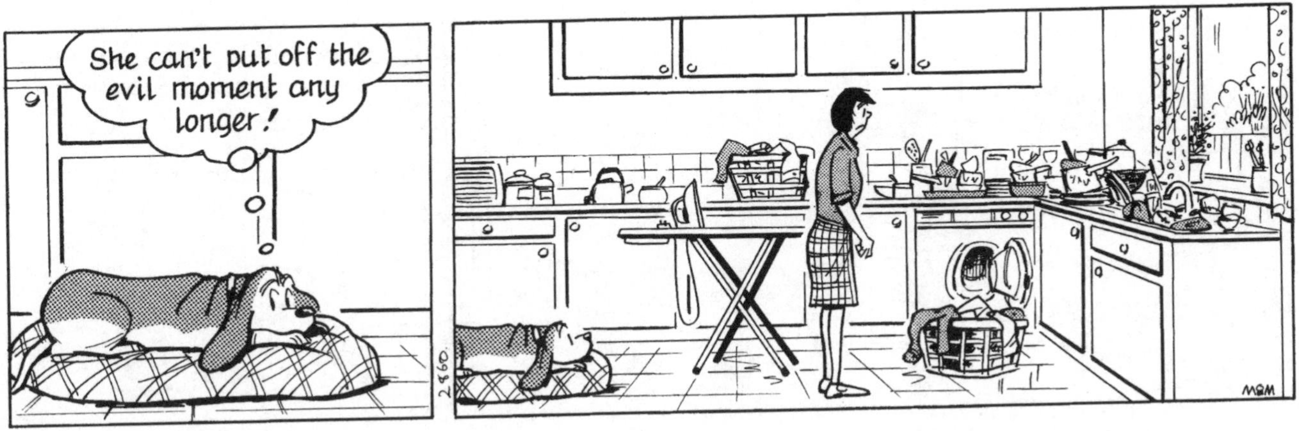
She can't put off the evil moment any longer!
2860

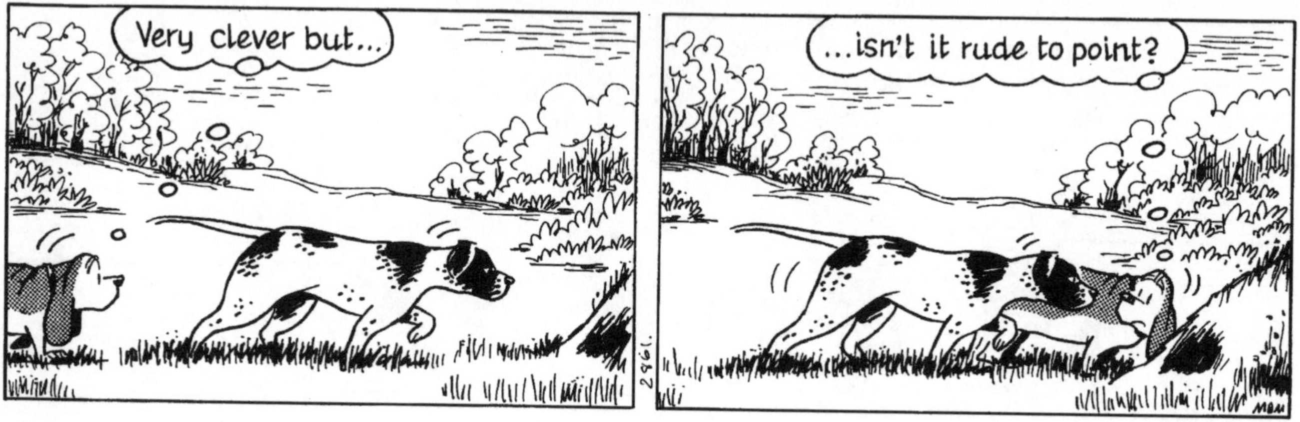
Very clever but...
...isn't it rude to point?
MBM

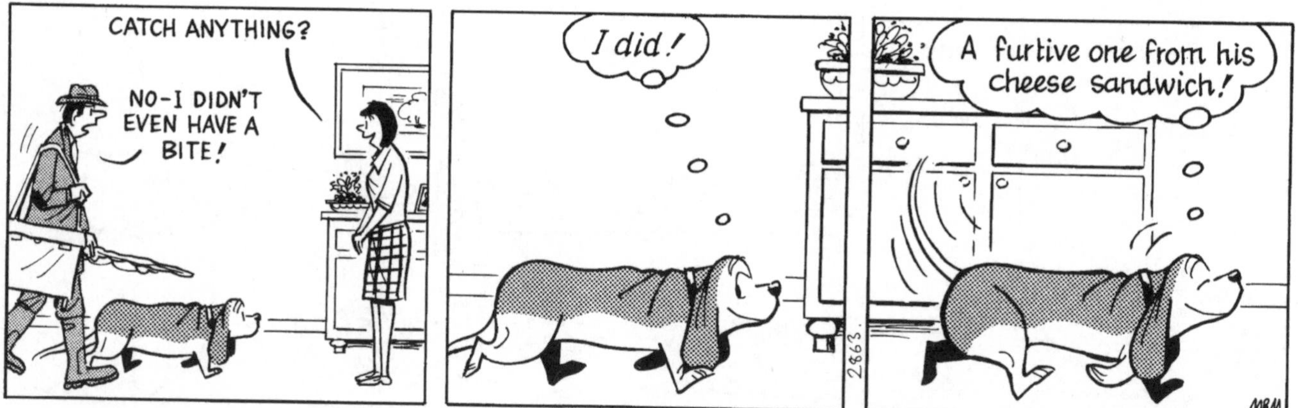
CATCH ANYTHING?
NO–I DIDN'T EVEN HAVE A BITE!
I did!
A furtive one from his cheese sandwich!
2863.
MBM

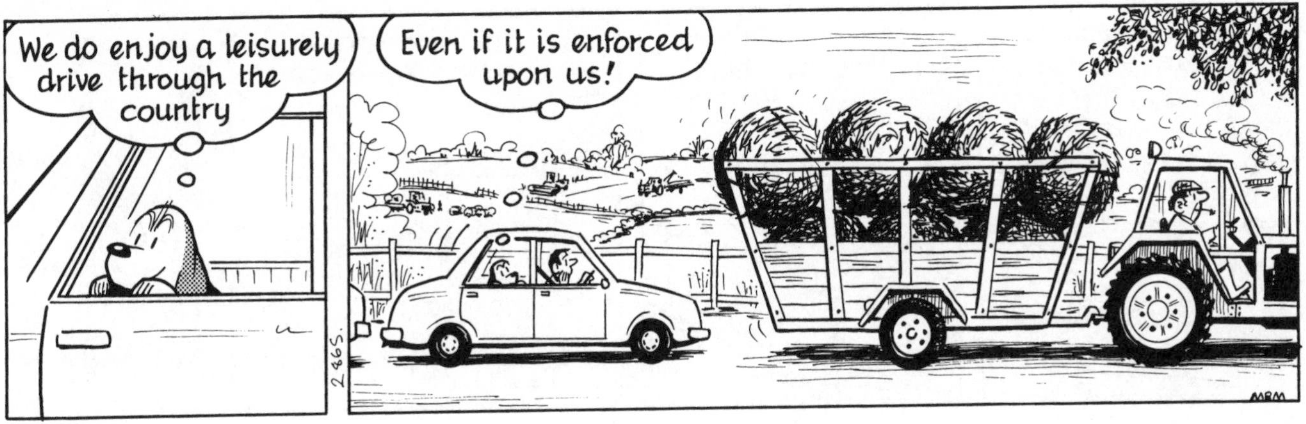
We do enjoy a leisurely drive through the country
Even if it is enforced upon us!

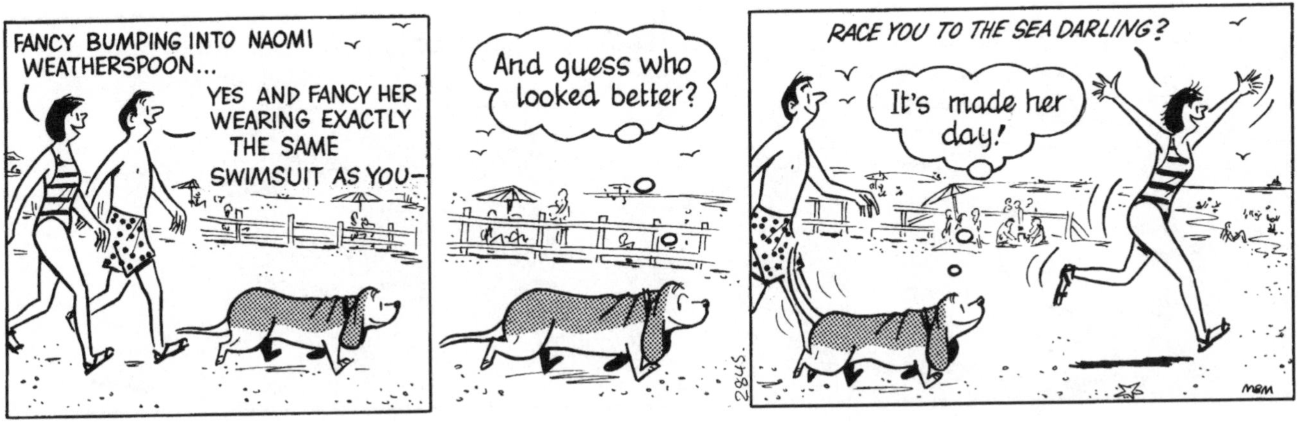
FANCY BUMPING INTO NAOMI WEATHERSPOON...
YES AND FANCY HER WEARING EXACTLY THE SAME SWIMSUIT AS YOU-
And guess who looked better?
RACE YOU TO THE SEA DARLING?
It's made her day!

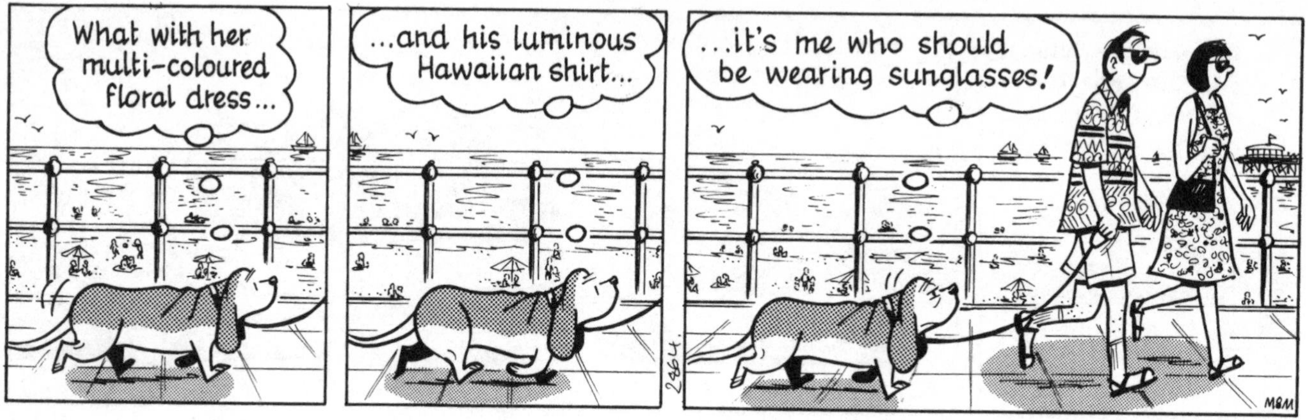
What with her multi-coloured floral dress...
...and his luminous Hawaiian shirt...
...it's me who should be wearing sunglasses!
2964.
MBM

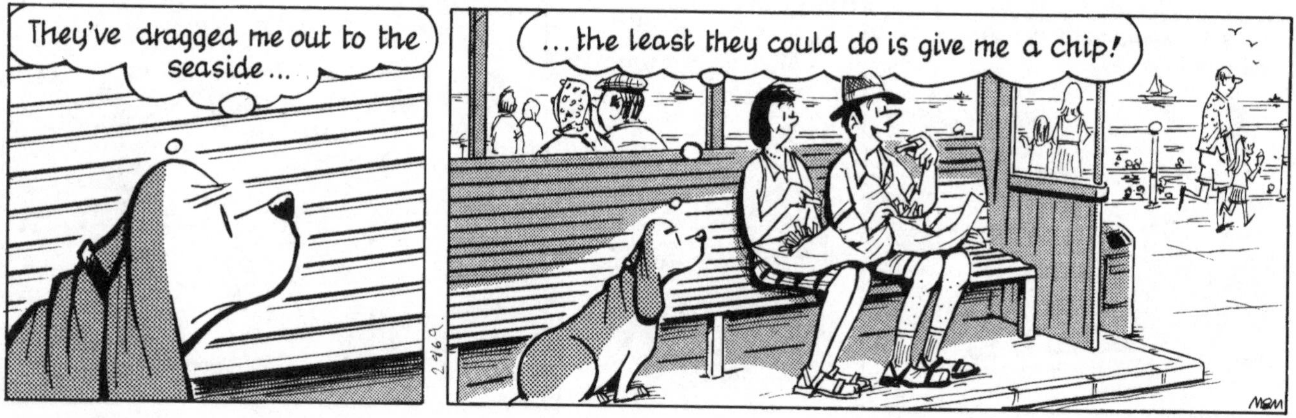
They've dragged me out to the seaside...
...the least they could do is give me a chip!
2969
MBM

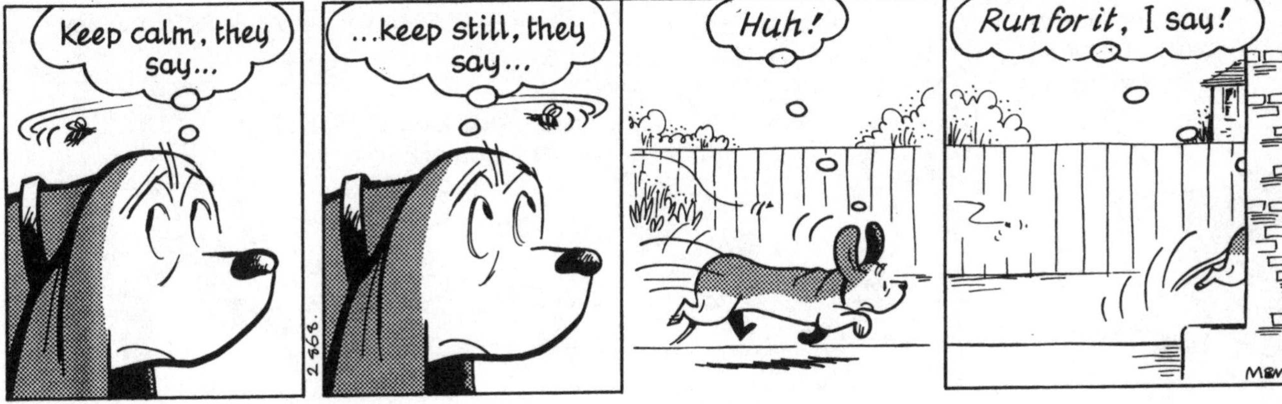
Keep calm, they say...
...keep still, they say...
Huh!
Run for it, I say!
2868.
M&M

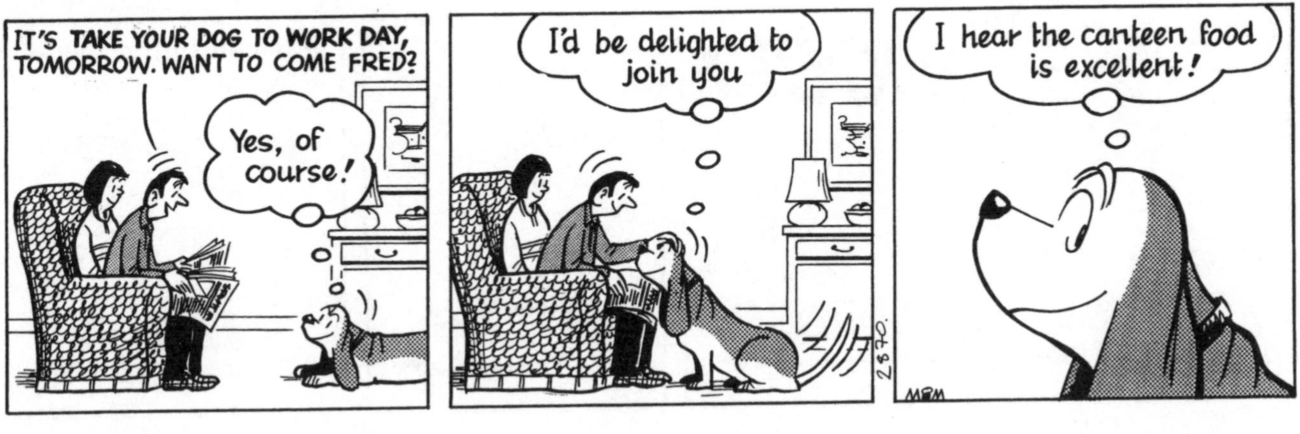
IT'S TAKE YOUR DOG TO WORK DAY, TOMORROW. WANT TO COME FRED?
Yes, of course!
I'd be delighted to join you
I hear the canteen food is excellent!
2870.
M&M

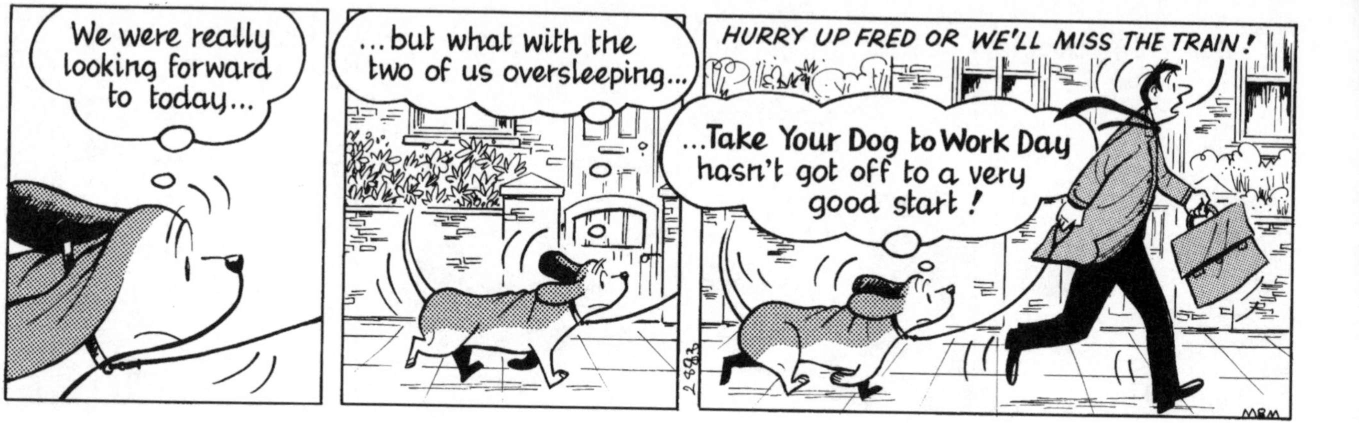
We were really looking forward to today...
...but what with the two of us oversleeping...
HURRY UP FRED OR WE'LL MISS THE TRAIN!
...Take Your Dog to Work Day hasn't got off to a very good start!

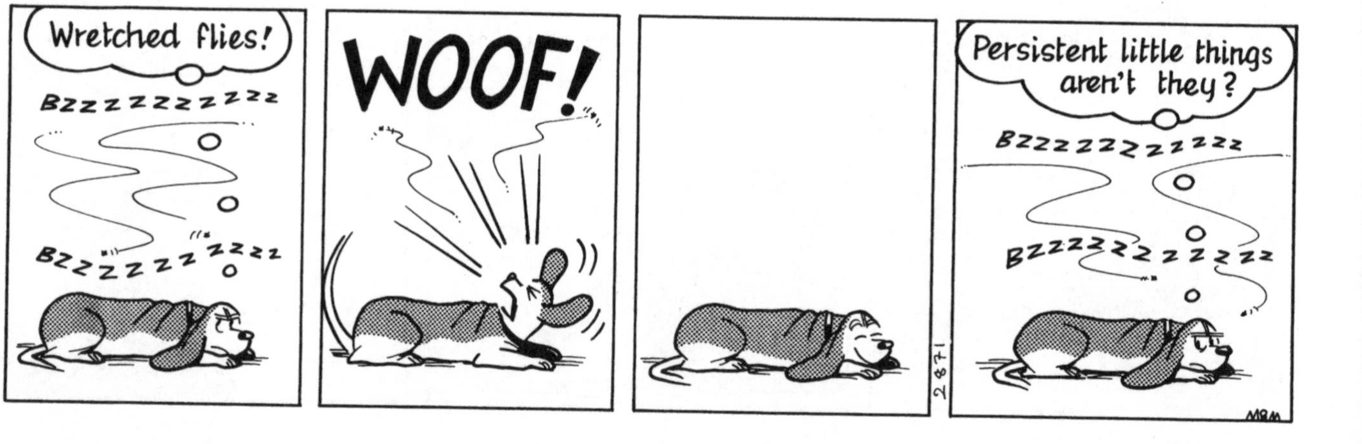
Wretched flies!
BZZZZZZZZZZZ
BZZZZZZZZZZZ
WOOF!
Persistent little things aren't they?
BZZZZZZZZZZZ
BZZZZZZZZZZZZ

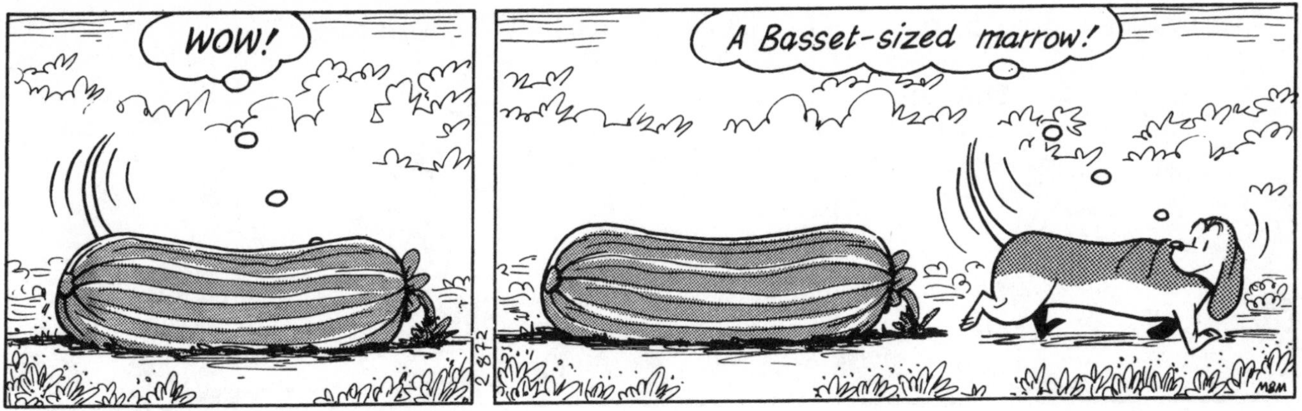
WOW!
A Basset-sized marrow!
2872
MBM

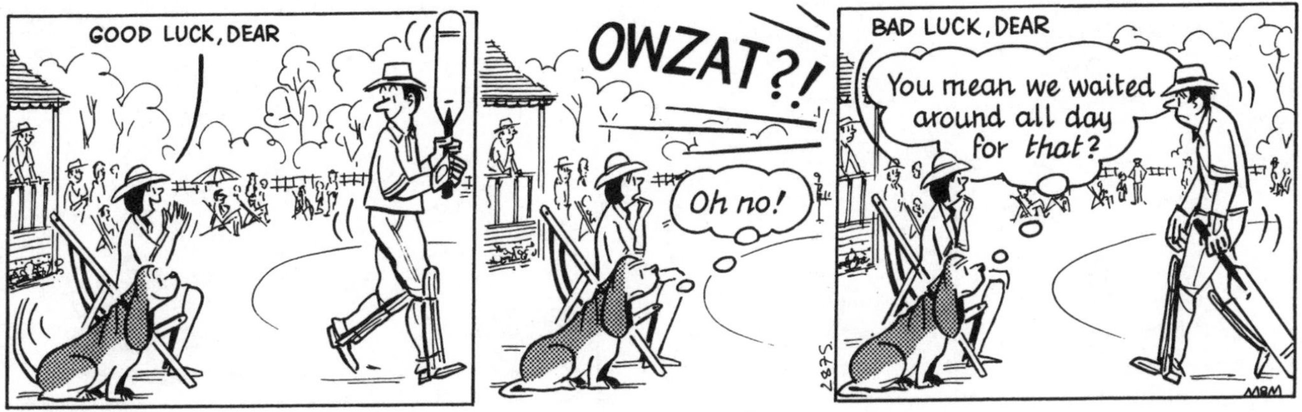
GOOD LUCK, DEAR
OWZAT?!
Oh no!
BAD LUCK, DEAR
You mean we waited around all day for *that*?
2875
MBM

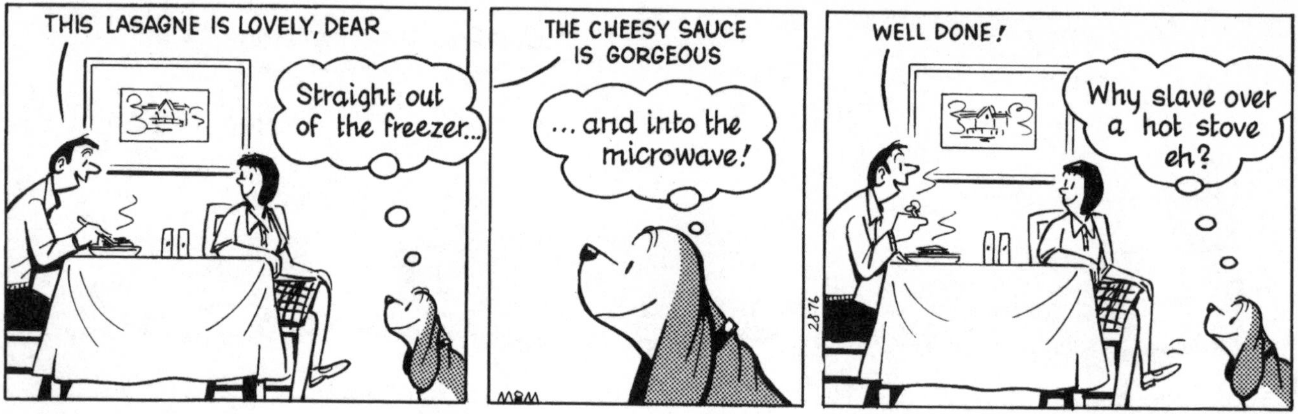
THIS LASAGNE IS LOVELY, DEAR
Straight out of the freezer...
THE CHEESY SAUCE IS GORGEOUS
... and into the microwave!
WELL DONE!
Why slave over a hot stove eh?

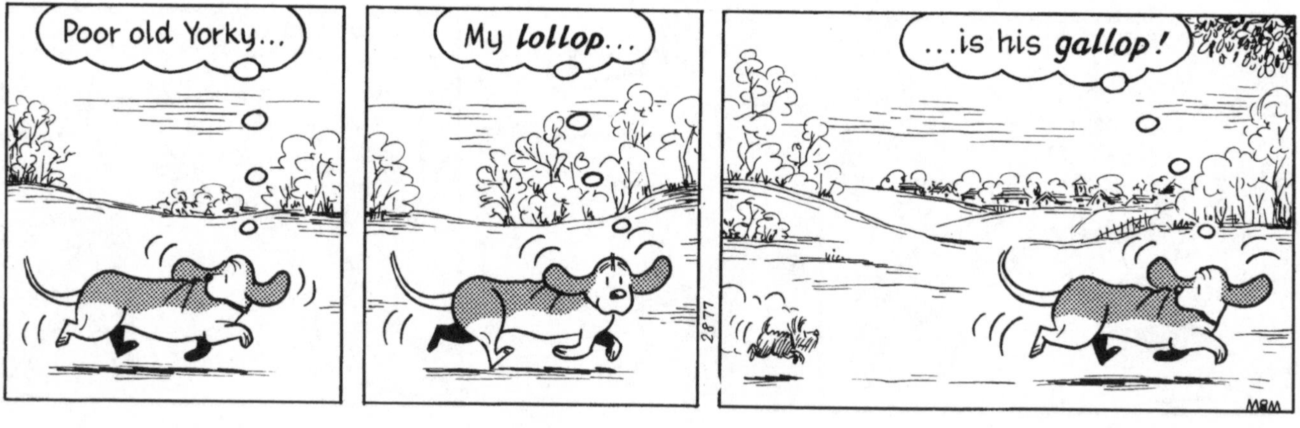
Poor old Yorky...
My **lollop**...
...is his **gallop**!

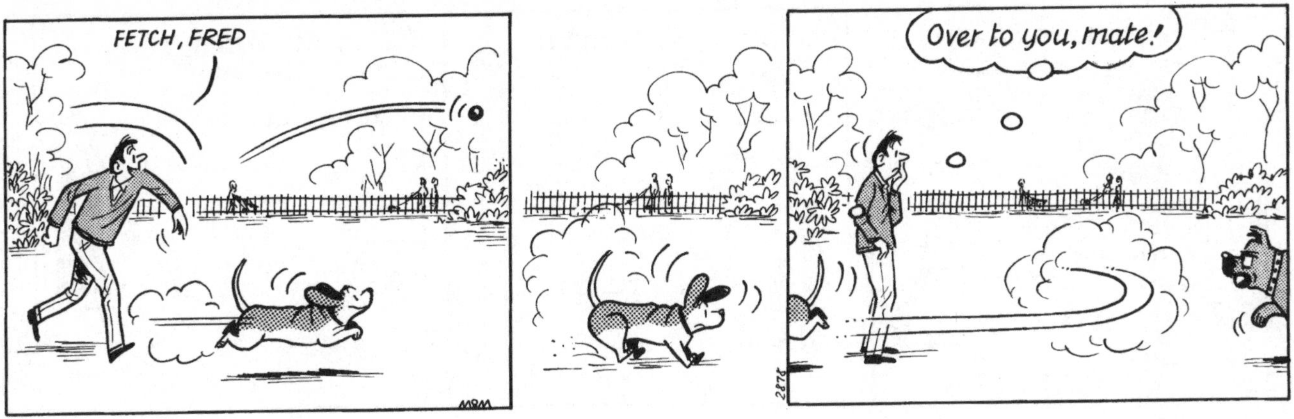
FETCH, FRED
Over to you, mate!

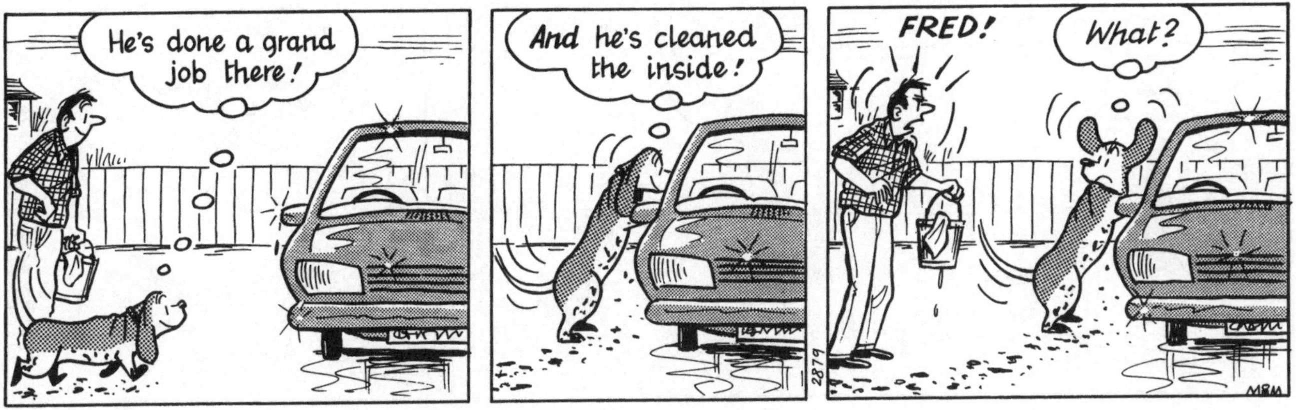
He's done a grand job there!
And he's cleaned the inside!
FRED!
What?

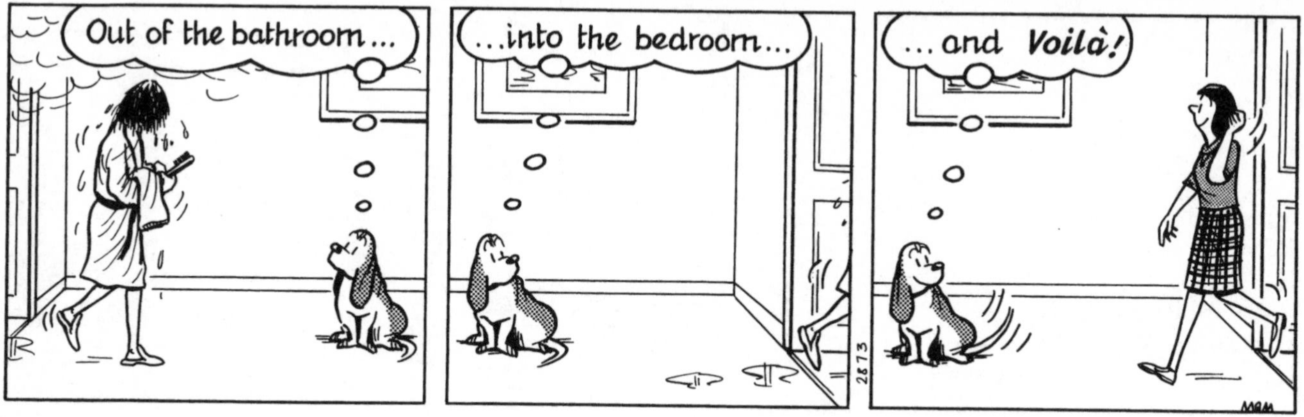

Out of the bathroom...
...into the bedroom...
...and Voilà!
2873
MGM

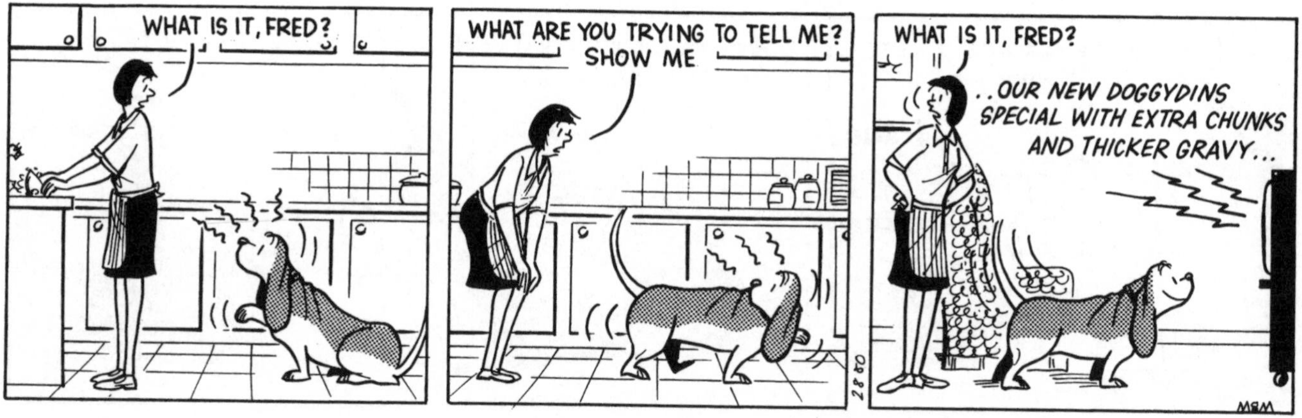

WHAT IS IT, FRED?
WHAT ARE YOU TRYING TO TELL ME? SHOW ME
WHAT IS IT, FRED?
..OUR NEW DOGGYDINS SPECIAL WITH EXTRA CHUNKS AND THICKER GRAVY...
2880
MGM

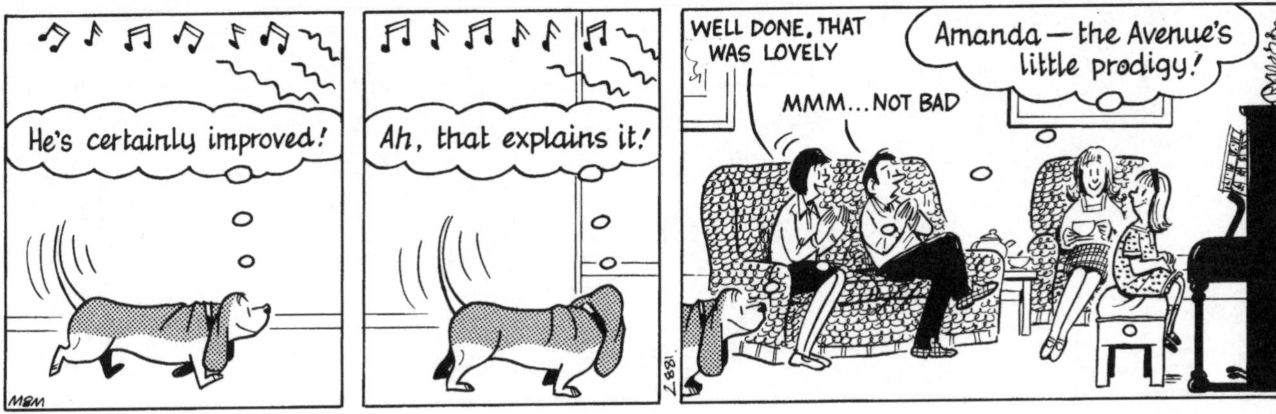
He's certainly improved!
Ah, that explains it!
WELL DONE. THAT WAS LOVELY
MMM...NOT BAD
Amanda—the Avenue's little prodigy!

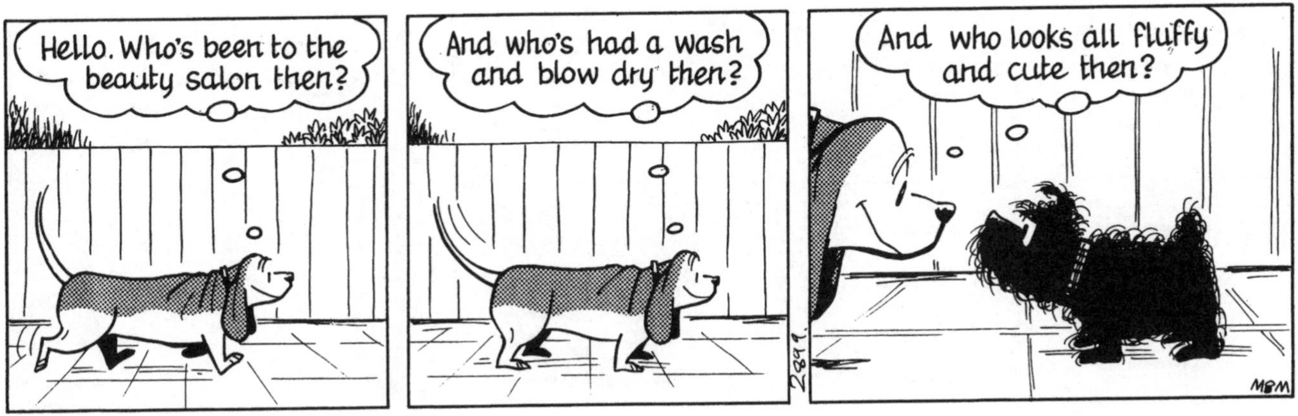
Hello. Who's been to the beauty salon then?
And who's had a wash and blow dry then?
And who looks all fluffy and cute then?

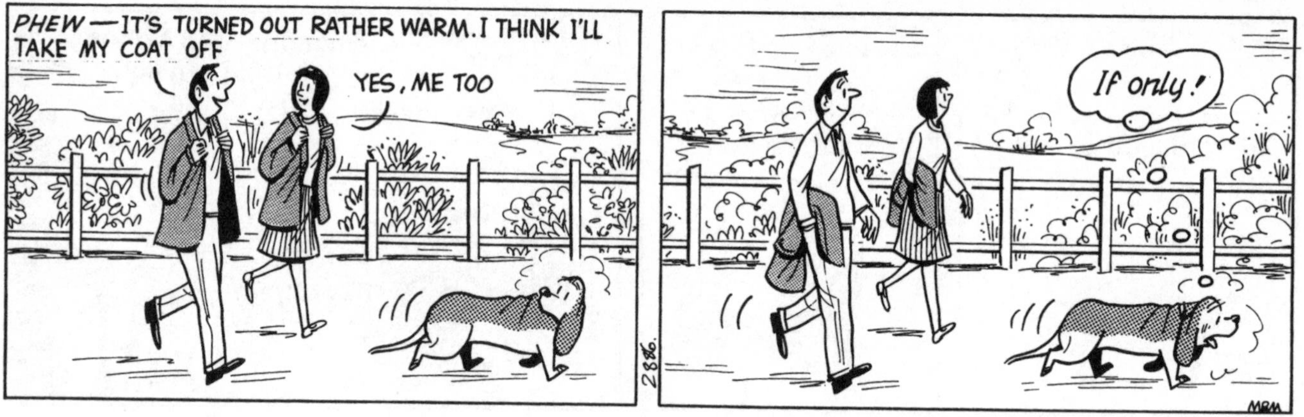
PHEW — IT'S TURNED OUT RATHER WARM. I THINK I'LL TAKE MY COAT OFF
YES, ME TOO
If only!
2886.
MRM

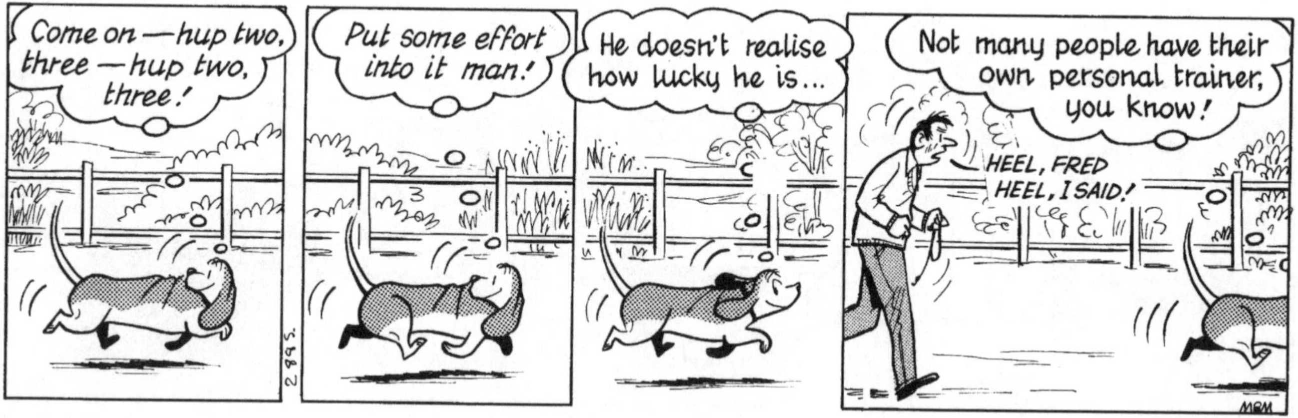
Come on — hup two, three — hup two, three!
2895.
Put some effort into it man!
He doesn't realise how lucky he is...
Not many people have their own personal trainer, you know!
HEEL, FRED
HEEL, I SAID!
MRM

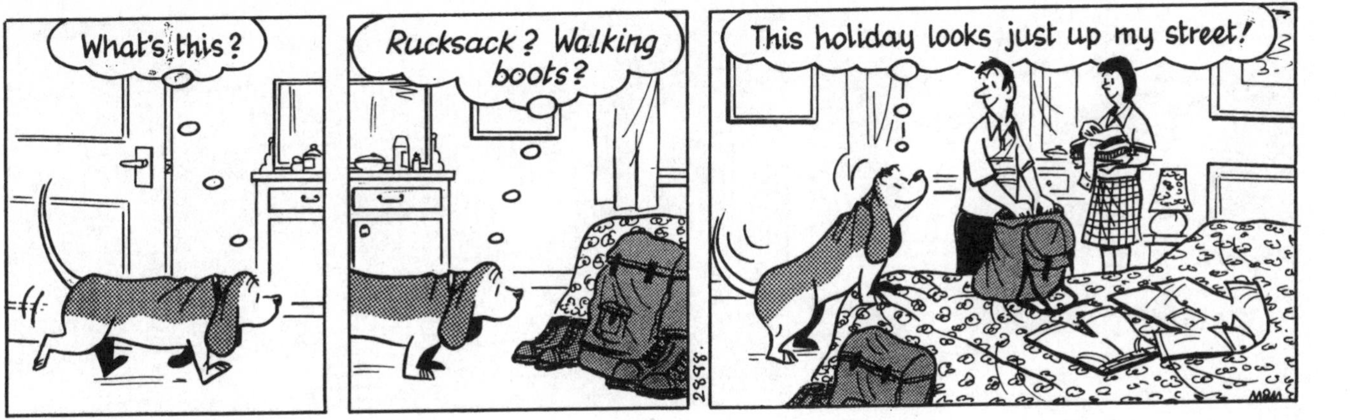
What's this?
Rucksack? Walking boots?
This holiday looks just up my street!

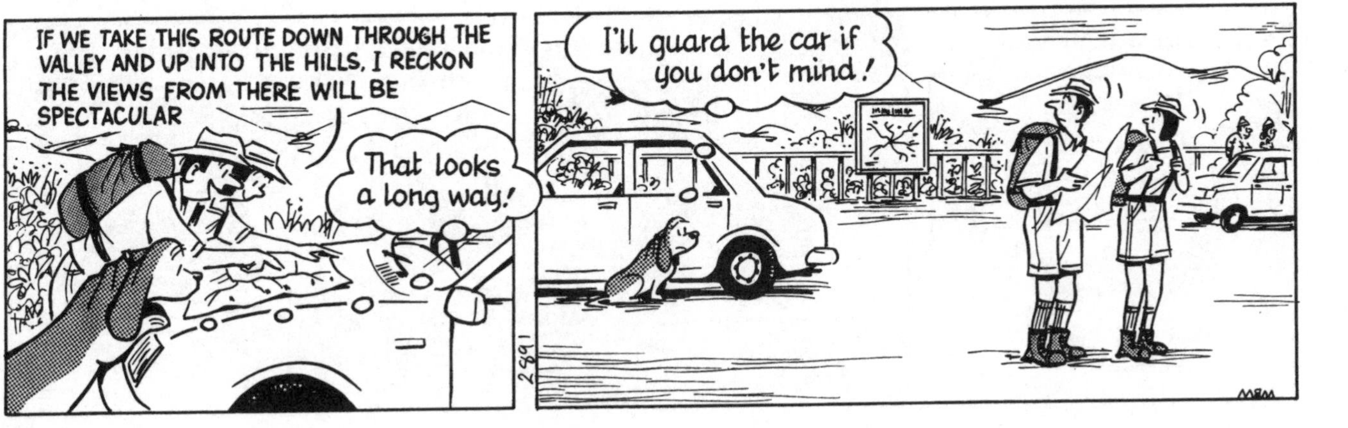
IF WE TAKE THIS ROUTE DOWN THROUGH THE VALLEY AND UP INTO THE HILLS, I RECKON THE VIEWS FROM THERE WILL BE SPECTACULAR
That looks a long way!
I'll guard the car if you don't mind!

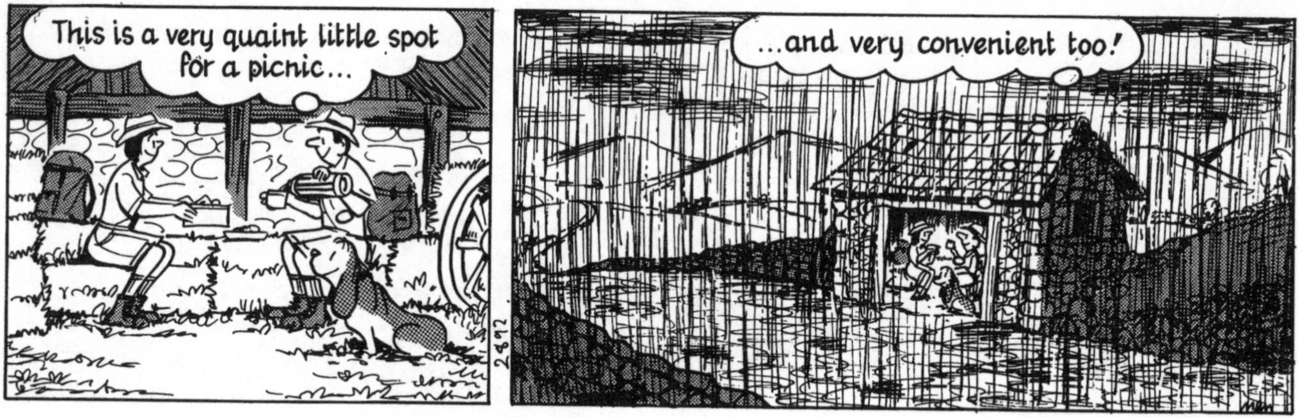
This is a very quaint little spot for a picnic...
...and very convenient too!
2892

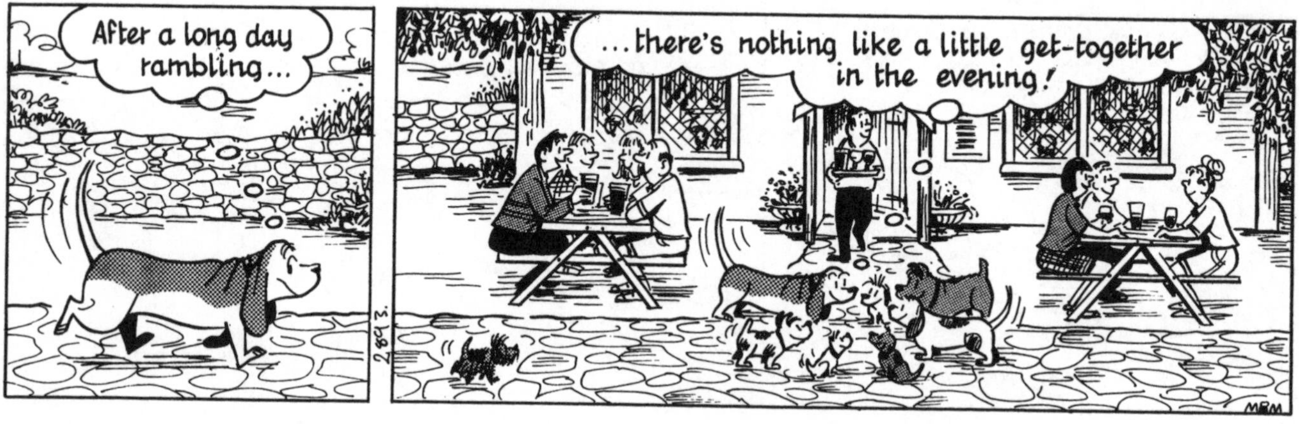
After a long day rambling...
...there's nothing like a little get-together in the evening!
2893
MRM

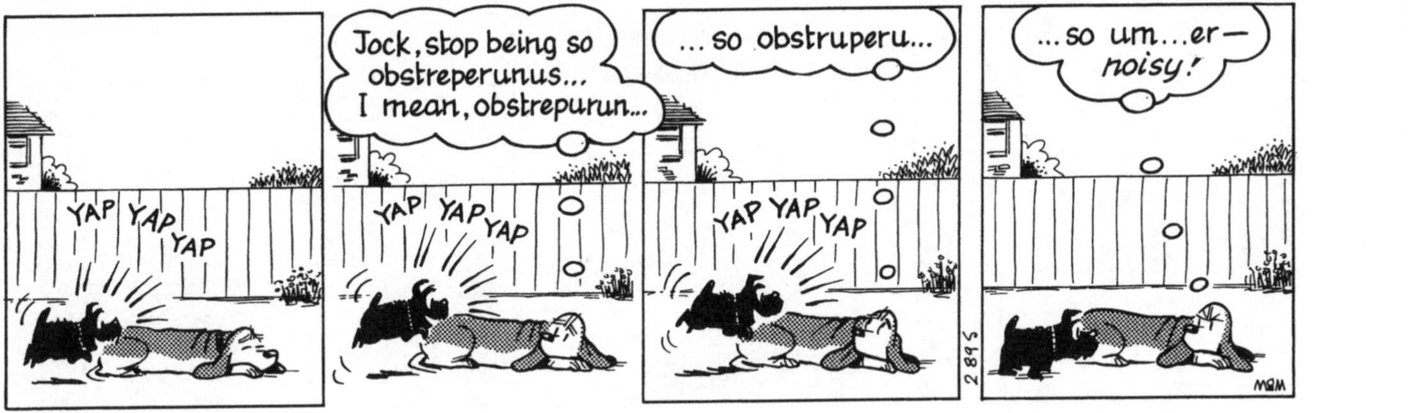

YAP YAP YAP
Jock, stop being so obstreperunus... I mean, obstrepurun...
YAP YAP YAP
... so obstruperu...
YAP YAP YAP
... so um... er— noisy!

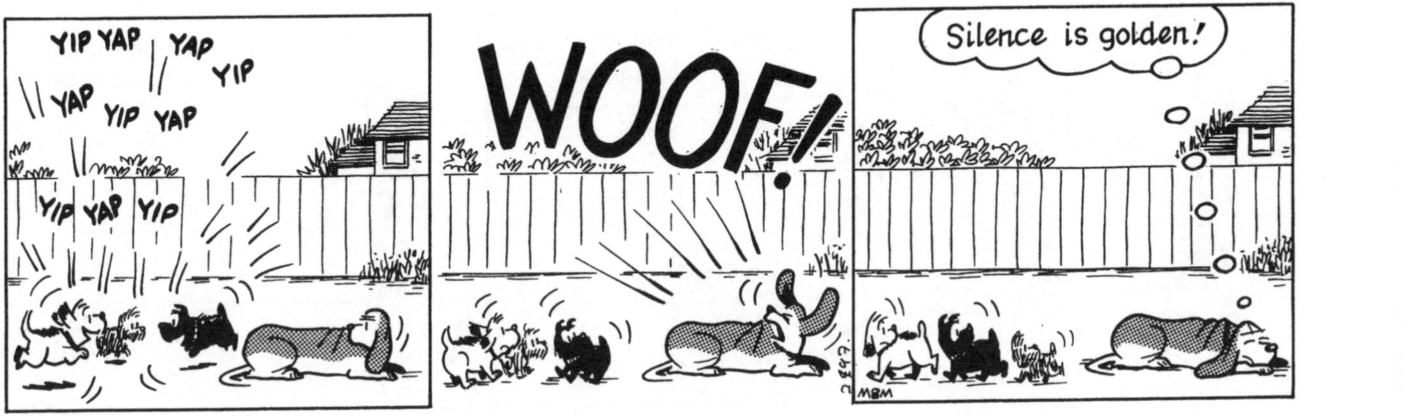

YIP YAP YAP YIP YAP YIP YAP YIP YAP YIP
WOOF!
Silence is golden!

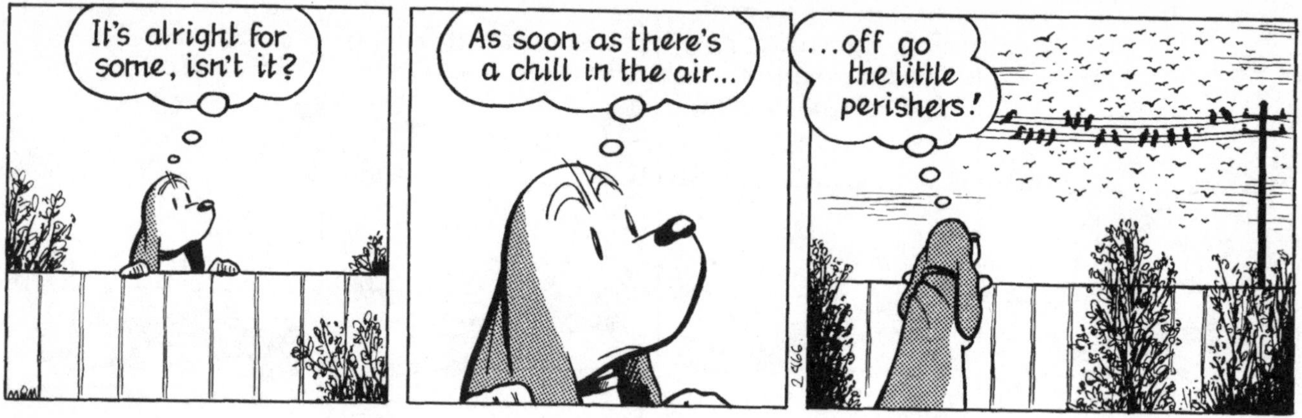
It's alright for some, isn't it?
As soon as there's a chill in the air...
...off go the little perishers!

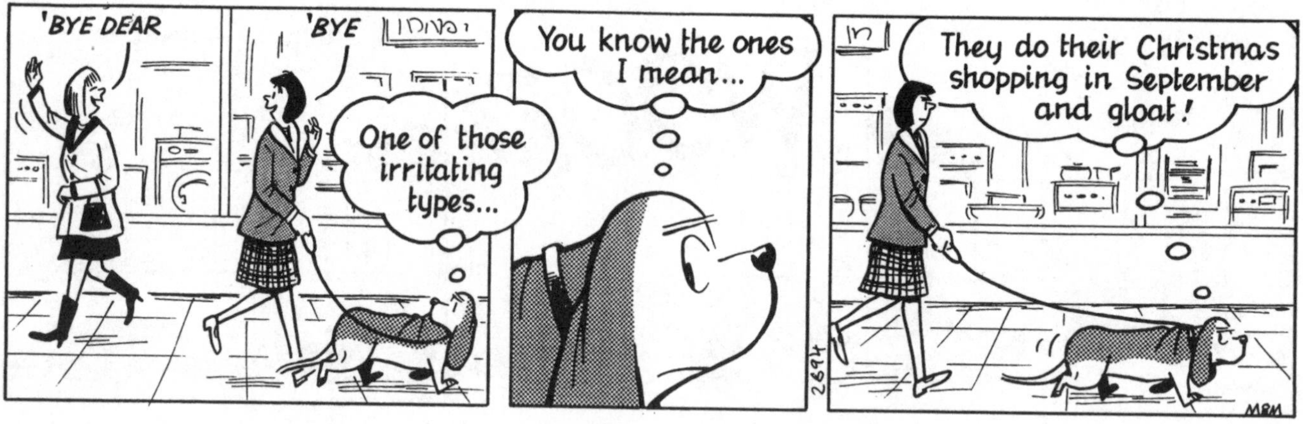
'BYE DEAR
'BYE
One of those irritating types...
You know the ones I mean...
They do their Christmas shopping in September and gloat!

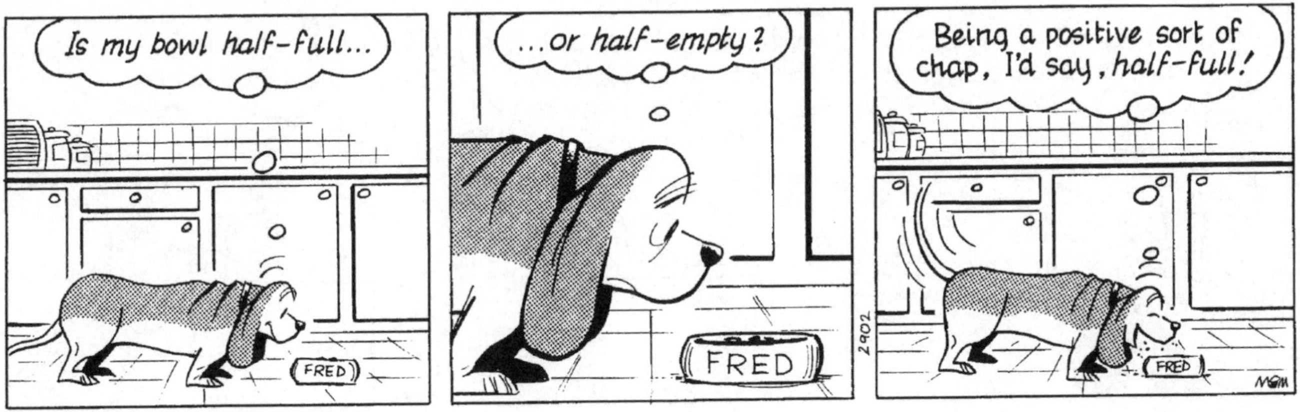
Is my bowl half-full...
FRED
...or half-empty?
FRED
Being a positive sort of chap, I'd say, half-full!
FRED

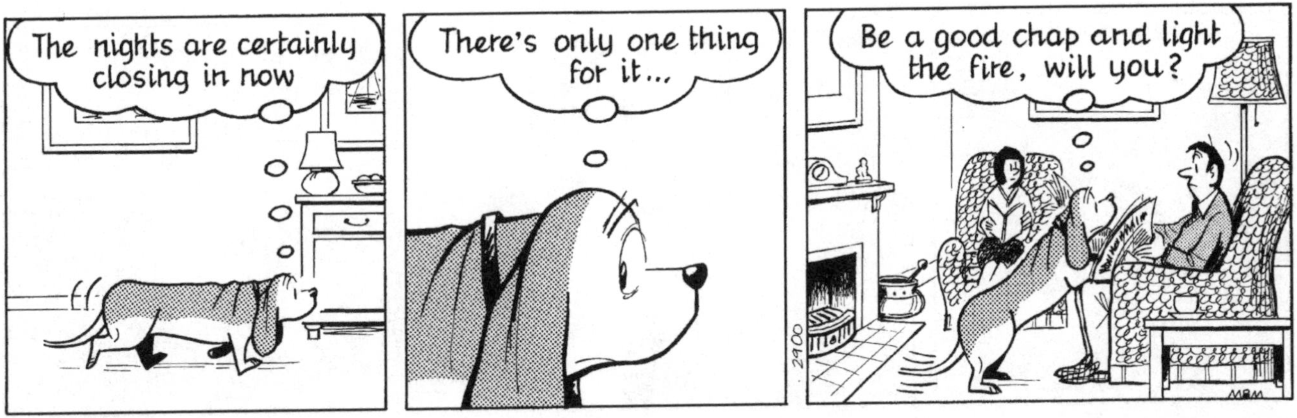
The nights are certainly closing in now
There's only one thing for it...
Be a good chap and light the fire, will you?

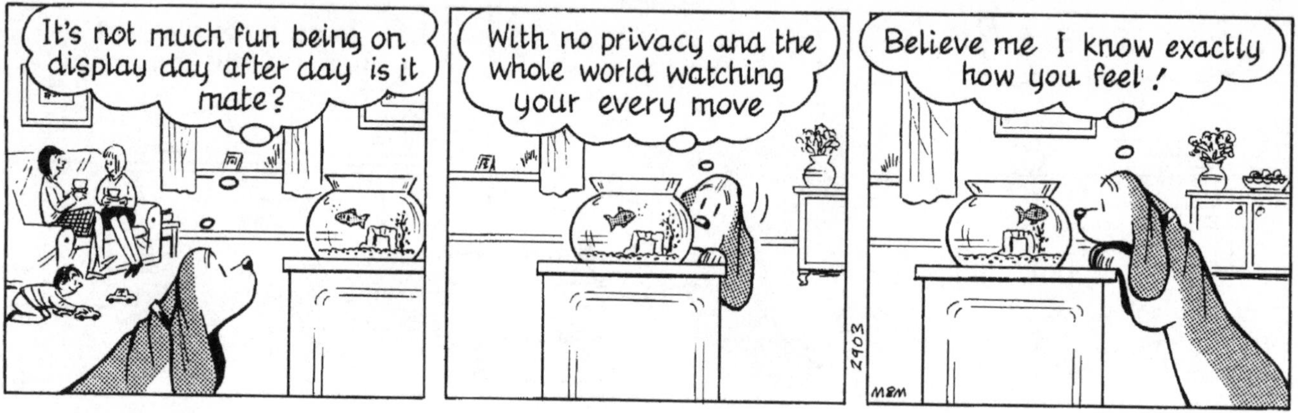
It's not much fun being on display day after day is it mate?
With no privacy and the whole world watching your every move
Believe me I know exactly how you feel!
2903

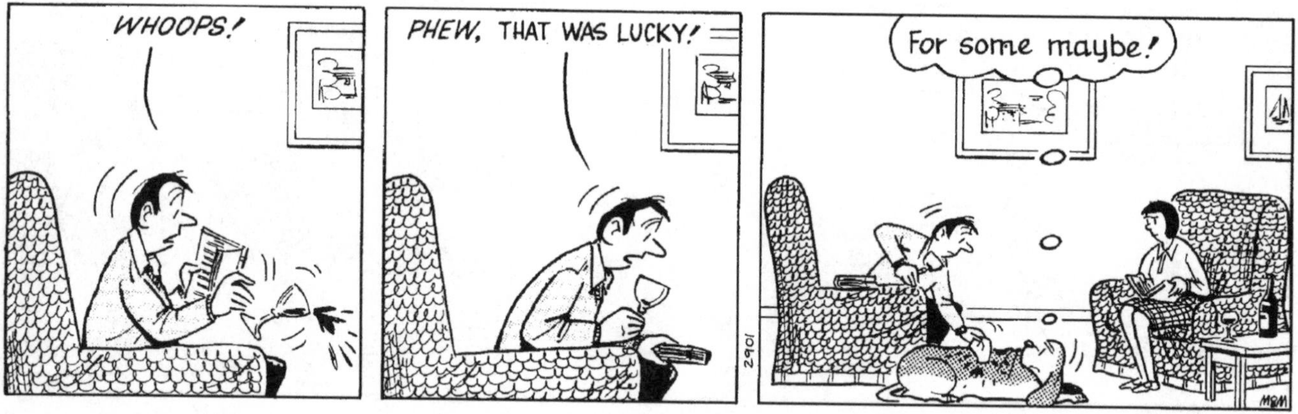
WHOOPS!
PHEW, THAT WAS LUCKY!
2901
For some maybe!

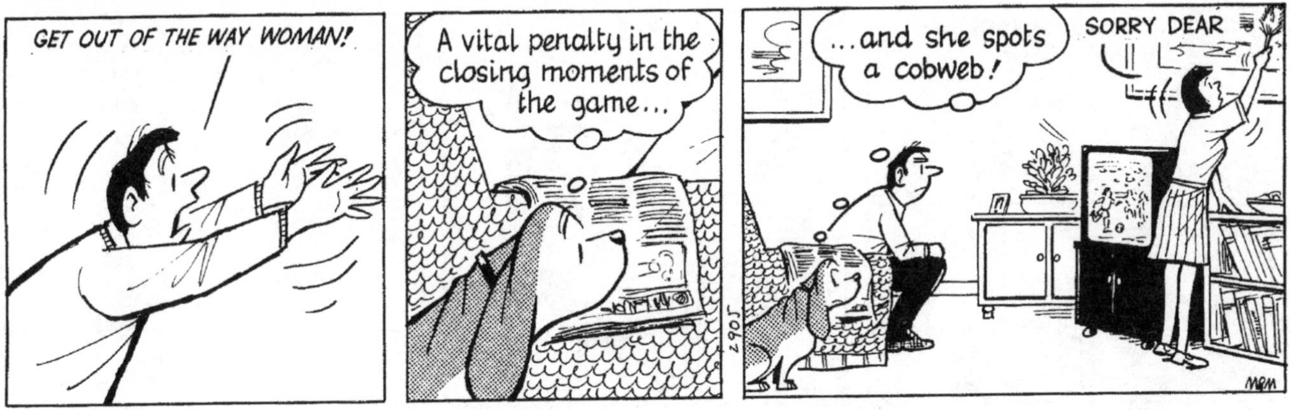
GET OUT OF THE WAY WOMAN!
A vital penalty in the closing moments of the game...
...and she spots a cobweb!
SORRY DEAR
2905
MBM

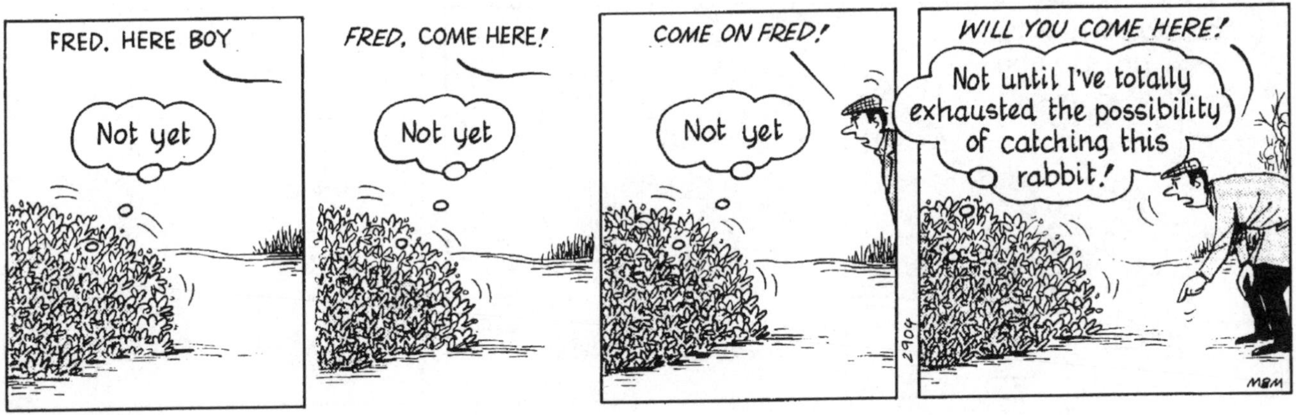
FRED, HERE BOY
Not yet
FRED, COME HERE!
Not yet
COME ON FRED!
Not yet
WILL YOU COME HERE!
Not until I've totally exhausted the possibility of catching this rabbit!
2904
MBM

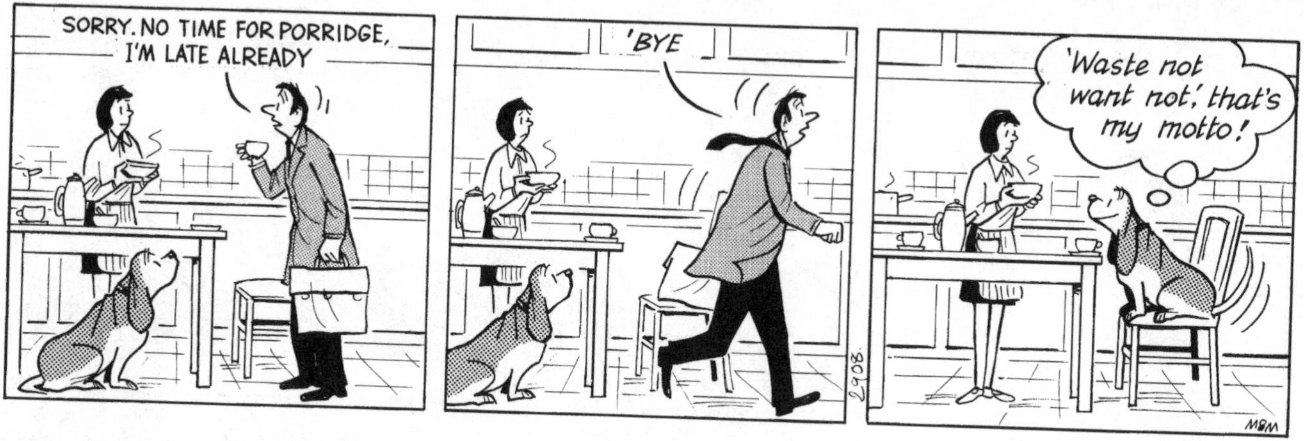
SORRY. NO TIME FOR PORRIDGE, I'M LATE ALREADY
'BYE
'Waste not want not,' that's my motto!

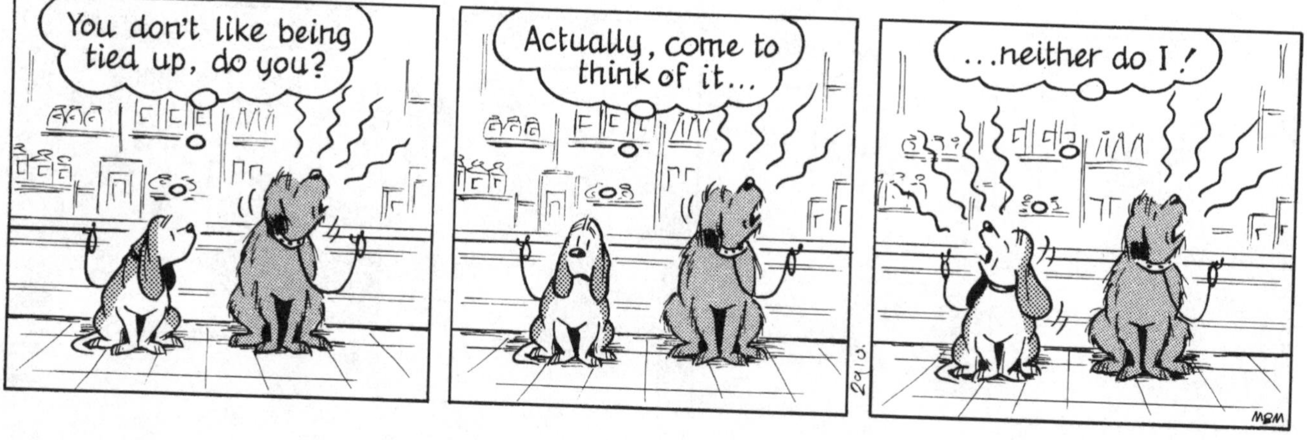
You don't like being tied up, do you?
Actually, come to think of it...
...neither do I!

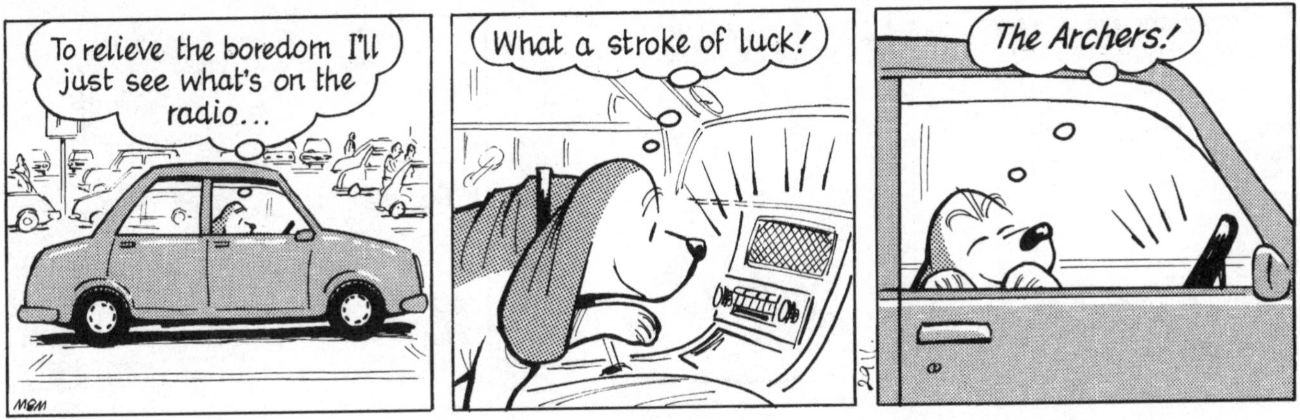
To relieve the boredom I'll just see what's on the radio...
What a stroke of luck!
The Archers!

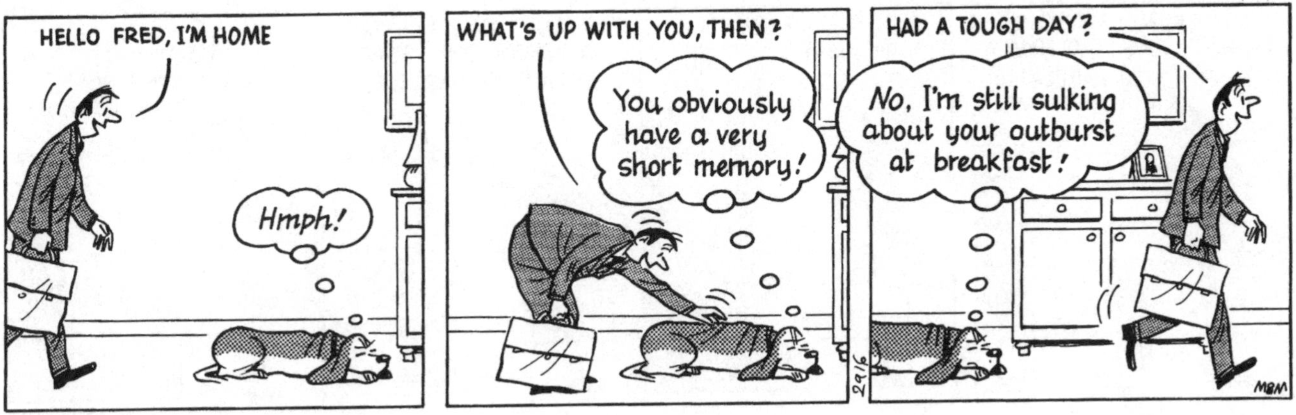
HELLO FRED, I'M HOME
Hmph!
WHAT'S UP WITH YOU, THEN?
You obviously have a very short memory!
HAD A TOUGH DAY?
No, I'm still sulking about your outburst at breakfast!

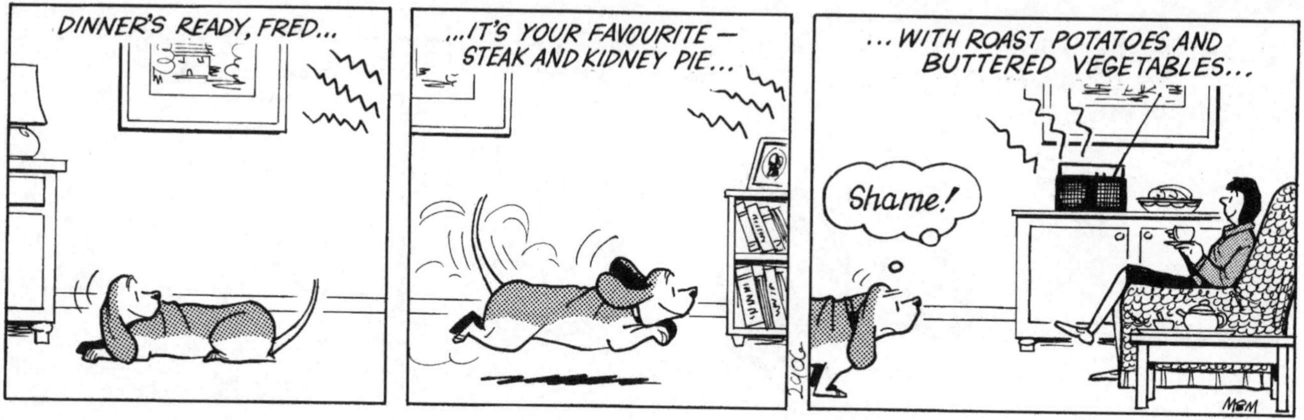
DINNER'S READY, FRED...
...IT'S YOUR FAVOURITE – STEAK AND KIDNEY PIE...
...WITH ROAST POTATOES AND BUTTERED VEGETABLES...
Shame!

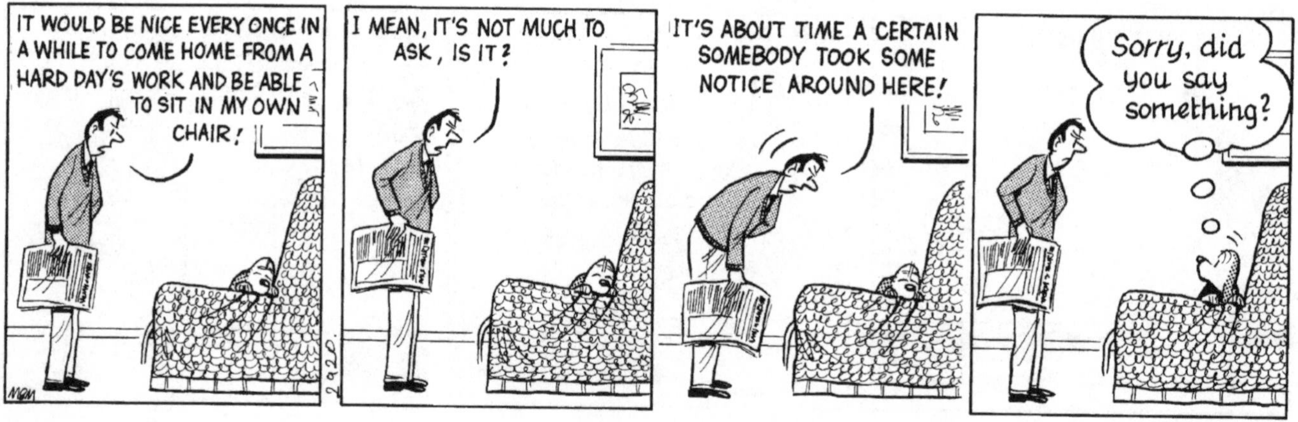
IT WOULD BE NICE EVERY ONCE IN A WHILE TO COME HOME FROM A HARD DAY'S WORK AND BE ABLE TO SIT IN MY OWN CHAIR!
I MEAN, IT'S NOT MUCH TO ASK, IS IT?
IT'S ABOUT TIME A CERTAIN SOMEBODY TOOK SOME NOTICE AROUND HERE!
Sorry, did you say something?

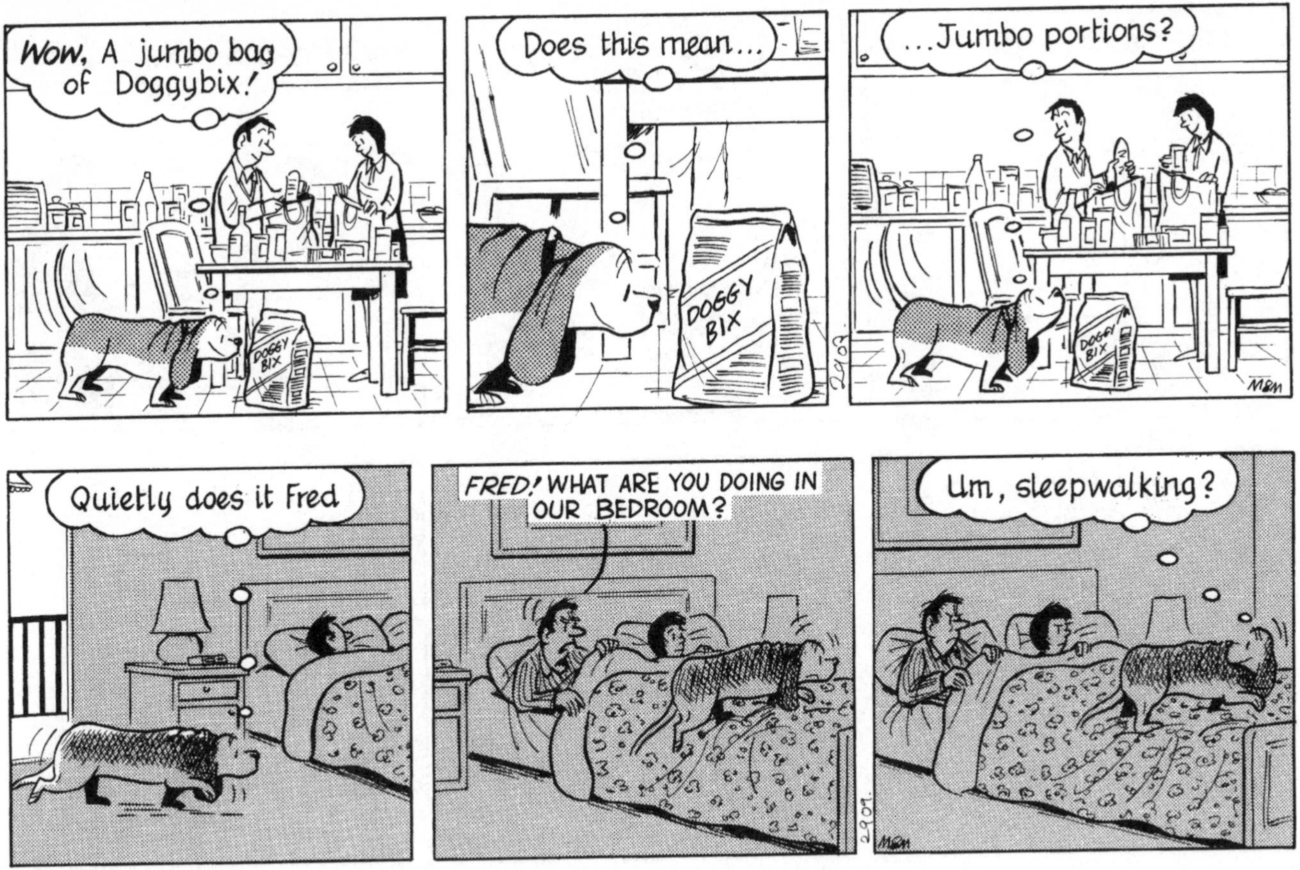

WOW, A jumbo bag of Doggybix!
DOGGY BIX
Does this mean...
DOGGY BIX
2903
...Jumbo portions?
DOGGY BIX
M&M
Quietly does it Fred
FRED! WHAT ARE YOU DOING IN OUR BEDROOM?
2909.
Um, sleepwalking?
M&M

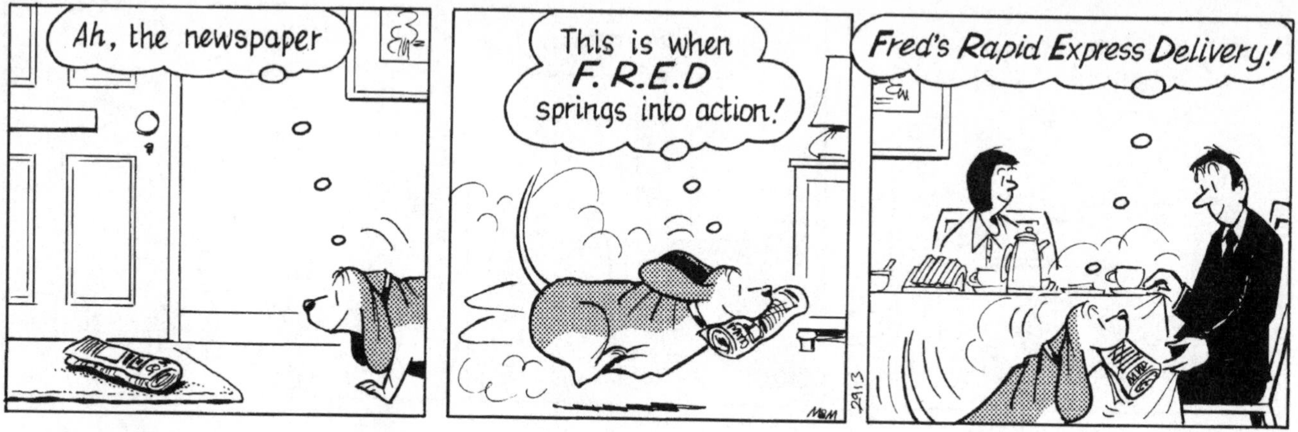
Ah, the newspaper
This is when F.R.E.D springs into action!
Fred's Rapid Express Delivery!

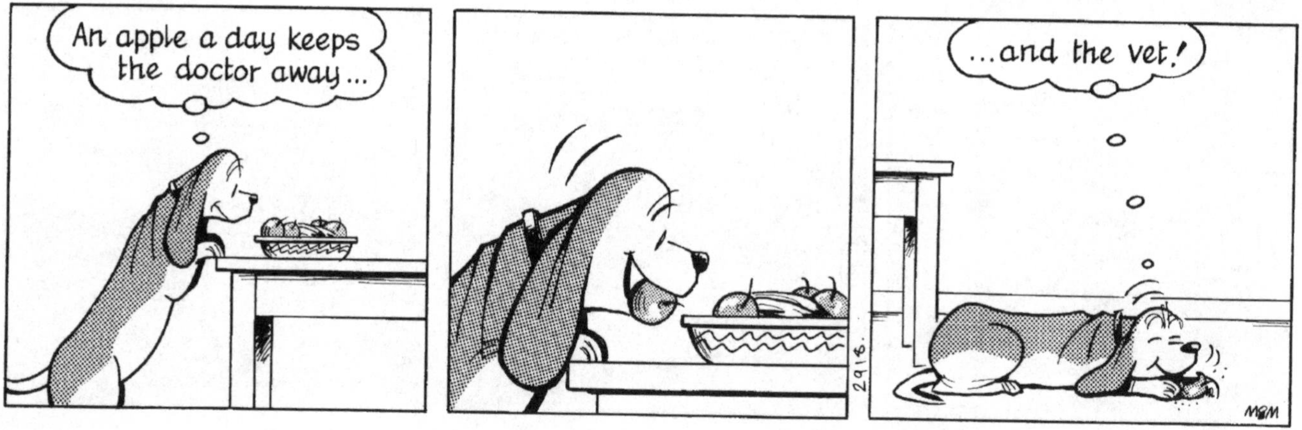
An apple a day keeps the doctor away...
...and the vet!

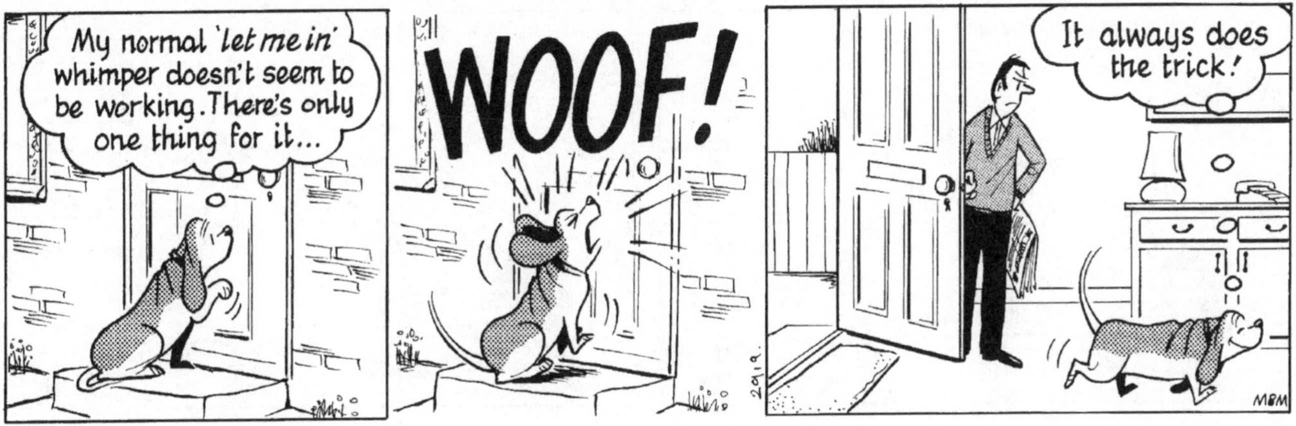
My normal 'let me in' whimper doesn't seem to be working. There's only one thing for it...
WOOF!
It always does the trick!
MBM

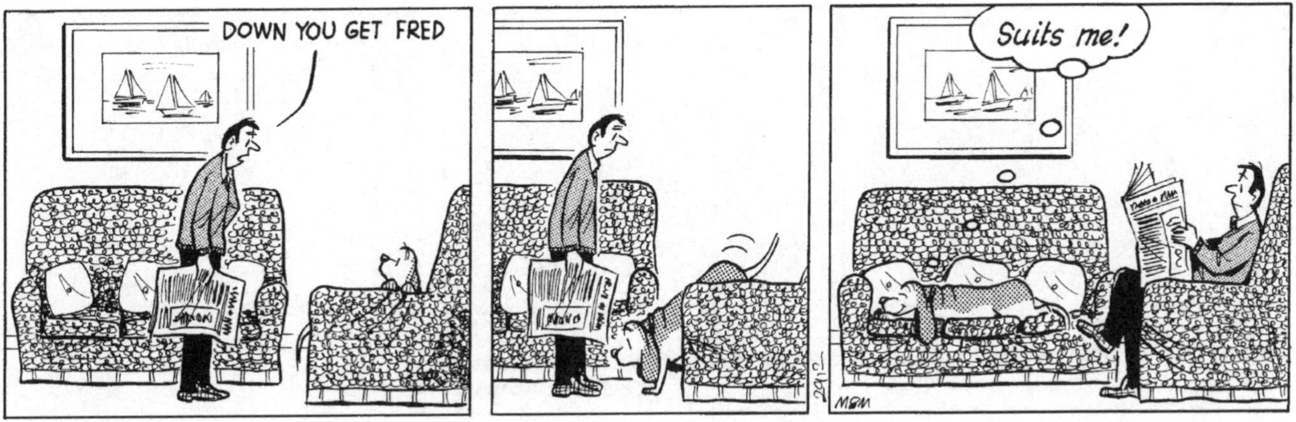
DOWN YOU GET FRED
Suits me!
MBM

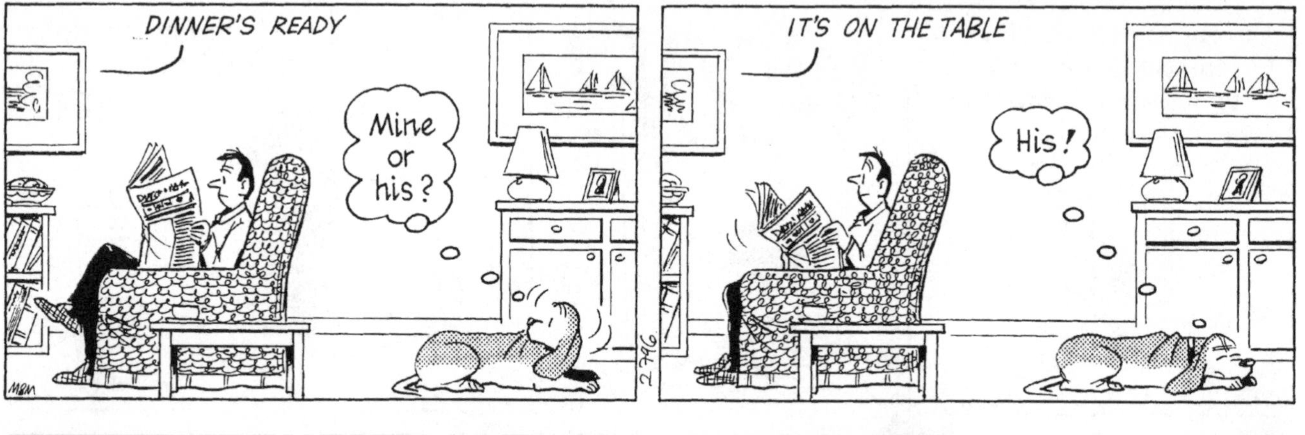
DINNER'S READY
Mine or his?
IT'S ON THE TABLE
His!

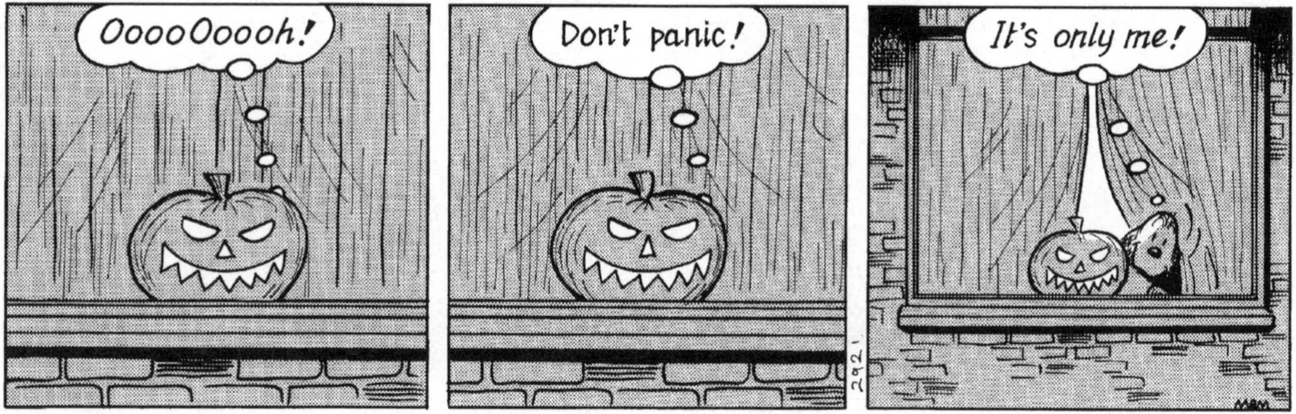
OoooOoooh!
Don't panic!
It's only me!

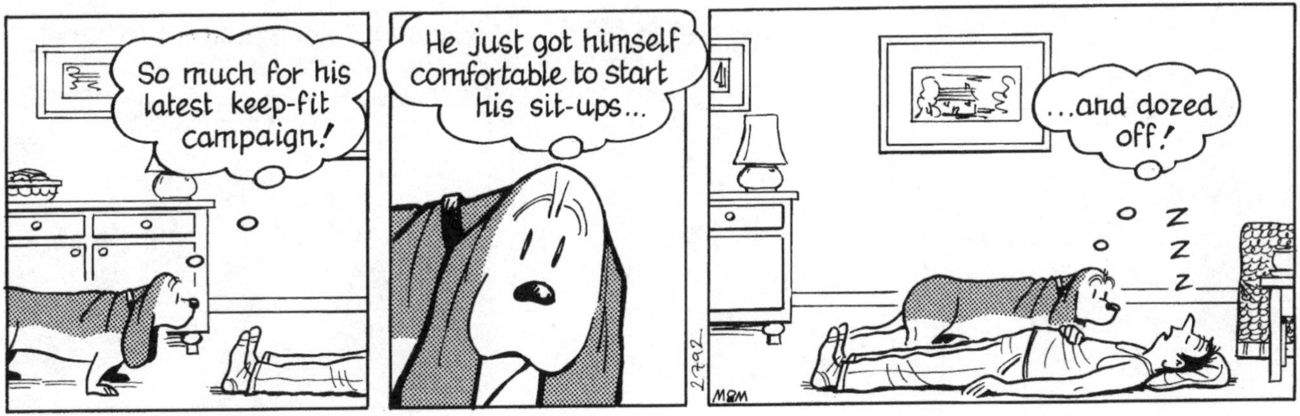
So much for his latest keep-fit campaign!
He just got himself comfortable to start his sit-ups...
...and dozed off!
Z Z Z

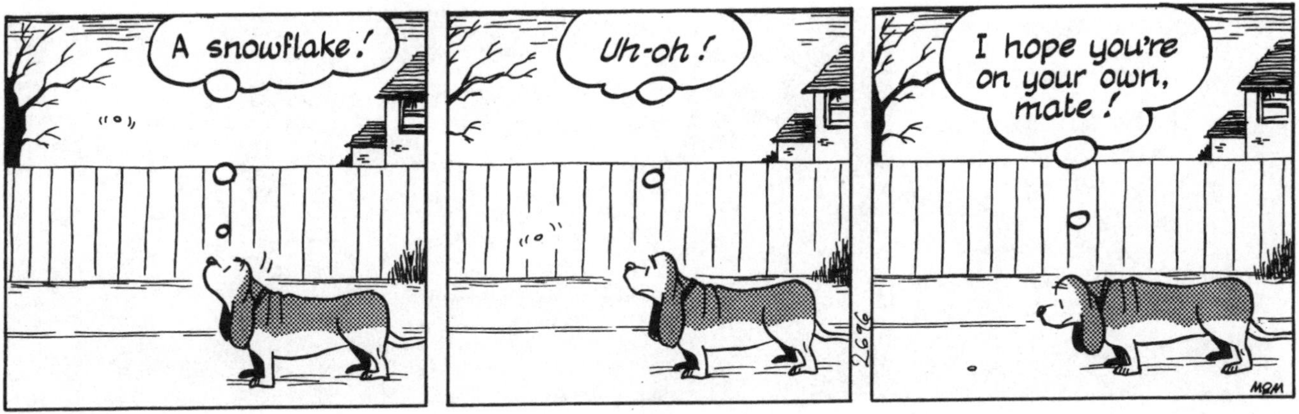
A snowflake!
Uh-oh!
I hope you're on your own, mate!

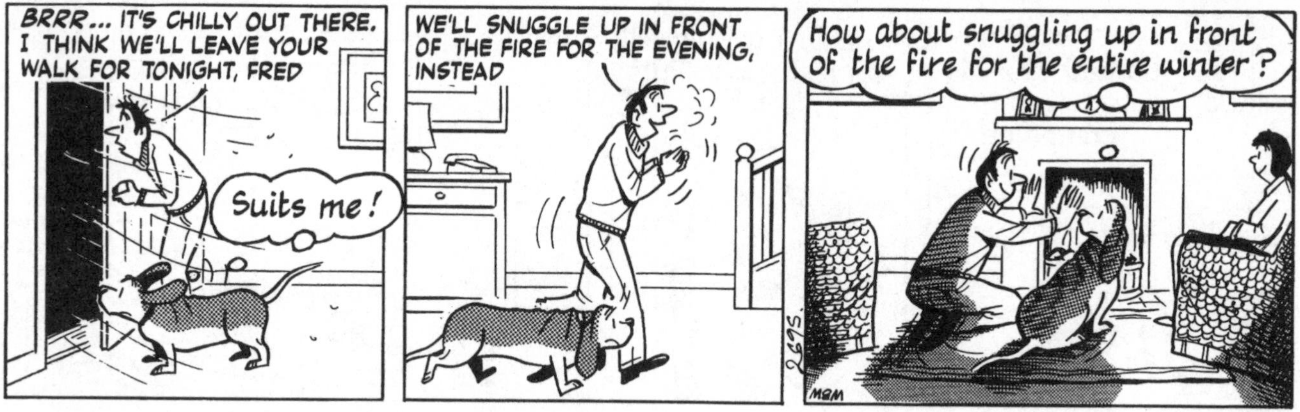
BRRR... IT'S CHILLY OUT THERE. I THINK WE'LL LEAVE YOUR WALK FOR TONIGHT, FRED
Suits me!
WE'LL SNUGGLE UP IN FRONT OF THE FIRE FOR THE EVENING, INSTEAD
How about snuggling up in front of the fire for the entire winter?

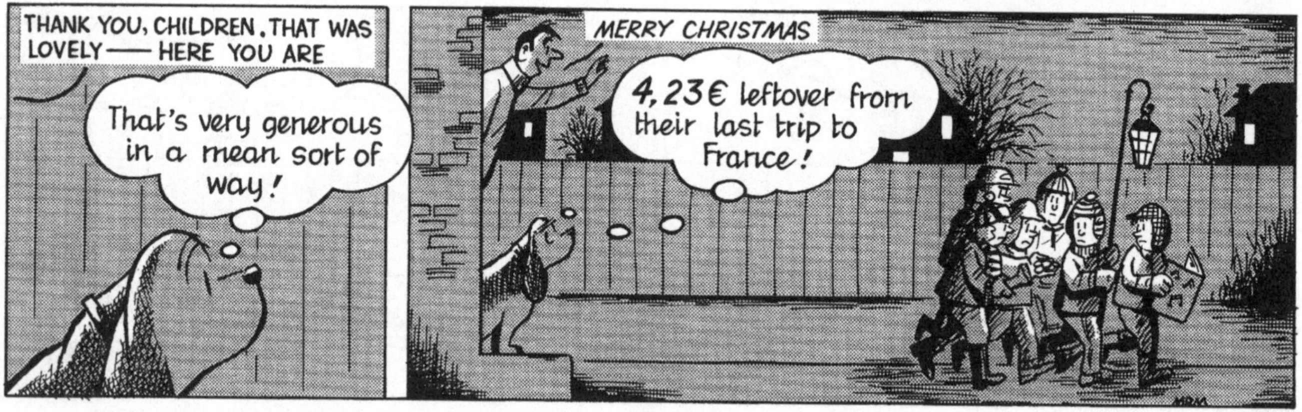
THANK YOU, CHILDREN. THAT WAS LOVELY — HERE YOU ARE
That's very generous in a mean sort of way!
MERRY CHRISTMAS
4,23€ leftover from their last trip to France!

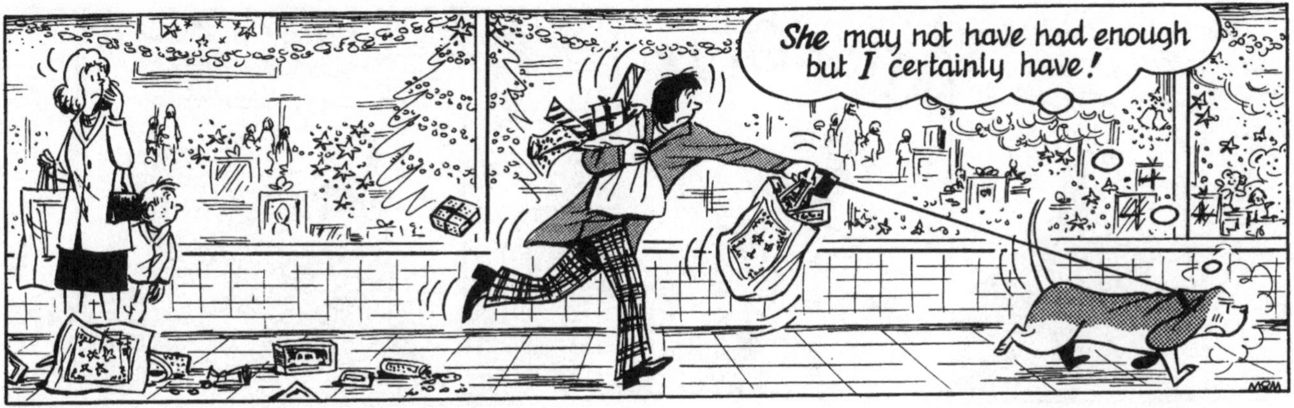
She may not have had enough but *I* certainly have!
MBM

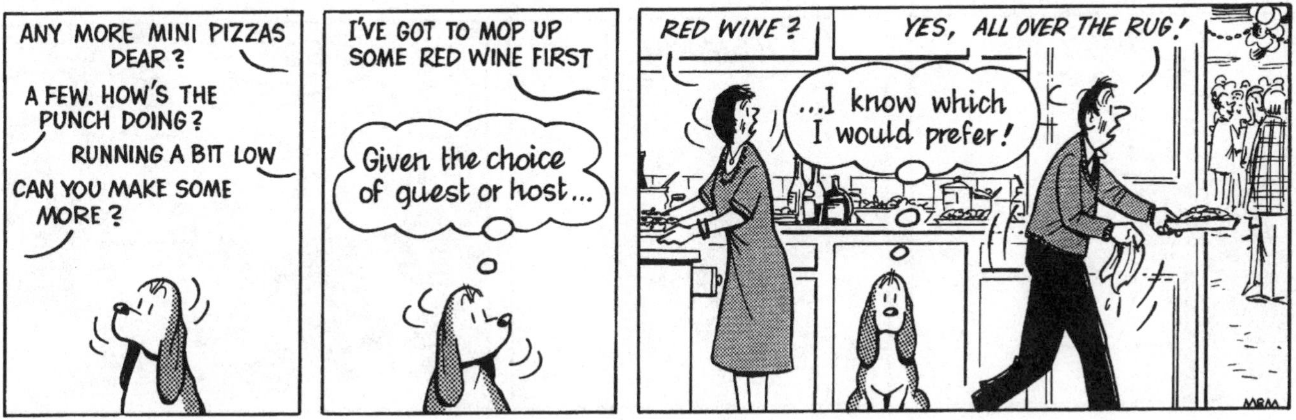
ANY MORE MINI PIZZAS DEAR?
A FEW. HOW'S THE PUNCH DOING?
RUNNING A BIT LOW
CAN YOU MAKE SOME MORE?
I'VE GOT TO MOP UP SOME RED WINE FIRST
Given the choice of guest or host...
RED WINE?
YES, ALL OVER THE RUG!
...I know which I would prefer!
MBM

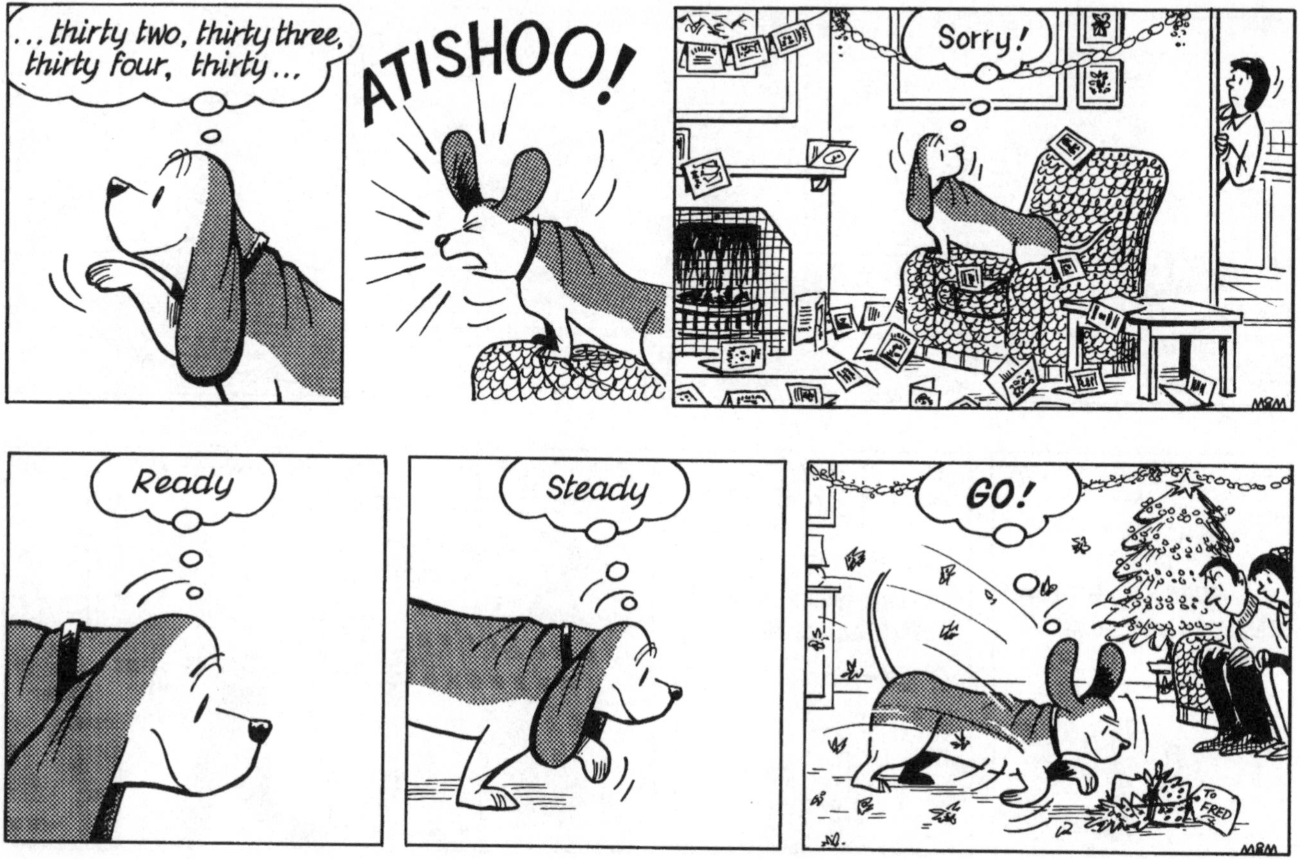
...thirty two, thirty three, thirty four, thirty...
ATISHOO!
Sorry!
MSM
Ready
Steady
GO!
TO FRED
MSM

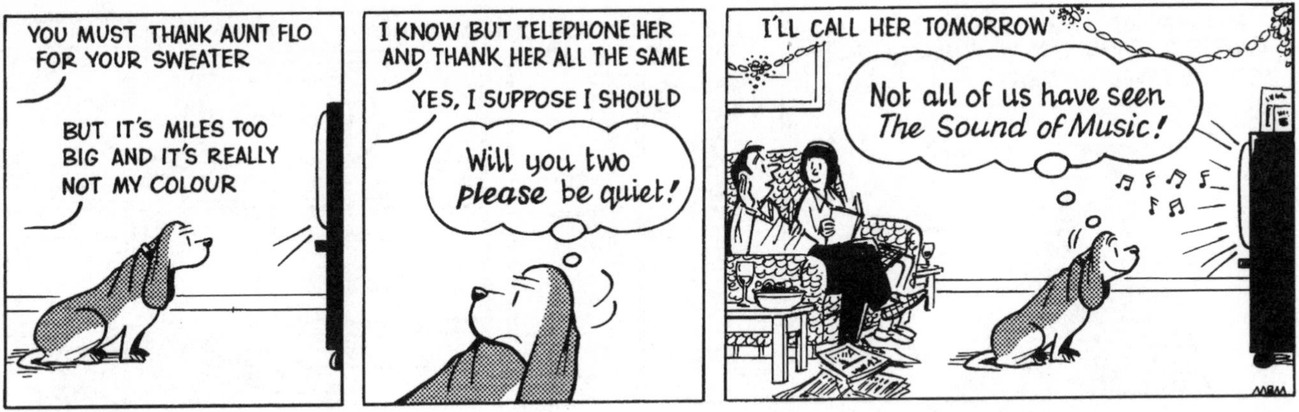
YOU MUST THANK AUNT FLO FOR YOUR SWEATER
BUT IT'S MILES TOO BIG AND IT'S REALLY NOT MY COLOUR
I KNOW BUT TELEPHONE HER AND THANK HER ALL THE SAME
YES, I SUPPOSE I SHOULD
Will you two please be quiet!
I'LL CALL HER TOMORROW
Not all of us have seen The Sound of Music!

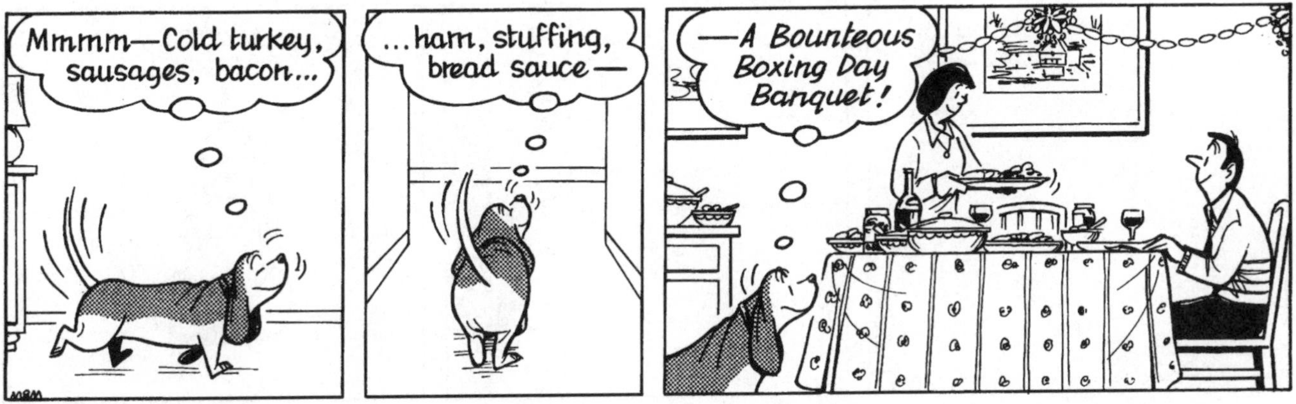
Mmmm—Cold turkey, sausages, bacon...
...ham, stuffing, bread sauce—
—A Bounteous Boxing Day Banquet!

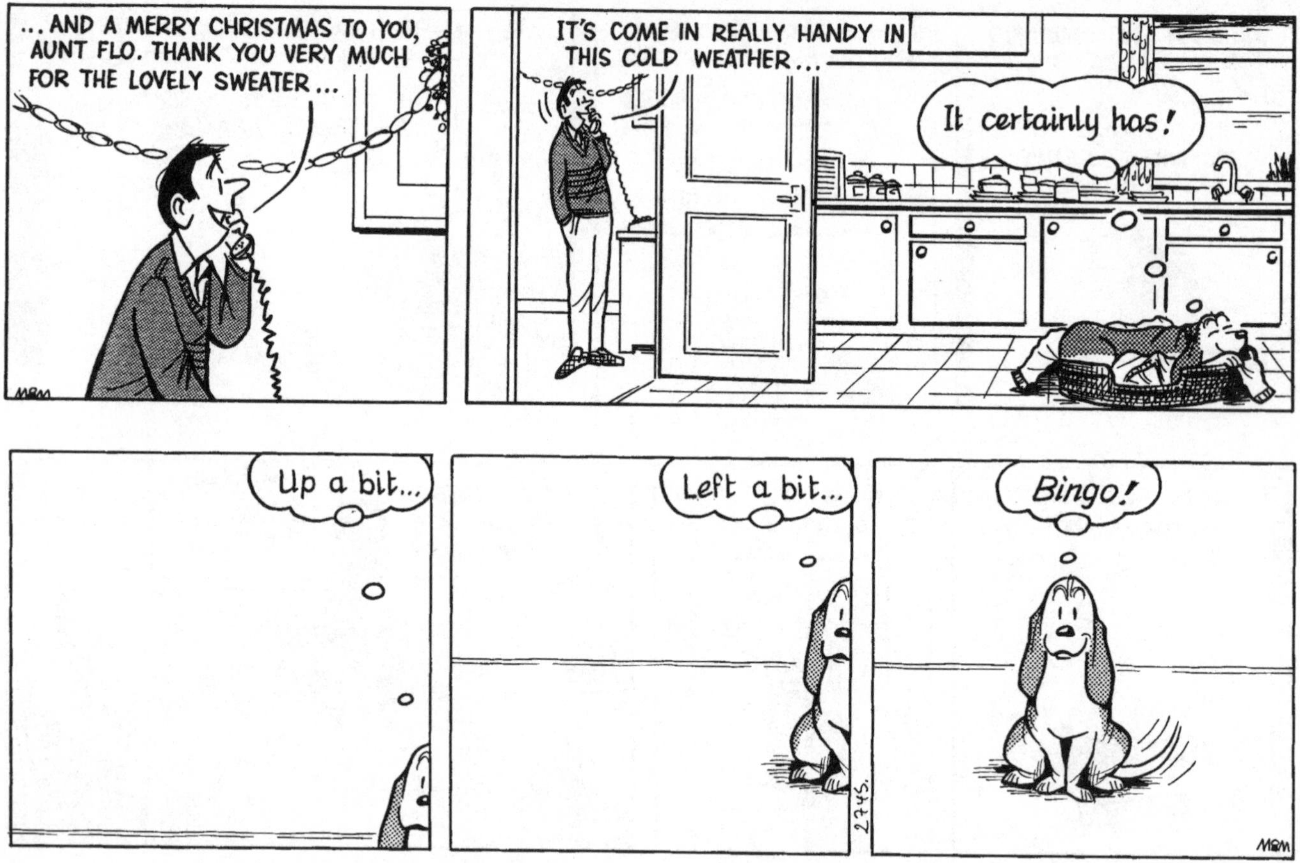
... AND A MERRY CHRISTMAS TO YOU, AUNT FLO. THANK YOU VERY MUCH FOR THE LOVELY SWEATER ...
IT'S COME IN REALLY HANDY IN THIS COLD WEATHER ...
It certainly has!
Up a bit...
Left a bit...
Bingo!
2745.